Cooking Up World History

COOKING UP WORLD HISTORY

Multicultural Recipes and Resources

Patricia C. Marden
and
Suzanne I. Barchers

1994

TEACHER IDEAS PRESS

A Division of
Libraries Unlimited, Inc.
Englewood, Colorado

TEACHER IDEAS PRESS
A Division of
Libraries Unlimited, Inc.
P.O. Box 6633
Englewood, CO 80155-6633

1-800-237-6124

Library of Congress Cataloging-in-Publication Data

Marden, Patricia C., 1948-
    Cooking up world history : multicultural recipes and resources / Patricia C. Marden and Suzanne I. Barchers.
        xv, 237 p. 22x28 cm.
        Includes bibliographical references and index.
        ISBN 1-56308-116-4
        1. Cookery, International--Study and teaching (Elementary)
    2. Cookery, International--Study and teaching (Secondary) 3. Food habits--Study and teaching (Elementary) 4. Food habits--Study and teaching (Secondary)   I. Barchers, Suzanne I. II. Title.
    TX725.A1M347   1994
    641.59'007--dc20   93-40457
                                                                              CIP

Dedicated to Chris, the certainty of my life,
and also to the myriad of wonderful people
in the world who create the fascinating
aspects of culture through their foods.

P.C.M.

Dedicated to Terry Rodriguez and Debbie Wilson,
whose courage is inspirational.

S.I.B.

Contents

xii / Contents

Introduction

Any study of world cultures or history can be enlivened by experiencing the foods of those peoples. Through foods, students appreciate the differences, as well as the commonalities, among peoples. Further, they strengthen their reading, math, cooperative, and problem-solving skills as they determine how to prepare, adapt, and serve a recipe. Teachers who regularly cook in the classroom find that cooking is often the highlight of a unit of study. *Cooking Up World History* provides elementary and middle school teachers with recipes, research suggestions, and resources appropriate for culinary exploration.

CHAPTER INTRODUCTIONS

Each chapter introduction includes a map of the country or region and a brief discussion about the role of food in the culture. These introductions merely provide an overview. An excellent source for more information is the series of books titled *Cooking the . . . Way.* (See "Bibliography: Resources in Series" on page 227.) This series includes background information on the country, recipes, and information about the recipes. The cookbook section in public and school libraries will have many resource books specific to various countries or regions. Encourage all students to explore both children's and adults' sections.

RECIPES

Because there are so many fascinating countries in our world, it was difficult to limit the choice of countries for a manageable book size. Selection of the countries was based on two criteria: the study of the country or region in standard social studies programs and the presence of the culture in the United States.

Recipes were chosen to reflect the traditions of the country or geographic area, as well as the important foods, such as corn, rice, or beans. The section for each country includes a variety of recipes that might make up a complete meal or breakfast and dinner. Many recipes were included for their simplicity, but others will require more planning and preparation. The number of servings generally reflects what one might serve four to six people. For the classroom, this would provide a sample taste; for a complete classroom meal, recipes will have to be increased or combined with other foods.

Before beginning any cooking project, review the safety notes on page xv. Information regarding measurement is included in appendix B and altitude adjustments are found in appendix C. Occasionally, it will be necessary to purchase specific spices or other ingredients at ethnic markets or shops. Consult students, parents, and the phone directory for help with finding unusual items. Whenever possible, enlist the help of a parent or volunteer from that culture to assist with the cooking.

LIBRARY LINKS

Each recipe concludes with a Library Link that is often a research question linked to history of the culture or the food. Many of the answers can be found in standard reference books. Others can be found in books about foods or the particular culture. Readers might prefer to refer to the answers found in appendix A, page 211.

BIBLIOGRAPHIES

The bibliographies for each chapter include fiction and nonfiction books, films, and videos. There are many wonderful nonfiction books in series, and these are listed in "Bibliography: Resources in Series," on page 227. Books in English about certain countries may not be widely available in the United States, and reading should be supplemented by the series books. General books about food and cultures are found in "Bibliography: Resources About Food and Cultures" on page 225. Happily, more books from various cultures are appearing each year, and readers are encouraged to look for additional titles.

It is difficult to indicate reading levels. Many books can be sampled for pertinent information by younger readers, and beautifully illustrated books should be enjoyed by all ages. If a reading level is indicated "grades 3 and up," it generally means that it could be read by third-graders and older students. Younger students may appreciate the book as a read-aloud. Teachers should provide a variety of books at many levels and let students discover what is most valuable. Even middle-school students will enjoy many of the books designated "grades kindergarten and up."

A FINAL WORD

Cooking Up World History should be your starting point for exploring world cultures. Begin your own collection of recipes, encourage your students to explore these cultures further, and begin to investigate cultures not included herein. Enjoy!

Cooking and Safety Tips

COOKING TIPS

1. Read recipe carefully before beginning.

2. Gather ingredients.

3. Gather all utensils, bowls, and other equipment.

4. Turn on the oven to preheat, if needed.

5. Measure exactly.

6. Make sure you have completed each step before going on to the next one.

7. Time any baking or cooking carefully. All baking temperatures are indicated in Fahrenheit.

FOR SAFETY'S SAKE

1. Ask for an adult's help before using the oven or stove. Always use thick, dry potholders to handle hot equipment.

2. Turn off stove and oven when cooking and baking are complete.

3. If grease should catch fire, pour baking soda on the fire. Do not pour water over the flames. If the fire is in a pan, put the lid on to smother the flames.

4. Always tie back long or loose hair when working around the oven or stove. This should also be done with loose sleeves or other clothing.

5. Keep hands and face away from steam when cooking liquids over a stove.

6. When cooking with saucepans, always turn the handles so they don't stick out over the edge of the stove.

7. During cooking, allow as few people as possible around hot items. It is best to designate an adult to remain in that area.

8. Sharp instruments should remain on tables when not in use and should be carefully carried to a sink for cleanup by an adult.

9. When peeling vegetables, always move the blade away from your hands.

10. When cutting or chopping, use a cutting board to protect counter or table tops. Always cut away from your hands.

11. Wash knives and other sharp instruments separately from other tools and be careful when wiping the blades.

12. Make sure that your hands are dry whenever plugging in or using electrical appliances.

13. Do not immerse electrical appliances in water when cleaning them. Refer to manufacturer's directions for cleaning.

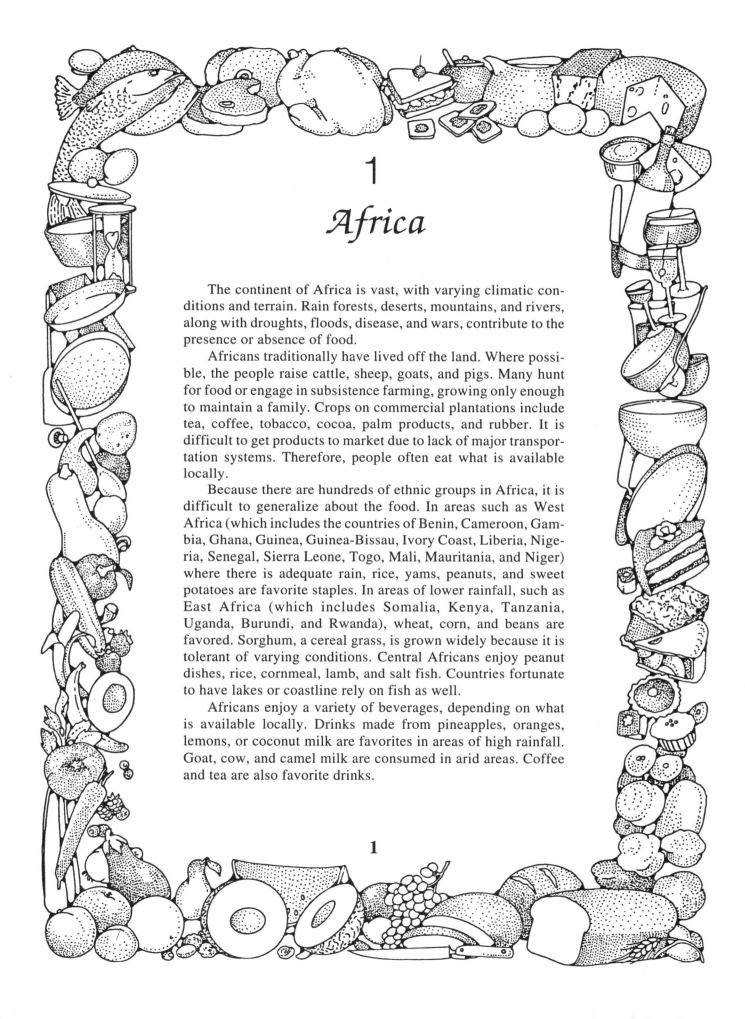

1

Africa

The continent of Africa is vast, with varying climatic conditions and terrain. Rain forests, deserts, mountains, and rivers, along with droughts, floods, disease, and wars, contribute to the presence or absence of food.

Africans traditionally have lived off the land. Where possible, the people raise cattle, sheep, goats, and pigs. Many hunt for food or engage in subsistence farming, growing only enough to maintain a family. Crops on commercial plantations include tea, coffee, tobacco, cocoa, palm products, and rubber. It is difficult to get products to market due to lack of major transportation systems. Therefore, people often eat what is available locally.

Because there are hundreds of ethnic groups in Africa, it is difficult to generalize about the food. In areas such as West Africa (which includes the countries of Benin, Cameroon, Gambia, Ghana, Guinea, Guinea-Bissau, Ivory Coast, Liberia, Nigeria, Senegal, Sierra Leone, Togo, Mali, Mauritania, and Niger) where there is adequate rain, rice, yams, peanuts, and sweet potatoes are favorite staples. In areas of lower rainfall, such as East Africa (which includes Somalia, Kenya, Tanzania, Uganda, Burundi, and Rwanda), wheat, corn, and beans are favored. Sorghum, a cereal grass, is grown widely because it is tolerant of varying conditions. Central Africans enjoy peanut dishes, rice, cornmeal, lamb, and salt fish. Countries fortunate to have lakes or coastline rely on fish as well.

Africans enjoy a variety of beverages, depending on what is available locally. Drinks made from pineapples, oranges, lemons, or coconut milk are favorites in areas of high rainfall. Goat, cow, and camel milk are consumed in arid areas. Coffee and tea are also favorite drinks.

BANANA FRITTERS

(West Africa)

INGREDIENTS

1½ cups flour

5 tablespoons sugar

3 eggs

1 cup milk

¼ teaspoon salt

5 medium bananas

Oil for deep fat frying

Cooking thermometer

Powdered sugar

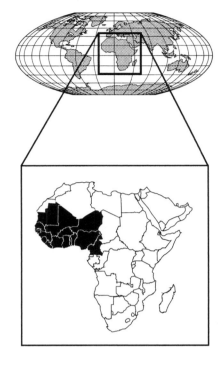

West Africa

STEPS

1. Put flour and sugar in a large bowl.
2. Beat in eggs, one at a time.
3. Stir in milk and salt. Stir well.
4. Peel bananas. Put in a small, deep bowl.
5. Mash bananas well.
6. Stir bananas into flour batter. Let sit for 20 minutes.
7. Pour oil 3 inches deep into a large saucepan. Heat until it reaches 375 degrees.
8. Put large spoonfuls of batter into oil. Fry until brown on both sides.
9. Remove from oil. Drain on paper towels.
10. Sprinkle with powdered sugar. Serve warm.

Serves 6.

📖 **Library Link 1:** What countries are the primary producers of bananas?

FUFU

(Yam Paste Balls)

(West Africa)

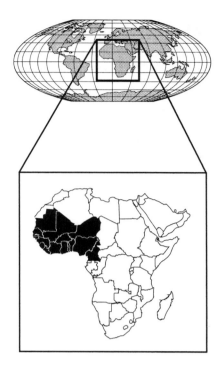

West Africa

INGREDIENTS

2 pounds yams

2¼ cups water

2 teaspoons salt

¼ teaspoon nutmeg

STEPS

1. Slice yams into 2½-inch-thick slices.

2. Peel skin from slices.

3. Put yams and water in a large saucepan.

4. Bring mixture to a boil over high heat.

5. Reduce heat to a simmer. Cover and cook for 45 minutes or until yams are soft.

6. Drain off water. Put yams in a bowl.

7. Mash yams thoroughly and add salt and nutmeg.

8. Using a pestle or wooden mallet, pound the yams with hard strokes for about 10 minutes or until they form a sticky paste. (Dip pestle in cold water whenever it begins to stick.)

9. Put some water in a small bowl and set it beside a plate.

10. Sprinkle water on the plate and on your hands.

11. Scoop up about ¼ cup of yams. Roll it on the plate until it is a smooth ball.

12. Repeat with rest of yams, being sure to wet hands and plate each time.

13. Fufu may be served immediately, with meat or chicken dishes, or wrapped and refrigerated first.

Serves 6.

📖 **Library Link 2:** What are the features of yams?

SPICED OKRA

(West Africa)

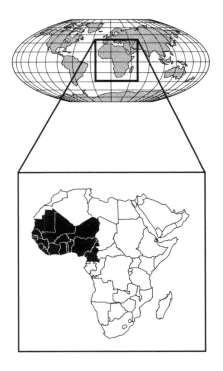

West Africa

INGREDIENTS

2 cups water

1½ tablespoons minced onions

½ teaspoon minced garlic

¼ teaspoon red cayenne pepper

½ teaspoon salt

¼ pound okra, washed, stemmed, and cut into large chunks

STEPS

1. Put the water, onions, garlic, red pepper, and salt in a medium, heavy saucepan.

2. Bring mixture to a boil over high heat.

3. Drop okra into boiling water.

4. Cook and stir for about 15 minutes or until okra is soft.

5. Pour mixture into a colander. Run cold water over it.

6. Let cool before serving.

Serves 3-4.

📖 **Library Link 3:** Research information about okra.

FISH AND SHRIMP STEW

(Mozambique)

INGREDIENTS

1 pound large shrimp

8 fish steaks (sea bass or snapper)

2 teaspoons salt

4 tablespoons olive oil

1 cup minced onions

2 green peppers

3 tomatoes, peeled and chopped

½ teaspoon red cayenne pepper

½ cup coconut milk

Mozambique

STEPS

1. Shell and devein shrimp.
2. Wash shrimp and pat dry.
3. Sprinkle fish steaks on both sides, using ½ to 1 teaspoon of the salt.
4. Put shrimp and fish on a plate. Cover with plastic wrap and refrigerate.
5. Heat oil over medium heat in a large, heavy skillet.
6. Add onions and peppers. Cook about 5 minutes or until soft.
7. Add tomatoes. Cook until most of the juice is gone.
8. Remove pan from heat. Stir in pepper and rest of salt.
9. Remove fish and shrimp from refrigerator.
10. Arrange 4 of the fish steaks in the bottom of a large saucepan.
11. Sprinkle half of the shrimp and half of the vegetable mixture over the fish.
12. Add the rest of the fish steaks. Then add the rest of the shrimp and vegetables.
13. Pour in the coconut milk. Simmer over low heat for 10-15 minutes or until fish flakes apart.
14. Serve hot.

Serves 4-6.

📖 **Library Link 4:** Research information about the coconut.

STEAMED PAPAYA

(East Africa)

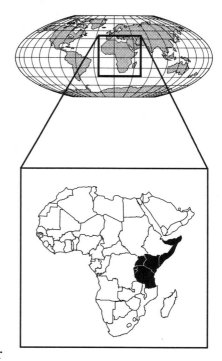

East Africa

INGREDIENTS

2 pounds slightly ripe papaya, peeled and cut into cubes

6 tablespoons butter

¼ teaspoon nutmeg

⅛ teaspoon cinnamon

¾ teaspoon salt

STEPS

1. Pour water into a steamer to within 1 inch of the steaming rack.
2. Spread papaya cubes on the rack. Bring water to a boil over medium heat.
3. Cover pan. Cook for 15-20 minutes or until papaya is soft.
4. Melt butter over medium heat in a large skillet.
5. Add papaya.
6. Stir in nutmeg, cinnamon, and salt.
7. Stir until papaya is well coated with spices.
8. Remove from heat. Serve hot.

Serves 6.

📖 **Library Link 5:** Research the history and nonfood uses of papaya.

KARKELINGE
(Figure Eight Cookies)
(South Africa)

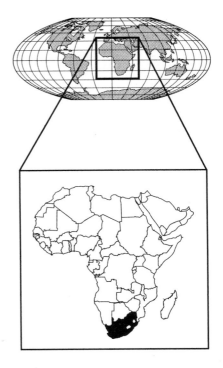

South Africa

INGREDIENTS

1½ cups flour

1 teaspoon baking powder

½ teaspoon cinnamon

⅛ teaspoon allspice

¼ teaspoon salt

1 stick butter, softened

1 cup sugar

1 egg, beaten

1 egg white beaten with 2 teaspoons water

½ cup almonds, chopped fine

STEPS

1. Mix flour, baking powder, cinnamon, allspice, and salt in a large mixing bowl.
2. Cream butter in a medium bowl.
3. Add ¾ cup sugar to butter. Mix well.
4. Stir in whole egg.
5. Add butter mixture to flour mixture.
6. Stir and knead mixture until dough is smooth.
7. Roll dough on floured board into a rectangle ¼-inch thick.
8. Cut dough into ½-inch-wide strips. Shape into cylinders.
9. Roll cylinders into figure eight shapes. Pinch ends together.
10. Brush egg white and water mixture over cookies.
11. Mix last ¼ cup sugar and almonds. Sprinkle over egg white.
12. Chill cookies in refrigerator for 30 minutes.
13. Bake in 400 degree oven for 10-12 minutes or until lightly browned.

Makes 10-15.

📖 **Library Link 6:** Research the word "cookie."

ANNOTATED BIBLIOGRAPHY

Aardema, Verna, reteller. *Bringing the Rain to Kapiti Plain: A Nandi Tale.* Illustrated by Beatriz Vidal. New York: Dial Books for Young Readers, 1981. Grades kindergarten and up.
   Ki-pat uses an eagle feather for an arrow that pierces the clouds, bringing rain to parched Kapiti Plain.

_____. *Traveling to Tondo: A Tale of the Nkundo of Zaire.* Illustrated by Will Hillenbrand. New York: Alfred A. Knopf, 1991. Grades 1 and up.
   Bowane, a civet cat, takes too long to return to his intended, losing her to another cat. The brief glossary and pronunciation guide are especially useful.

_____. *What's So Funny, Ketu? A Nuer Tale.* Illustrated by Marc Brown. New York: Dial Press, 1982. Grades kindergarten and up.
   A snake rewards Ketu's kindness with a secret gift of magic, hearing the animals' thoughts, which threatens everything Ketu loves.

_____. *Who's in Rabbit's House?* Illustrated by Leo and Diane Dillon. New York: Dial Press, 1977. Grades 1 and up.
   This Masai tale of rabbit, who is prevented from entering his house by the Long One, is perfect for dramatic interpretation.

_____. *Why Mosquitoes Buzz in People's Ears.* Illustrated by Leo and Diane Dillon. New York: Scholastic, 1975. Grades 2 and up.
   This West African cumulative tale explains why mosquitoes are swatted.

Abrahams, Roger D., reteller. *African Folktales: Traditional Stories of the Black World.* New York: Pantheon Books, 1983. Grades 4 and up.
   This collection includes tales of wonder, stories to discuss, trickster tales, tales of praise, and stories of life.

Alexander, Lloyd. *The Fortune-Tellers.* Illustrated by Trina Schart Hyman. New York: Dutton Children's Books, 1992. Grades kindergarten and up.
   In this richly illustrated tale set in Cameroon, a carpenter learns he will marry his true love and be happy if he avoids misery.

Appiah, Sonia. *Amoko and Efua Bear.* Illustrated by Carol Easmon. New York: Macmillan, 1988. Grades preschool and up.
   Amoko, a five-year-old girl who lives in Ghana, temporarily loses her beloved teddy bear.

Brown, Marcia, translator. *Shadow.* New York: Aladdin Books, 1982. Grades 2 and up.
   Shadow appears everywhere: in nature, in a mask, with man.

Bryan, Ashley. *Beat the Story-Drum, Pum-Pum.* New York: Atheneum, 1980. Grades 1 and up.
   Five African tales are illustrated with striking woodcuts.

Case, Dianne. *Love, David.* Illustrated by Dan Andreasen. New York: Lodestar Books, 1991. Grades 4 and up.
   The harsh realities of life in South Africa are portrayed through the day-to-day lives of Anna and her beloved half-brother, David.

Dee, Ruby, reteller. *Tower to Heaven*. Illustrated by Jennifer Bent. New York: Henry Holt, 1991. Grades 1 and up.
Onyankopon, the sky god, gets tired of Yaa and returns to the sky. When the villagers build a tower to heaven out of mortars, the tower is one mortar short.

Dobkins, Lucy M. *Daddy, There's a Hippo in the Grapes*. Illustrated by Kirk Botero. Gretna, LA: Pelican, 1992. Grades 3 and up.
Twelve-year-old Ibrahim has the responsibility of keeping animals from eating the garden that supplies the family's only income. When animals from a Kenyan game preserve begin to invade, he has to convince the adults of the real problem.

Feelings, Muriel. *Jambo Means Hello: Swahili Alphabet Book*. Illustrated by Tom Feelings. New York: Dial Books for Young Readers, 1974. Grades 1 and up.
The simple text explains the letters of the Swahili alphabet.

_____. *Moja Means One: Swahili Counting Book*. Illustrated by Tom Feelings. New York: Dial Press, 1971. Grades preschool and up.
Children not only can learn to count in Swahili but also can explore Eastern African life.

French, Fiona. *Anancy and Mr. Dry-Bone*. Boston: Little, Brown, 1991. Grades preschool and up.
Both Anancy and Mr. Dry-Bone use humor to win Miss Louise's hand in marriage.

Gray, Nigel. *A Balloon for Grandad*. Illustrated by Jane Ray. New York: Orchard Books, 1988. Grades preschool and up.
When Sam's balloon floats away, he hopes it will fly to Grandad Abdulla's home across the sea.

Grifalconi, Ann. *Darkness and the Butterfly*. Boston: Little, Brown, 1987. Grades kindergarten and up.
In this tale from Cameroon, Osa's fear of the dark is diminished when the Wise Woman shares that the butterfly flies in the dark.

_____. *The People Could Fly: American Black Folktales*. Illustrated by Leo and Diane Dillon. New York: Alfred A. Knopf, 1985. Grades 4 and up.
This collection includes tales of animals, the supernatural, freedom, and the real, the extravagant, and the fanciful.

_____. *The Village of Round and Square Houses*. Boston: Little, Brown, 1986. Grades kindergarten and up.
A child from Cameroon relates why the village has round houses for women and square houses for men.

Isadora, Rachel. *The Crossroads*. New York: Greenwillow Books, 1991. Grades 1 and up.
In South Africa, everyone rejoices when the fathers return from the mines.

_____. *Over the Green Hills*. New York: Greenwillow Books, 1992. Grades kindergarten and up.
As Zolani and his mother cross the Transkei countryside, the reader learns about the beautiful country of South Africa.

Knutson, Barbara, reteller. *How the Guinea Fowl Got Her Spots: A Swahili Tale of Friendship*. Minneapolis, MN: Carolrhoda Books, 1990. Grades kindergarten and up.
After Guinea Fowl saves Cow's life, Cow gives a gift of life to Guinea Fowl.

_____. *Why the Crab Has No Head*. Minneapolis, MN: Carolrhoda Books, 1987. Grades kindergarten and up.
The crab brags about the head it will receive and is punished with having to see from eyes on its body.

Lester, Julius. *How Many Spots Does a Leopard Have? And Other Tales*. Illustrated by David Shannon. New York: Scholastic, 1989. Grades 2 and up.
Ten African and two Jewish tales explain, inspire, and caution readers. Illustrations are bold and rich.

Lewin, Hugh. *Jafta—The Journey*. Illustrated by Lisa Kopper. Minneapolis, MN: Carolrhoda Books, 1984. Grades preschool and up.
Jafta journeys from his rural South African village to the town where his father works in the factory.

Lottridge, Celia Barker, reteller. *The Name of the Tree*. Illustrated by Ian Wallace. New York: Margaret K. McElderry Books, 1989. Grades 1 and up.
In this Bantu tale, various animals try to learn the name of the tree that will save them during a drought.

Maartens, Maretha. *Paperbird*. New York: Clarion Books, 1989. Grades 4 and up.
Adam's job selling newspapers in a nearby city supports his entire family. When political conflict, newborn twins, and Adam's illness threaten to consume the family's meager resources, friends provide support.

Mennen, Ingrid, and Niki Daly. *Somewhere in Africa*. Illustrated by Nicolaas Maritz. New York: Dutton Children's Books, 1990. Grades preschool and up.
Ashraf, who lives in the city, ponders the lions, crocodiles, and zebras that he reads about in a library book.

Mollel, Tololwa M. *The Orphan Boy*. Illustrated by Paul Morin. New York: Clarion Books, 1990. Grades 2 and up.
Venus is embodied in a young boy who comes to earth to help an old man in this African story.

Williams, Karen Lynn. *When Africa Was Home*. Illustrated by Floyd Cooper. New York: Orchard Books, 1991. Grades 1 and up.
Peter, a young white boy, loves living in an African village while his dad works there and misses his friends and the country when he must return to America.

VIDEOS

Kenya Safari: Essence of Africa. Society for Visual Education. 45 minutes. Grades 4 and up.
Travel from a game reserve to a Masai village to a plantation.

Mandela: Free at Last. Society for Visual Education. 79 minutes. Grades 6 and up.
Produced by JCI Video, this includes footage smuggled out of South Africa, interviews, and Mandela's first speech upon his release from prison.

Oh Kojo! How Could You! Society for Visual Education. 18 minutes. Grades 3 and up.
In Marc Brown's version of this Ashanti folktale, a young boy outwits a wily trickster.

Sub-Saharan Africa: The Land. Society for Visual Education, 1991. 13.30 minutes each. Grades 4 and up.
Titles include "Africa's Geography and Climate," "The African People: Past and Present," "Africa's Natural Resources," and "Africa's Changing Occupations." Skill sheets available.

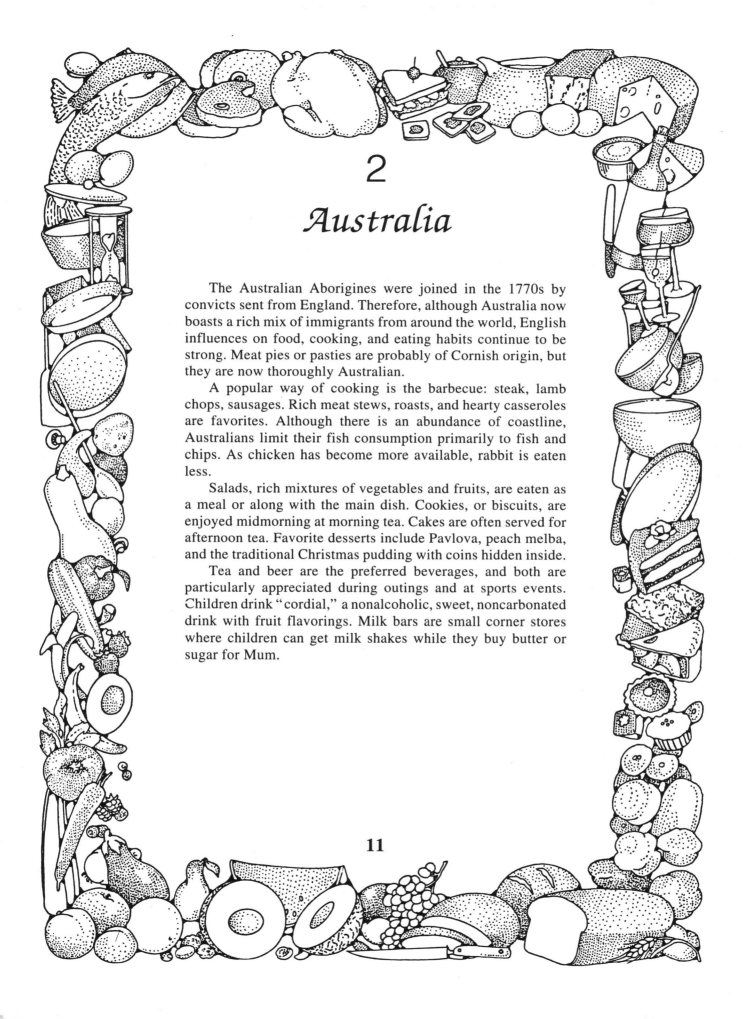

2

Australia

The Australian Aborigines were joined in the 1770s by convicts sent from England. Therefore, although Australia now boasts a rich mix of immigrants from around the world, English influences on food, cooking, and eating habits continue to be strong. Meat pies or pasties are probably of Cornish origin, but they are now thoroughly Australian.

A popular way of cooking is the barbecue: steak, lamb chops, sausages. Rich meat stews, roasts, and hearty casseroles are favorites. Although there is an abundance of coastline, Australians limit their fish consumption primarily to fish and chips. As chicken has become more available, rabbit is eaten less.

Salads, rich mixtures of vegetables and fruits, are eaten as a meal or along with the main dish. Cookies, or biscuits, are enjoyed midmorning at morning tea. Cakes are often served for afternoon tea. Favorite desserts include Pavlova, peach melba, and the traditional Christmas pudding with coins hidden inside.

Tea and beer are the preferred beverages, and both are particularly appreciated during outings and at sports events. Children drink "cordial," a nonalcoholic, sweet, noncarbonated drink with fruit flavorings. Milk bars are small corner stores where children can get milk shakes while they buy butter or sugar for Mum.

DAMPER BREAD

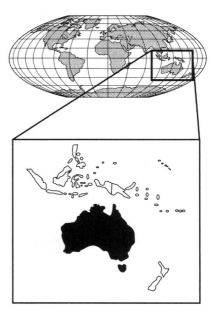

Australia

INGREDIENTS

2¼ cups flour

2 teaspoons baking powder

½ teaspoon salt

¾ cup buttermilk

2 eggs, beaten

3 tablespoons butter, melted

STEPS

1. Put flour, baking powder, and salt in a mixing bowl. Stir well.

2. Stir in buttermilk, eggs, and butter.

3. Pour batter into a greased loaf pan.

4. Bake in a 350-degree oven for 45 minutes or until top is browned and toothpick comes out clean.

5. Remove loaf from pan. Cool and cut into slices.

Serves 6-8.

📖 **Library Link 1:** Research how damper bread is cooked in the Outback.

KANGAROO TAIL SOUP

INGREDIENTS

2½ tablespoons butter

2 large onions, sliced

4 carrots, peeled and sliced

2 potatoes, peeled and sliced

3 celery stalks, sliced

1 kangaroo tail, skinned and cut into large chunks

5 pints beef stock

4 tablespoons barley, washed

2 bay leaves

1 whole nutmeg

Salt and pepper to taste

1 tablespoon Worcestershire sauce

Chopped parsley

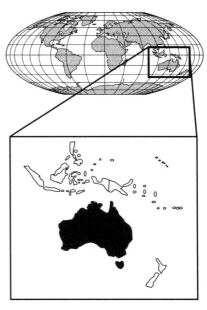

Australia

STEPS

1. Melt butter in a large saucepan over medium-high heat.
2. Add onions, carrots, potatoes, and celery. Fry for 10 minutes or until browned.
3. Add tail, stock, barley, bay leaves, and nutmeg. Bring to a boil.
4. Reduce heat. Cover pan and simmer for 3 hours.
5. Remove from heat and cool.
6. Skim fat from soup.
7. Strain soup.
8. Rinse pan and return soup to it.
9. Sprinkle with salt and pepper. Add Worcestershire sauce.
10. Bring soup to a boil.
11. Remove from heat. Pour into bowls and sprinkle with parsley.

Serves 6.

📖 **Library Link 2:** Research which kangaroo species are protected and why some kangaroos are considered pests.

Note: To purchase kangaroo tail, look in the Yellow Pages for a supplier of exotic meats or contact Dale's Exotic Game Meats, 1961 W. 64th Ave., Denver, CO 80221; 800-BUY-WILD.

From *Cooking Up World History*. Copyright © 1994. Teacher Ideas Press, P.O. Box 6633, Englewood, CO 80155-6633.

PINEAPPLE CABBAGE SALAD

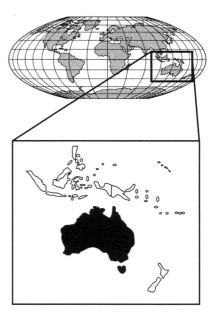

Australia

INGREDIENTS

1 pineapple, peeled, cored, and cubed

1 grapefruit, peeled and cut into segments

1 orange, peeled and cut into segments

½ medium cabbage, shredded

½ cucumber, peeled and sliced

8 ounces cooked ham, cut into cubes

Grated rind of ½ lemon

4 tablespoons oil

2 tablespoons vinegar

2 tablespoons mayonnaise

2 tablespoons cream

Salt and sugar to taste

STEPS

1. Put all fruit, vegetables, and ham in a large bowl. Mix together.
2. Put grated lemon, oil, vinegar, mayonnaise, cream, salt, and sugar in a small bowl. Mix well.
3. Pour the dressing mixture over the salad. Stir gently to combine.
4. Chill in refrigerator before serving.

Serves 4-6.

📖 **Library Link 3:** Research challenges with rabbits in Australia: population, crop damage, and so forth.

CARPETBAGGER STEAK

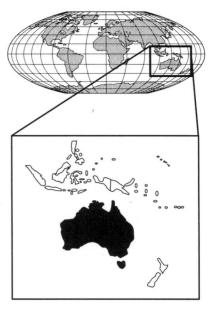

Australia

INGREDIENTS

4 thick steak fillets

Salt and pepper

1 tablespoon minced shallots

8 raw oysters

Melted butter

2 tablespoons fresh, chopped parsley

STEPS

1. Use a knife to cut a horizontal slit in each steak fillet to make a pocket. Don't cut it all the way through.

2. Sprinkle salt, pepper, and shallots in the pocket of each fillet.

3. Put 2 oysters in each pocket.

4. Use skewers to close the pockets.

5. Preheat a grill to high.

6. Brush each fillet with melted butter. Sprinkle with more pepper.

7. Grill fillets until cooked as you like them, 3-6 minutes on each side.

8. Brush with more melted butter when you turn fillets.

9. Sprinkle with parsley. Serve hot.

Serves 4.

📖 **Library Link 4:** Research why the English sent convicts to Australia.

CRAB AND ASPARAGUS

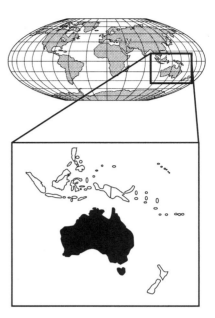

Australia

INGREDIENTS

3 teaspoons butter

⅓ cup onion, chopped

¼ cup celery, chopped

2 tablespoons carrot, minced finely

1 clove garlic, minced finely

1 tablespoon flour

2 cups light cream

1 bay leaf

½ teaspoon salt

1 teaspoon Worcestershire sauce

⅛ teaspoon pepper

¼ teaspoon thyme

4 ounces crab meat

⅔ cup sliced asparagus spears

STEPS

1. Put butter in a saucepan over medium-high heat.
2. Add onion, celery, carrot, and garlic. Cook about 3 minutes until vegetables are soft.
3. Stir in flour.
4. When flour mixture bubbles, slowly stir in cream.
5. Stir and cook until sauce is smooth and thickened.
6. Stir in bay leaf, salt, Worcestershire sauce, pepper, and thyme.
7. Reduce heat to low. Add crab and asparagus.
8. Cover pan and simmer about 25 minutes or until vegetables are tender.
9. Remove bay leaf. Serve hot.

Serves 2-4.

📖 **Library Link 5:** Research Australia's Aborigines.

PAVLOVA

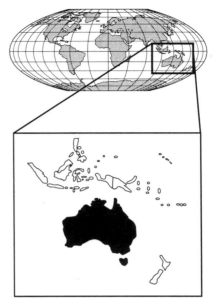

Australia

INGREDIENTS

4 large egg whites at room temperature

½ teaspoon salt

1 cup sugar

2 teaspoons cornstarch

2 teaspoons vinegar

2 bananas, peeled and sliced

2 kiwi fruit, peeled and sliced

10 ounces heavy cream, whipped

STEPS

1. Beat egg whites in a large mixing bowl until foamy.
2. Add salt. Continue to beat until egg whites form stiff peaks.
3. Gradually add sugar, beating well after each addition.
4. Combine cornstarch with vinegar. Gently fold it into egg whites.
5. Grease an 8-inch round cake pan. Cover the bottom with waxed paper. Grease waxed paper also.
6. Pour egg white mixture into pan. Smooth out toward edges. Make indentation in the center.
7. Put pan into a 300-degree oven. Reduce heat to 250 degrees.
8. Bake for 1 hour and 15 minutes.
9. Remove the meringue from the oven. Let it cool in the pan.
10. Carefully remove meringue from the pan. Place it on a serving dish.
11. Place sliced fruit carefully in center.
12. Cover with whipped cream and serve.

Serves 6.

📖 **Library Link 6:** Research the animals native to Australia.

ANNOTATED BIBLIOGRAPHY

Barbalet, Margaret. *The Wolf*. Illustrated by Jane Tanner. New York: Macmillan, 1992. Grades 1 and up.
  Tal and his family cope with an ongoing nightmare, the threat of a howling wolf. Finally, Tal overcomes his fears through acceptance of the wolf.

Beatty, Patricia. *Jonathan Down Under*. New York: William Morrow, 1982. Grades 5 and up.
  Jonathan and his father change from a ship bound to China to a ship full of hopeful gold miners heading to Australia.

Cox, David. *Bossyboots*. New York: Crown, 1985. Grades preschool and up.
  Abigail's bossiness comes to the rescue when a stagecoach is being robbed.

Fox, Mem. *Possum Magic*. Nashville, TN: Abingdon Press, 1987. Grades preschool and up.
  Grandma Poss makes Hush invisible, but she struggles to make him visible again.

Klein, Robin. *All in the Blue Unclouded Weather*. New York: Viking, 1991. Grades 4 and up.
  Four sisters enjoy the Australian summer during the late 1940s.

_____. *Tearaways*. New York: Viking, 1990. Grades 5 and up.
  This collection of short stories, peopled with interesting, sinister, and clever characters, is excellent for reading aloud.

Park, Ruth. *Playing Beatie Bow*. New York: Atheneum, 1982. Grades 6 and up.
  While Abigail deals with family difficulties in the present, she discovers life and love from 100 years ago.

Pople, Maureen. *The Other Side of Family*. New York: Henry Holt, 1986. Grades 5 and up.
  Until World War II ends, Kate must stay with relatives in Australia where she makes surprising discoveries about her family.

Roughsey, Dick. *The Rainbow Serpent*. Milwaukee, WI: Gareth Stevens, 1975. Grades kindergarten and up.
  This creation story features Goorialla, a huge rainbow serpent.

Thiele, Colin. *Shadow Shark*. New York: HarperCollins, 1985. Grades 5 and up.
  Joe is living with his cousin on an island off southern Australia when they join fishermen in pursuit of a huge shark.

Trezise, Percy, and Mary Haginikitas. *Black Duck and Water Rat*. Milwaukee, WI: Gareth Stevens, 1988. Grades kindergarten and up.
  When Water Rat takes Black Duck for his wife, their children are two strange creatures, the platypuses.

Trezise, Percy, and Dick Roughsey. *Gidja the Moon*. Milwaukee, WI: Gareth Stevens, 1988. Grades kindergarten and up.
  This tale explains the moon's origin and its role in the world.

Trezise, Percy. *The Peopling of Australia*. Milwaukee, WI: Gareth Stevens, 1987. Grades kindergarten and up.
  The development of the ancient civilization of the Aborigines is explored in art and simple text.

Trezise, Percy, and Dick Roughsey. *Turramulli the Giant Quinkin*. Milwaukee, WI: Gareth Stevens, 1982. Grades 1 and up.
  This is an Aboriginal myth about a family that is pursued by the fierce Turramulli.

Vaughan, Marcia D. *Wombat Stew*. Illustrated by Pamela Lofts. Englewood Cliffs, NJ: Silver Burdett Press, 1984. Grades preschool and up.

In this rollicking tale, the animals outsmart a dingo that is trying to make stew from a captured wombat.

Wrightson, Patricia. *Moon Dark*. New York: Margaret K. McElderry Books, 1987. Grades 5 and up.

This is the story of the effect settlers have on a community of animals: kangaroos, bush rats, bandicoots, goanna, possums, fly foxes, and a dog.

_____. *The Nargun and the Stars*. New York: Atheneum, 1974. Grades 5 and up.

Young orphan Simon must live with relatives on a sheep farm in northern Australia, where he is challenged by the country's spirits.

_____. *An Older Kind of Magic*. Illustrated by Noela Young. San Diego, CA: Harcourt Brace Jovanovich, 1972. Grades 4 and up.

Three children encounter fantasy and magic when they try to save the botanical gardens from being turned into a parking lot.

VIDEOS

Australia: The Land and People. Filmfair Communications, 1983. 20 minutes. Grades kindergarten and up.

This video depicts the Australian society as ready to tackle new ventures.

Australia's Animal Wonders. National Geographic Society, 1983. 15 minutes. Grades kindergarten and up.

A look at the birds, mammals, and reptiles unique to Australia.

The Greedy Frog. Churchill Films, 1989. 9 minutes. Grades kindergarten and up.

An animated Australian Aboriginal folktale about a frog who drinks all the water while the other animals try to get it back.

Where the Forest Meets the Sea. Films, Inc., 1988. 7 minutes. Grades kindergarten and up.

An animated journey through the Diantree Tropical Rainforest, by Jeannie Baker.

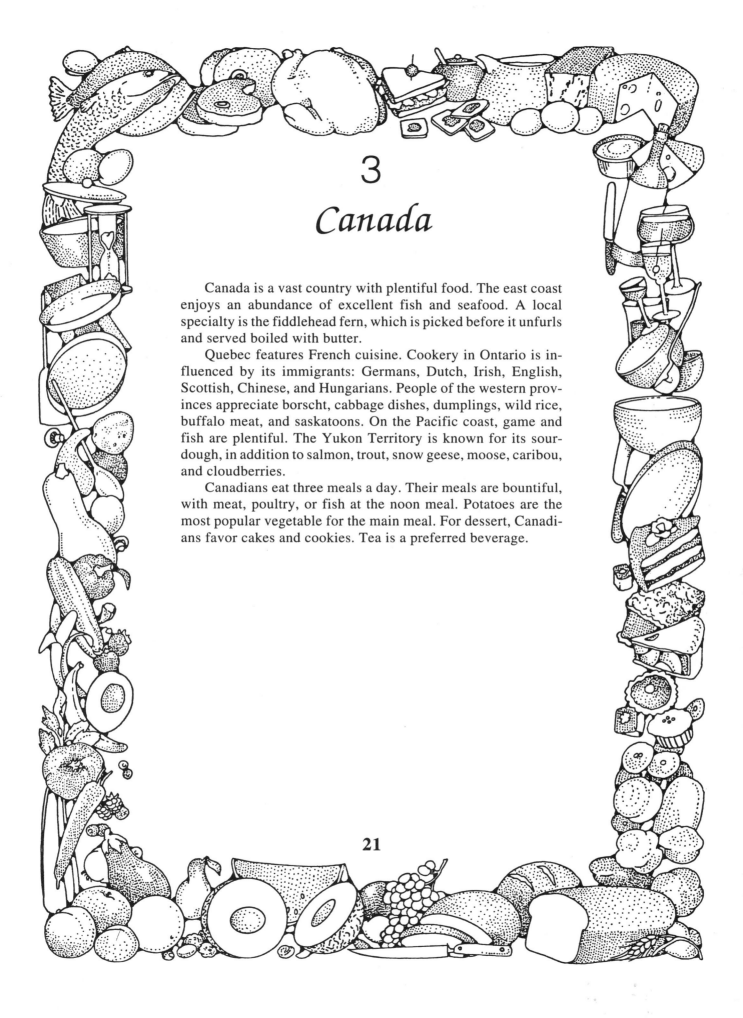

3

Canada

Canada is a vast country with plentiful food. The east coast enjoys an abundance of excellent fish and seafood. A local specialty is the fiddlehead fern, which is picked before it unfurls and served boiled with butter.

Quebec features French cuisine. Cookery in Ontario is influenced by its immigrants: Germans, Dutch, Irish, English, Scottish, Chinese, and Hungarians. People of the western provinces appreciate borscht, cabbage dishes, dumplings, wild rice, buffalo meat, and saskatoons. On the Pacific coast, game and fish are plentiful. The Yukon Territory is known for its sourdough, in addition to salmon, trout, snow geese, moose, caribou, and cloudberries.

Canadians eat three meals a day. Their meals are bountiful, with meat, poultry, or fish at the noon meal. Potatoes are the most popular vegetable for the main meal. For dessert, Canadians favor cakes and cookies. Tea is a preferred beverage.

HABITANT PEA SOUP

INGREDIENTS

1 pound yellow split peas

Water

1 large onion, sliced thinly

1 pound salt pork

½ teaspoon celery salt

½ teaspoon savory

¼ teaspoon thyme

1 tablespoon chopped parsley

3½ pints water

Salt and pepper to taste

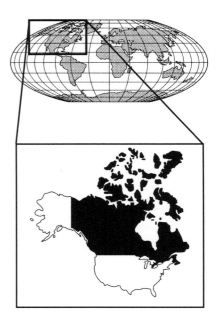

Canada

STEPS

1. Put peas in a large pan. Cover with water and soak overnight.

2. Drain peas. Put in a 4½-quart casserole dish or soup kettle.

3. Add onion, salt pork, celery salt, savory, thyme, parsley, and 3½ pints water.

4. Bring to a boil over high heat.

5. Cover. Reduce and simmer for 3 hours.

6. Add salt and pepper to taste.

7. Serve hot.

Serves 6-8.

📖 **Library Link 1:** Research peas.

CANADIAN PASTRY

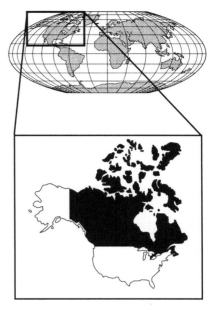

Canada

INGREDIENTS

⅔ cup plus 2 tablespoons shortening, softened

2 cups flour

1 teaspoon salt

3-4 tablespoons cold water

1 egg yolk, beaten

STEPS

1. Put shortening in a large bowl.

2. Mix flour and salt. Cut into shortening.

3. Using a fork, stir in water slowly until a soft dough forms. Work with dough as little as possible.

4. Wrap dough in plastic wrap to keep from drying out.

5. When ready to use dough, roll out onto floured board.

6. Brush dough with egg yolk before baking.

Makes 1 double crust pastry.

Library Link 2: What countries have most influenced Canadian cookery? Research other dishes they have inspired.

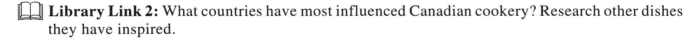

TOURTIÈRE
(Canadian Pork Pie)

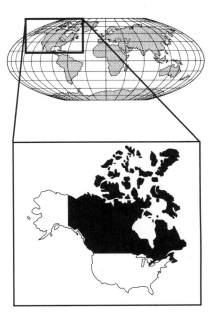

Canada

INGREDIENTS

1 pound ground pork

½ pound ground beef

1 onion, chopped

2 cloves garlic, minced finely

½ cup water

2 teaspoons salt

½ teaspoon thyme

¼ teaspoon sage

½ teaspoon pepper

¼ teaspoon cloves

Canadian pastry (see recipe on page 23)

STEPS

1. Put all ingredients except pastry in a large saucepan over medium-high heat.
2. Bring to a boil. Cook 5-7 minutes or until meat is browned.
3. Heat oven to 425 degrees.
4. Divide Canadian pastry in half.
5. Roll one piece out onto a floured board about 1½ inches wider than a pie pan.
6. Put dough in pie pan.
7. Pour meat mixture into crust in pan.
8. Roll other piece of dough onto a floured board 1½ inches wider than pie pan.
9. Put dough on top of meat filling.
10. Fold top crust edge over bottom edge and pinch all around.
11. Cut a few slits in top.
12. Brush top crust with egg yolk. Bake 10 minutes.
13. Reduce oven to 350 degrees. Bake for 25 minutes more or until crust is golden brown.
14. Let stand 10 minutes before cutting and serving.

Serves 6-8.

📖 **Library Link 3:** A tourtière is also a name for a pie dish for making *tourtes*. Research sweet *tourtes*.

BEEF DAUBE

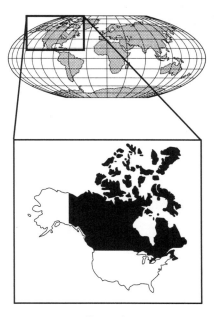

Canada

INGREDIENTS

1 cup dried beans, northern or navy

Water

2 tablespoons oil

1 onion, chopped

2 pounds beef round steak, cut into cubes

1 tablespoon flour

2 tablespoons tomato paste

1⅓ cups beef broth

2 teaspoons red vinegar

1 bay leaf

¼ teaspoon thyme

1 teaspoon salt

¼ teaspoon pepper

STEPS

1. Put beans in medium pot. Cover with water and soak overnight.
2. Put oil in large stovetop casserole over medium-high heat.
3. Add onion. Cook until soft.
4. Add beef. Cook until browned.
5. Sprinkle flour over beef. Stir and cook for 3 minutes.
6. Stir in tomato paste, broth, vinegar, bay leaf, thyme, salt, and pepper.
7. Bring to a boil.
8. Add beans and soaking water to meat mixture.
9. Cover and put into a 400-degree oven.
10. Bake about 1 hour or until beef and beans are tender.
11. Remove bay leaf. Serve hot.

Serves 4-6.

📖 **Library Link 4:** Native Canadians include the Huron and Iroquois Indians. What foods did they prefer before colonial times?

PRINCE EDWARD ISLAND WARM POTATO SALAD

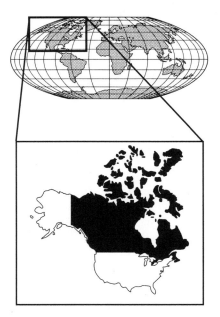

Canada

INGREDIENTS

8 medium potatoes

8 slices bacon

2 stalks celery, sliced

1 onion, sliced

½ teaspoon celery seed

¾ cup vinegar

¼ teaspoon prepared mustard

1½ teaspoons salt

½ teaspoon pepper

3 tablespoons chopped parsley

STEPS

1. Put unpeeled potatoes in large saucepan. Cover with water.
2. Bring to a boil over high heat.
3. Reduce heat. Simmer until potatoes are tender but still firm.
4. Drain well. Let potatoes cool.
5. Peel potatoes. Slice into 1-inch-thick slices. Set aside.
6. Put bacon in a large skillet over medium-high heat. Fry until crisp.
7. Drain bacon slices on paper towels. Keep grease in pan.
8. Put potatoes in a large bowl.
9. Crumble bacon and add to potatoes.
10. Add celery, onion, and celery seed. Toss lightly.
11. Add vinegar, mustard, salt, and pepper to bacon grease in skillet.
12. Heat through over medium heat.
13. Pour over potato mixture. Toss well.
14. Sprinkle with parsley. Serve warm.

Serves 6-8.

📖 **Library Link 5:** Find Prince Edward Island on a map. What provinces are nearby?

BLUEBERRY CRISP

INGREDIENTS

4 cups blueberries

2 tablespoons lemon juice

¼ cup brown sugar

¼ cup white sugar

2 teaspoons cornstarch

⅔ cup oats

½ cup flour

½ cup brown sugar

⅛ teaspoon salt

½ cup butter, softened

Vanilla ice cream, optional

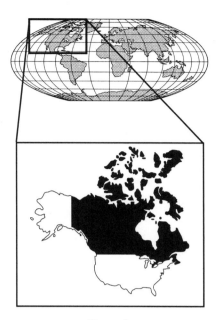

Canada

STEPS

1. Put blueberries in a large bowl. Add lemon juice and toss lightly.

2. Mix in ¼ cup brown and ¼ cup white sugar and cornstarch.

3. Pour into a 1½-quart casserole dish.

4. Put oats, flour, ½ cup brown sugar, and salt in a medium bowl. Stir well.

5. Cut in butter with a fork.

6. Sprinkle mixture over blueberries.

7. Bake in a 350-degree oven for 35-45 minutes or until mixture is brown.

8. Serve warm, with or without ice cream on top.

Serves 6.

📖 **Library Link 6:** Research saskatoons.

From *Cooking Up World History*. Copyright © 1994. Teacher Ideas Press, P.O. Box 6633, Englewood, CO 80155-6633.

ANNOTATED BIBLIOGRAPHY

Andrews, Jan. *Very Last First Time*. Illustrated by Ian Wallace. New York: Atheneum, 1985. Grades kindergarten and up.
Eva collects mussels on the sea ice while the tide is out and decides it will be her last *first* time for such an adventure.

Blades, Ann. *Mary of Mile 18*. Montreal: Tundra Books, 1971. Grades kindergarten and up.
Mary's life in Canada is routine until a wolf pup appears at her home.

Buchanan, Dawna Lisa. *The Falcon's Wing*. New York: Orchard Books, 1992. Grades 4 and up.
Bryn has many new adjustments: her mother's death, moving to her aunt's farm in Canada, her mentally retarded cousin, a new school, and becoming a young woman.

Holling, Holling Clancy. *Paddle-to-the-Sea*. Boston: Houghton Mifflin, 1941. Grades 3 and up.
Paddle, a carved figure of an Indian, is set on a journey through the Great Lakes and down the Saint Lawrence River to the Atlantic Ocean.

Moak, Allan. *Big City ABC*. Montreal: Tundra Books, 1984. Grades preschool and up.
This brightly illustrated book takes the reader on a tour of Toronto.

Norman, Howard. *The Owl-Scatterer*. Illustrated by Michael McCurdy. Boston: Atlantic Monthly Press, 1986. Grades 1 and up.
When the village of Big Footprint Lake has too many owls, an old hermit must scatter them.

Speare, Jean. *A Candle for Christmas*. Illustrated by Ann Blades. New York: Margaret K. McElderry Books, 1986. Grades preschool and up.
It is Christmas Eve in the Canadian Northwest, and Tomas anxiously awaits the return of his parents.

Tanobe, Miyuki. *Quebec: I Love You*. Montreal: Tundra Books, 1976. Grades 2 and up.
Tanobe's lush color illustrations and text in English and French describe her delight in discovering the people and culture of French Canada.

Ward, Lynn. *The Biggest Bear*. Boston: Houghton Mifflin, 1952. Grades preschool and up.
Though Johnny's bear has grown too big and mischievous to keep, every effort to make him return to the wild fails. When the bear is captured in a trap, Johnny realizes that the zoo is a fine place for his friend.

VIDEOS

Canada: Portrait of a Nation. Society for Visual Education, 1992. 2 videos, 38 minutes each. Grades 4 and up.
    Learn about the challenges Canadians face, their resources, and the culture. Skill sheets available.

Canadians: Their Cities. Encyclopedia Britannica, 1974. 16 minutes. Grades 4 and up.
    Canadians discuss what life is like in different cities.

Canadians: Their Land. Encyclopedia Britannica, 1974. 16 minutes. Grades 4 and up.
    Canadians discuss what life is like in different areas of Canada.

The Cap. Beacon Films. 26 minutes. Grades 2 and up.
    When Steve loses his cap signed by a Montreal Expos star, it is found in the possession of a wealthy man's son. Steve is disappointed when his father accepts $100 for the cap.

One's a Heifer. Beacon Films. 26 minutes. Grades 2 and up.
    Peter, a farm boy living on the Canadian plains, searches for his missing calves.

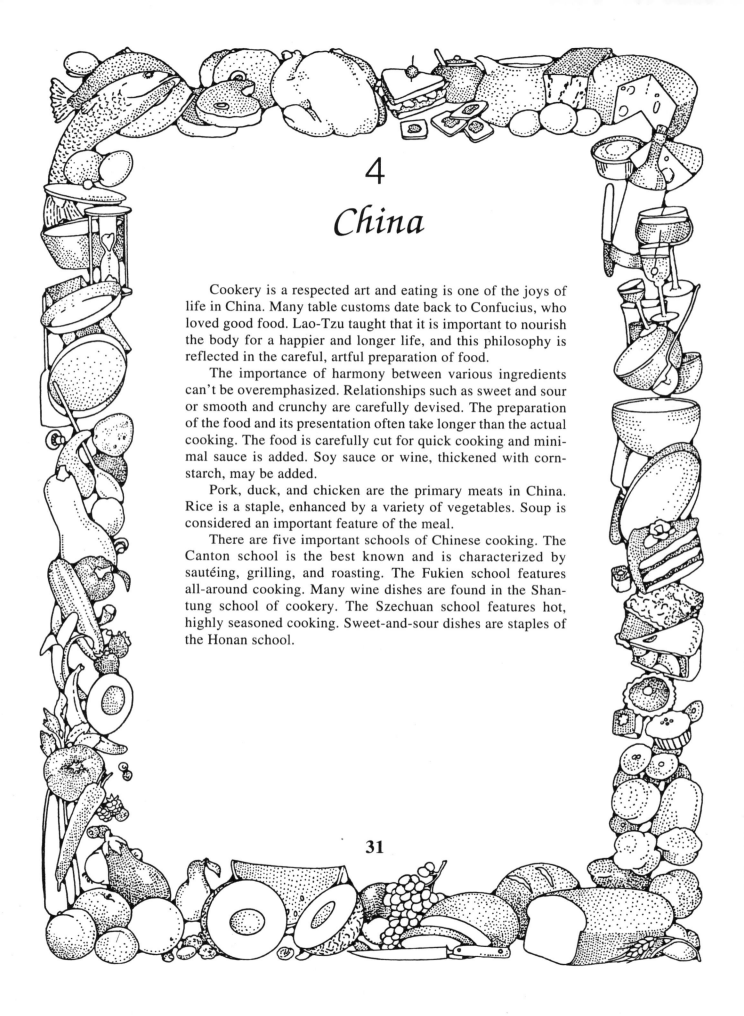

4

China

Cookery is a respected art and eating is one of the joys of life in China. Many table customs date back to Confucius, who loved good food. Lao-Tzu taught that it is important to nourish the body for a happier and longer life, and this philosophy is reflected in the careful, artful preparation of food.

The importance of harmony between various ingredients can't be overemphasized. Relationships such as sweet and sour or smooth and crunchy are carefully devised. The preparation of the food and its presentation often take longer than the actual cooking. The food is carefully cut for quick cooking and minimal sauce is added. Soy sauce or wine, thickened with cornstarch, may be added.

Pork, duck, and chicken are the primary meats in China. Rice is a staple, enhanced by a variety of vegetables. Soup is considered an important feature of the meal.

There are five important schools of Chinese cooking. The Canton school is the best known and is characterized by sautéing, grilling, and roasting. The Fukien school features all-around cooking. Many wine dishes are found in the Shantung school of cookery. The Szechuan school features hot, highly seasoned cooking. Sweet-and-sour dishes are staples of the Honan school.

CRABMEAT PUFFS

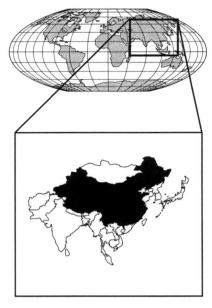

China

INGREDIENTS

6 ounces crabmeat

6 ounces cream cheese, softened

½ teaspoon salt

⅛ teaspoon garlic salt

40 wonton skins

1 egg, beaten

Vegetable oil

Cooking thermometer

STEPS

1. Chop crabmeat.
2. Mix crabmeat, cream cheese, salt, and garlic salt in a bowl.
3. Brush a wonton skin with some of the egg.
4. Place a teaspoonful of crab mixture in center of wonton skin.
5. Top with another wonton skin. Press edges to seal.
6. Brush egg on center of each side of wonton puff.
7. Pinch each of the 4 sides.
8. Put 1½ inches of oil in a wok. Heat to 350 degrees on a cooking thermometer.
9. Fry puffs in oil until golden brown on both sides.
10. Drain on paper towels.
11. Repeat until all puffs are made. Keep puffs covered with plastic wrap to keep from drying out.
12. Serve with sweet-and-sour sauce.

Serves 8.

📖 **Library Link 1:** Research the role of religion in Chinese cookery.

EGG DROP SOUP

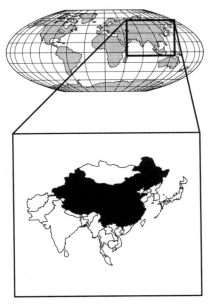

China

INGREDIENTS

2 10½-ounce cans chicken broth

2 eggs, well beaten

5 spinach leaves

STEPS

1. Put chicken broth in a medium saucepan.

2. Cook over medium-high heat until it boils.

3. Dribble egg slowly into boiling broth while stirring constantly.

4. Slice spinach into strips.

5. Add spinach. Heat thoroughly.

6. Serve hot.

Serves 4.

📖 **Library Link 2:** Research Chinese 100-year eggs.

FU JUNG TAN

(Egg Fu Jung)

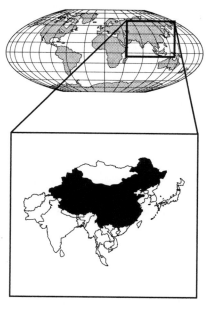

China

INGREDIENTS

6 dried mushrooms

5 tablespoons peanut or corn oil

⅓ cup bamboo shoots cut in strips

½ cup roast pork cut in strips

1¾ cups bean sprouts

1 scallion, finely chopped

6 large eggs

1½ teaspoons salt

Dash pepper

½ teaspoon sesame oil

STEPS

1. Soak mushrooms in ½ cup warm water until soft.
2. Drain off the water. Chop the mushrooms finely.
3. Heat 2 tablespoons of the peanut or corn oil in a wok over high heat.
4. Stir in mushrooms, bamboo shoots, pork, bean sprouts, and scallion.
5. Cook and stir for 2 minutes.
6. Remove pork mixture from wok. Put in a large bowl.
7. Beat eggs well. Stir into pork mixture.
8. Add rest of the ingredients. Stir well.
9. Heat wok until very hot. Add 3 tablespoons peanut or corn oil.
10. Pour mixture into the wok.
11. Push mixture around the sides of the wok. Flip and turn them so the outside is brown and the inside is soft.
12. Serve hot.

Serves 4.

📖 **Library Link 3:** Research what might be served at a large Chinese banquet.

SZECHUAN PORK

INGREDIENTS

1 pound boneless pork, cut into strips (across the grain)

2 teaspoons cornstarch

½ teaspoon salt

½ teaspoon sugar

Dash pepper

2 green onions

1 green bell pepper

1 red bell pepper

8 ounces sliced bamboo shoots

2 tablespoons vegetable oil

2½ teaspoons garlic, chopped finely

1 teaspoon ginger root, chopped finely

2 teaspoons chili paste

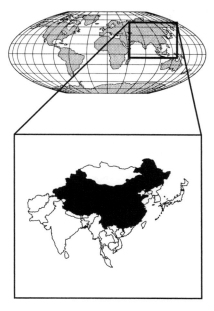

China

STEPS

1. Put pork, cornstarch, salt, sugar, and pepper in medium bowl. Stir well.
2. Cover bowl. Put in refrigerator for 30 minutes.
3. Cut green onions diagonally into 2-inch pieces.
4. Cut both peppers and bamboo shoots into ⅛-inch strips.
5. Heat wok until very hot.
6. Add oil.
7. Add pork, garlic, and ginger root. Stir for 2 minutes or until pork is no longer pink.
8. Add peppers and bamboo shoots. Cook 1 more minute.
9. Stir in green onions and chili paste.
10. Serve hot. May serve over rice.

Serves 4.

📖 **Library Link 4:** What do pigs symbolize in China?

HUO TUI TAN CH'AO FAN
(Ham and Egg Fried Rice)

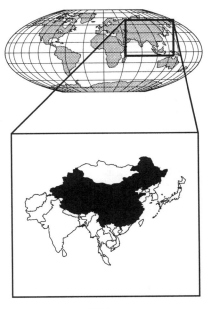

China

INGREDIENTS

3 tablespoons peanut or corn oil

2 tablespoons chopped onion

3 cups cold, cooked rice

2 eggs, well beaten

1 teaspoon salt

⅓ cup ham, chopped finely

Soy sauce to taste

STEPS

1. Heat oil in skillet over medium heat.
2. Cook onions in oil until clear.
3. Stir in rice, eggs, salt, and ham.
4. Cook about 5 minutes until all ingredients are heated through.
5. Stir in soy sauce.
6. Serve hot.

Serves 6.

📖 **Library Link 5:** Research "red" cooking.

COCONUT ANISE RICE CAKES

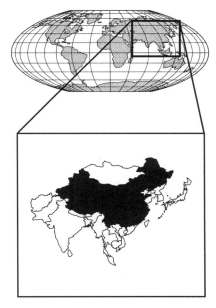

China

INGREDIENTS

1 pound glutinous rice

3 cups water for each 2 cups of rice

½ cup sweetened flaked coconut

2 tablespoons anise seed

¾ cup sugar

3 tablespoons margarine

STEPS

1. Wash and drain rice in cold water several times.

2. Soak rice in cold water at least 4 hours. Drain.

3. Put rice in a 3-quart saucepan with 3 cups water for each 2 cups rice. Cook over medium heat until it boils.

4. Continue cooking until small holes appear in the rice.

5. Cover saucepan. Turn heat to lowest setting. Cook for 10 minutes.

6. Remove saucepan from heat. Keep covered for 15 minutes. Do not lift lid.

7. While rice is hot, stir in coconut, anise seed, sugar, and margarine. Mix well.

8. Grease an 8-or 9-inch-square pan.

9. Press rice mixture evenly in pan.

10. Cool. Cut into squares.

11. Serve at room temperature.

Serves 6-8.

📖 **Library Link 6:** Research other favorite desserts in China.

ANNOTATED BIBLIOGRAPHY

Alexander, Lloyd. *The Remarkable Journey of Prince Jen*. New York: Dutton Children's Books, 1991. Grades 5 and up.
Jen sets out in search of the court of T'ienkuo with the help of six gifts and a faithful servant.

Andersen, Hans Christian. *The Nightingale*. Illustrated by Beni Montresor. New York: Crown, 1984. Grades 2 and up.
A Chinese emperor is saved by a nightingale.

Birdseye, Tom, adapter. *A Song of Stars*. Illustrated by Ju-Hong Chen. New York: Holiday House, 1990. Grades 2 and up.
When Princess Chauchau, a weaver, and Newlang, a herdsman, fall in love, they neglect their work. The Emperor of the Heavens decrees that they will be allowed to meet only on the seventh night of the seventh moon. This Asian legend is the inspiration for the Festival of the Milky Way in China and the Weaving Loom Festival in Japan.

Demi. *The Empty Pot*. New York: Henry Holt, 1990. Grades kindergarten and up.
Ping becomes heir to the emperor because he is honest about his failure to grow beautiful flowers.

_____. *Liang and the Magic Paintbrush*. New York: Holt, Rinehart & Winston, 1980. Grades preschool and up.
An old man gives Liang a paintbrush that brings his paintings to life.

Goldstein, Peggy. *Lóng Is a Dragon: Chinese Writing for Children*. San Francisco: China Books and Periodicals, 1991. Grades 2 and up.
Goldstein introduces 75 Chinese characters.

Hearn, Lafcadio. *The Voice of the Great Bell*. Retold by Margaret Hodges. Illustrated by Ed Young. Boston: Little, Brown, text 1963, illustrations 1989. Grades 2 and up.
The emperor orders a bell to be strengthened with gold, silver, and brass. When the bell makers fail, his daughter sacrifices her life for the bell.

Heyer, Marilee. *The Weaving of a Dream*. New York: Viking Kestrel, 1986. Grades 2 and up.
When the wind blows away a widow's carefully woven brocade, she enlists the help of her sons to retrieve it. Heyer's rich illustrations of this ancient Chinese legend are stunning.

Hsien-Yi and Gladys Yang, translators. *The Man Who Sold a Ghost: Chinese Tales of the 3rd-6th Centuries*. 2nd ed. Beijing, China: Foreign Languages Press, 1990. Grades 5 and up.
This collection of a vast variety of Chinese tales includes an appendix of source books.

Morris, Winifred. *The Future of Yen-tzu*. Illustrated by Friso Henstra. New York: Atheneum, 1992. Grades 2 and up.
When Yen-tzu leaves his farm he faces many twists of fate. Mistaken for a wise man, he inadvertently advises the emperor on important matters.

_____. *The Magic Leaf*. Illustrated by Ju-Hong Chen. New York: Atheneum, 1987. Grades 1 and up.
Lee Foo loves to study books, but his scholarly solutions to problems often turn to foolishness.

Tan, Amy. *The Moon Lady*. Illustrated by Gretchen Schields. New York: Macmillan, 1992. Grades 3 and up.
Tan has adapted this tale of a young Chinese girl's adventure and wish for the Moon Lady from her novel *The Joy Luck Club*.

Thomson, Peggy. *City Kids in China*. Photographs by Paul S. Conklin. New York: HarperCollins, 1991. Grades
    2 and up.
    The Chinese city of Changsha is the site for this fascinating glimpse of life in China.

Torre, Betty L., reteller. *The Luminous Pearl*. Illustrated by Carol Inouye. New York: Orchard Books, 1990.
    Grades 2 and up.
    Princess Mai Li wants only to marry an honest and brave man in this retelling of a rich folktale.

Wang, Rosalind, reteller. *The Fourth Question: A Chinese Tale*. Illustrated by Ju-Hong Chen. New York:
    Holiday House, 1991. Grades 2 and up.
    When Yee-Lee journeys to ask the wise man why he is hardworking yet still poor, three people he meets
on the journey have questions as well. Upon arrival, he learns he can have only three questions answered, and
he must make a difficult choice.

Waters, Kate, and Madeline Slovenz-Low. *Lion Dancer: Ernie Wan's Chinese New Year*. Photographs by
    Martha Cooper. New York: Scholastic, 1990. Grades kindergarten and up.
    Lush color photographs enhance this nonfiction account of preparing for and celebrating the Chinese New
Year.

Werner, Edward T. C. *Ancient Tales and Folklore of China*. London: Bracken Books, 1986. Grades 4 and up.
    In addition to a large collection of myths and legends, this book contains color illustrations and background
information on the Chinese.

Wolkstein, Diane, reteller. *The Magic Wings*. Illustrated by Robert Andrew Parker. New York: E.P. Dutton,
    1983. Grades 1 and up.
    When a goose girl decides she wants to grow wings, the village girls and women join in her desire.

Xi, Can, and Jian Wen, adapters. *Little Chen and the Dragon Brothers*. Illustrated by Gan Wuyan and Zhang
    Daping. Beijing, China: Foreign Languages Press, 1980. Grades 1 and up.
    Little Chen convinces the dragons to leave.

Yacowitz, Caryn, adapter. *The Jade Stone*. Illustrated by Ju-Hong Chen. New York: Holiday House, 1992.
    Grades 1 and up.
    Chan Lo risks the emperor's displeasure by carving jade into fish instead of a dragon.

Yee, Paul. *Tales from Gold Mountain: Stories of the Chinese in the New World*. Illustrated by Simon Ng. New
    York: Macmillan, 1989. Grades 4 and up.
    These original stories, with a folktale flavor, tell of the struggles of the Chinese who came to North
America.

Yen, Clara, reteller. *Why Rat Comes First: A Story of the Chinese Zodiac*. Illustrated by Hideo C. Yoshida. San
    Francisco: Children's Book Press. Grades 1 and up.
    The Jade King invites the animals to become the 12 months' symbols, but the children choose the rat to
be the first.

Yep, Laurence. *The Rainbow People*. Illustrated by David Weisner. New York: Harper & Row, 1989. Grades
    3 and up.
    Yep retells stories of tricksters, fools, virtues and vices, Chinese America, and love.

_____. *The Star Fisher*. New York: Morrow Junior Books, 1991. Grades 3 and up.
  Joan Lee and her family encounter prejudice and challenges when they move from Ohio to a small town in West Virginia to open a laundry in 1927.

Yolen, Jane. *The Emperor and the Kite*. Illustrated by Ed Young. Cleveland, OH: World Publishing, 1967. Grades 1 and up.
  The emperor's youngest daughter, Djeow Seow, braids her hair into a rope, attaches it to a kite, and saves her father.

_____. *The Seventh Mandarin*. Illustrated by Ed Young. New York: Seabury Press, 1970. Grades 2 and up.
  When the Seventh Mandarin flies the king's kite, it leads him outside the kingdom, where he learns the truth of poverty and suffering.

Young, Ed. *Lon Po Po: A Red-Riding Hood Story from China*. New York: Philomel, 1989. Grades kindergarten and up.
  Clever children outwit the wolf in a variant of this traditional folktale.

Yuan, Tian. *Chinese Folk Toys and Ornaments*. Beijing, China: Foreign Languages Press, 1980. Grades preschool and up.
  Soft watercolors plus the Chinese characters make this volume a treasure.

Ziner, Feenie, reteller. *Cricket Boy*. Illustrated by Ed Young. Garden City, NY: Doubleday, 1977. Grades 3 and up.
  Scholar Hu and his son enjoy the cricket fights, but their fame leads to a match with the emperor with near-tragic results.

VIDEO

Modern China. Society for Visual Education, 1985. 28:30 minutes. Grades 7 and up.
  Describes urban and rural life in China. Lesson plans available.

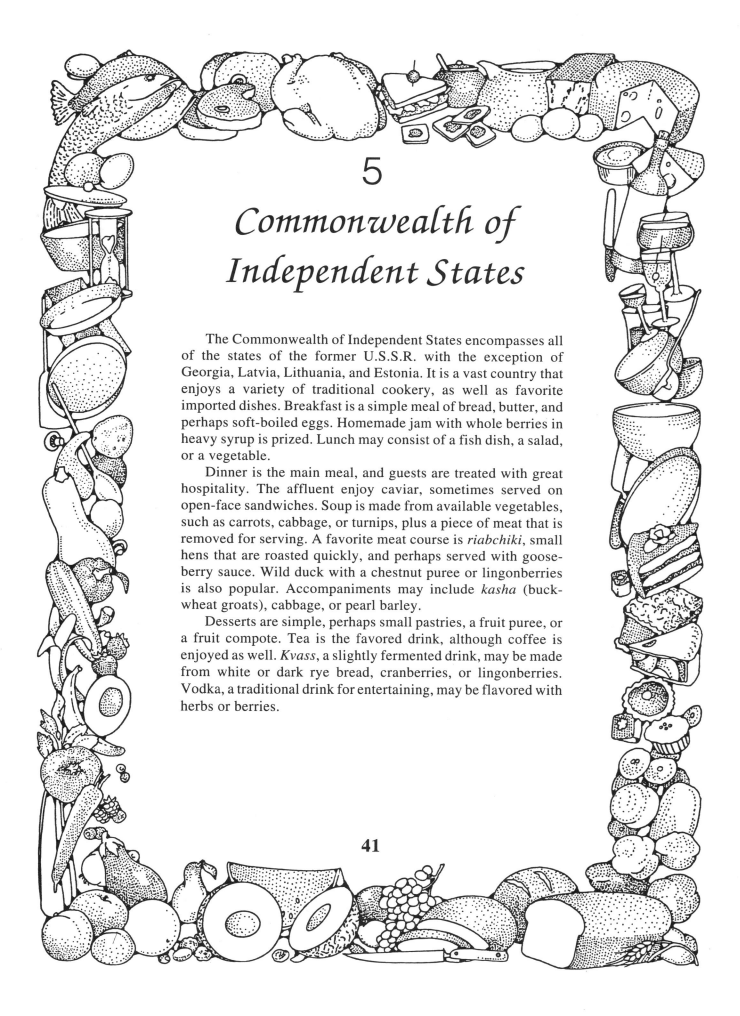

5

Commonwealth of Independent States

The Commonwealth of Independent States encompasses all of the states of the former U.S.S.R. with the exception of Georgia, Latvia, Lithuania, and Estonia. It is a vast country that enjoys a variety of traditional cookery, as well as favorite imported dishes. Breakfast is a simple meal of bread, butter, and perhaps soft-boiled eggs. Homemade jam with whole berries in heavy syrup is prized. Lunch may consist of a fish dish, a salad, or a vegetable.

Dinner is the main meal, and guests are treated with great hospitality. The affluent enjoy caviar, sometimes served on open-face sandwiches. Soup is made from available vegetables, such as carrots, cabbage, or turnips, plus a piece of meat that is removed for serving. A favorite meat course is *riabchiki*, small hens that are roasted quickly, and perhaps served with gooseberry sauce. Wild duck with a chestnut puree or lingonberries is also popular. Accompaniments may include *kasha* (buckwheat groats), cabbage, or pearl barley.

Desserts are simple, perhaps small pastries, a fruit puree, or a fruit compote. Tea is the favored drink, although coffee is enjoyed as well. *Kvass*, a slightly fermented drink, may be made from white or dark rye bread, cranberries, or lingonberries. Vodka, a traditional drink for entertaining, may be flavored with herbs or berries.

41

BLINI

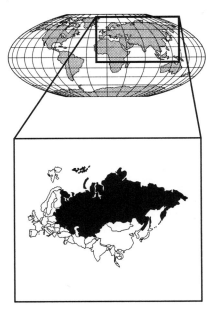

C.I.S.

INGREDIENTS

1⅓ cups wheat flour

1⅓ cups buckwheat flour

4 teaspoons yeast

5 tablespoons sugar

½ teaspoon salt

2⅔ cups milk

½ cup butter, cut into pieces

4 eggs, beaten

¼ cup melted butter

Smoked fish or caviar

½ cup sour cream

STEPS

1. Put flours, yeast, sugar, and salt in a large bowl.
2. Heat milk and ½ cup butter in a saucepan over medium heat until very warm and butter is melted (115 degrees).
3. Stir milk and butter and eggs into flour mixture.
4. Beat about 1 minute or until smooth with an electric mixer.
5. Cover bowl. Set in a warm place for 1 to 1½ hours or until mixture has risen to double its size.
6. Put a greased griddle over medium heat. Spoon about 2-3 tablespoons of mixture onto griddle.
7. Cook about 1 minute or until bottom is browned and top is bubbly.
8. Flip over to brown other side.
9. Keep blini in warm oven while cooking the rest.
10. To serve, brush with melted butter, top with smoked fish, and then top with sour cream.

Serves 6.

📖 **Library Link 1:** What is caviar? What is the origin of its name?

KASHA

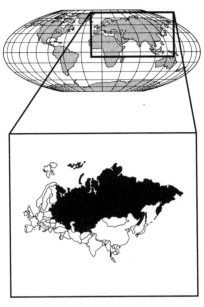

C.I.S.

INGREDIENTS

1 egg, beaten

1 cup kasha (buckwheat groats)

¼ cup butter, cut in pieces

2¼ cups chicken broth

¾ teaspoon salt

¼ teaspoon pepper

STEPS

1. Put egg and kasha in a medium bowl. Mix well.
2. Put a large frying pan over medium heat. Add kasha.
3. Cook, stirring constantly, until kasha is toasted and dried out.
4. Add rest of ingredients. Reduce heat to low.
5. Cover pan. Simmer for 15 minutes.
6. Stir occasionally.
7. Cook until kasha has absorbed liquid and is tender but not mushy. Add water if necessary.
8. Fluff with a fork. Serve hot.

Serves 6.

📖 **Library Link 2:** Research buckwheat.

PIROSHKI

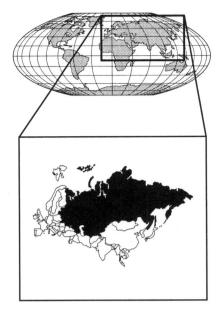

C.I.S.

INGREDIENTS

1½ cups flour

1 teaspoon salt

⅓ cup shortening

4 tablespoons sour cream

1 cup cooked ground beef

1 egg, beaten

2 eggs, hard-boiled and chopped

4 tablespoons chopped onion

½ teaspoon dillweed

¾ teaspoon salt

¼ teaspoon pepper

2 drops Tabasco

STEPS

1. Mix flour and salt in a large bowl.

2. Cut in shortening and sour cream.

3. With clean hands form into a soft dough. Add cold water if necessary.

4. Refrigerate dough for 30 minutes.

5. Combine beef, half of beaten egg, hard-boiled eggs, onion, dillweed, salt, pepper, and Tabasco in a medium bowl. Mix well.

6. Preheat oven to 400 degrees.

7. Roll dough out onto a floured board to ¼-inch thick.

8. Cut dough into 3-inch circles.

9. Put a small amount of meat mixture into center of each circle and fold dough over into a half circle.

10. Press edges together and brush top with saved beaten egg.

11. Bake on a greased baking sheet for 15 minutes or until lightly browned.

12. Serve hot.

Serves 8.

📖 **Library Link 3:** Research early Russian rulers and their favorite foods. Suggested rulers include Catherine the Great, Ivan the Terrible, Peter the Great, or various czars.

HOT BORSCHT

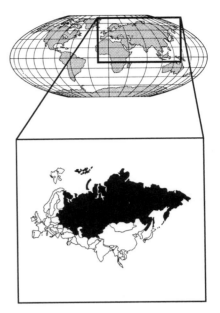

C.I.S.

INGREDIENTS

6 cups beef consommé

1 cup tomato sauce

1⅔ cups shredded cabbage

½ cup sliced celery

¾ cup shredded carrots

⅔ cup onions, sliced thinly

1 teaspoon sugar

1½ cups beets, cut into thin strips

Salt and pepper to taste

¼ cup dillweed

Sour cream

STEPS

1. Put consommé in a large saucepan.
2. Add tomato sauce, cabbage, celery, carrots, and onions.
3. Bring to a boil over medium-high heat.
4. Turn heat to low. Simmer for about 10 minutes until vegetables are tender, but not mushy.
5. Skim grease off soup.
6. Stir in sugar and beets.
7. Simmer for 10 more minutes.
8. Add salt and pepper to taste.
9. Put into soup bowls. Sprinkle with dillweed.
10. Serve hot with sour cream on the side.

Serves 6.

📖 **Library Link 4:** Research the historical agricultural role of root foods, such as beets.

CUCUMBER SALAD

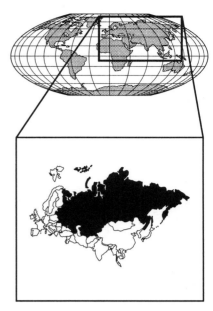

C.I.S.

INGREDIENTS

4 cucumbers, peeled and sliced thinly

2½ teaspoons salt

5 tablespoons sour cream

1 tablespoon lemon juice

1 teaspoon sugar

¼ teaspoon pepper

STEPS

1. Layer cucumbers in a shallow dish, sprinkling some of the salt between layers.

2. Let cucumbers sit at room temperature for 1 hour. Drain off liquid and dry with a paper towel.

3. Put sour cream, lemon juice, sugar, and pepper in a medium bowl. Beat together.

4. Stir in cucumbers.

5. Add the rest of the salt to taste.

6. Cover and chill.

7. Serve cold.

Serves 6.

📖 **Library Link 5:** Research cucumbers.

KISEL
(Apple Pudding)

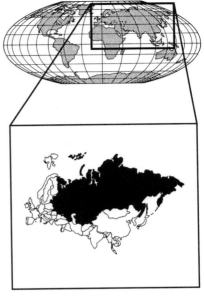

C.I.S.

INGREDIENTS

4 tart apples, peeled, cored, and sliced

1½ cups water

4 tablespoons sugar

1½ teaspoons cornstarch

¼ cup cream

STEPS

1. Put apples and water in a medium saucepan. Bring to a boil.

2. Reduce heat to a simmer. Simmer 15 minutes or until apples are tender.

3. Put apples and water in a sieve over a bowl.

4. Push apples through sieve. Return to saucepan.

5. Stir in sugar and bring to a boil.

6. Dissolve cornstarch in cream.

7. Stir in cornstarch and cream mixture. Cook, stirring constantly, about 3 minutes, until thick.

8. Remove from heat. Cool to lukewarm.

9. Pour into dessert dishes. Refrigerate.

10. Serve cold.

Serves 2-4.

📖 **Library Link 6:** Pastries are often served with tea. Research the Russian use of tea.

ANNOTATED BIBLIOGRAPHY

Afanasyev, Alexander Nikolayevich. *The Fool and the Fish.* Retold by Lenny Hort. Illustrated by Gennady Spirin. New York: Dial Books for Young Readers, 1990. Grades 1 and up.
A fish grants Ivan the Fool's every wish, and soon he marries the czar's daughter.

_____. *Russian Fairy Tales.* Translated by Norbert Guterman. Illustrated by Alexander Alexeieff. New York: Pantheon Books, 1945. Grades 3 and up.
This large volume provides a fascinating variety of Russian tales.

Asch, Frank, and Vladimir Vagin. *Here Comes the Cat!* New York: Scholastic, 1989. Grades preschool and up.
In Paul Revere style, a mouse warns the others of a cat's arrival. The Russian/English text repeats the warning "Here comes the cat!" leading the reader to a surprise ending.

Black, Algernon D., reteller. *The Woman of the Wood.* Illustrated by Evaline Ness. New York: Holt, Rinehart & Winston, 1973. Grades 1 and up.
A woodcarver, a tailor, and a teacher argue over who should own a jointly made creation.

Bogard, Larry. *The Kolokol Papers.* New York: Farrar, Straus & Giroux, 1981. Grades 6 and up.
Sixteen-year-old Lev speaks out against the former Soviet government after his father's arrest and faces pressures from the officials. Lev tells his story in *The Kolokol Papers* for release in the West.

Brett, Jan, adapter. *The Mitten.* New York: G.P. Putnam's Sons, 1989. Grades kindergarten and up.
Nicki drops his white mitten in the snow, and a variety of animals share it as a temporary home.

Brown, Marcia. *The Bun.* New York: Harcourt Brace Jovanovich, 1972. Grades kindergarten and up.
In this variant of "The Gingerbread Boy," a bun is eaten by the fox.

Cole, Joanna. *Bony-Legs.* Illustrated by Dirk Zimmer. New York: Macmillan, 1983. Grades kindergarten and up.
Sasha outwits the witch with help from a gate, a dog, and a cat.

Croll, Carolyn, adapter. *The Little Snowgirl.* New York: G.P. Putnam's Sons, 1989. Grades 1 and up.
A childless couple, delighted with their daughter of snow, almost lose her through their devotion.

Dolphin, Laurie. *Georgia to Georgia: Making Friends in the U.S.S.R.* Illustrations by E. Alan McGee. New York: Tambourine Books, 1991. Grades 2 and up.
Leslie Schulten's letter-writing campaign from students in Georgia to the Republic of Georgia results in a trip to Tbilisi, which is depicted in text and color photographs.

Ginsburg, Mirra, adapter. *Striding Slippers.* Illustrated by Sal Murdocca. New York: Macmillan, 1978. Grades 1 and up.
A clever shepherd's magic slippers are repeatedly stolen, to the dismay of the thieves.

Gogol, Nikolai. *Sorotchintzy Fair.* Illustrated by Gennadij Spirin. Translated by Daniel Reynolds. Boston: David R. Godine, 1990. Grades 2 and up.
Paraska goes to the fair for the first time and encounters exciting adventures.

Hastings, Selina, reteller. *Peter and the Wolf*. Illustrated by Reg Cartwright. New York: Henry Holt, 1987. Grades kindergarten and up.
   In this pictorial version of Sergei Prokofiev's musical tale, Peter disobeys his grandfather and must defeat the wolf.

Helprin, Mark. *Swan Lake*. Illustrated by Chris Van Allsburg. Boston: Houghton Mifflin, 1989. Grades 3 and up.
   Colorful illustrations enhance this classic ballet.

Kimmel, Eric A. *Baba Yaga: A Russian Folktale*. Illustrated by Megan Lloyd. New York: Holiday House, 1991. Grades 1 and up.
   Like Cinderella, Marina is mistreated by her stepmother and must also escape from Baba Yaga, a witch in the forest.

_____. *Bearhead*. Illustrated by Charles Mikolaycak. New York: Holiday House, 1991. Grades 1 and up.
   Madame Hexaba is so frustrated by Bearhead's literal interpretation of her directives that she sends him home with a wagon full of gold.

Levine, Arthur A. *All the Lights in the Night*. Illustrated by James E. Ransome. New York: Tambourine Books, 1991. Grades 2 and up.
   When the tsar makes life difficult for Jews, two young boys keep their spirits up with tales of Hanukkah as they travel to Palestine.

Mintz, Mary, translator. *The Millstones*. Illustrated by T. Berezenskaya. USSR: Minsk Yunatstva, 1985. Grades 2 and up.
   The landlord steals a couple's magic millstones in this Byelorussian folktale.

Morgan, Pierr. *The Turnip*. New York: Philomel, 1990. Grades preschool and up.
   It takes all the family plus the animals to pull up the turnip.

Murphy, Claire Rudolf. *Friendship Across Arctic Waters: Alaskan Cub Scouts Visit Their Soviet Neighbors*. Photographs by Charles Mason. New York: Lodestar Books, 1991. Grades 3 and up.
   Eleven Cub Scouts from Nome, Alaska, visit with Young Pioneers of Provideniya, where they live with Soviet families, celebrate the Fourth of July, and learn about Russia.

Polacco, Patricia. *Rechenka's Eggs*. New York: Philomel, 1988. Grades kindergarten and up.
   Babushka rescues an injured goose, Rechenka, which ruins her beautifully painted eggs. But the next morning she discovers the first of several miracles.

Pushkin, Alexander. *The Tale of Czar Saltan or The Prince and the Swan Princess*. Translated and retold by Patricia Tracy Lowe. Illustrated by I. Bilibin. New York: Thomas Y. Crowell, 1975. Grades 3 and up.
   Despite the treachery of her sisters, the czarina and her son are rewarded for their faithfulness.

_____. *The Tale of the Golden Cockerel*. Translated and retold by Patricia Tracy Lowe. Illustrated by I. Bilibin. New York: Thomas Y. Crowell, 1975. Grades 3 and up.
   An aging czar makes desperate promises to keep peace and must sacrifice all he loves.

Sherman, Josepha, reteller. *Vassilisa the Wise: A Tale of Medieval Russia*. Illustrated by Daniel San Souci. San Diego, CA: Harcourt Brace Jovanovich, 1989. Grades 1 and up.
   Vassilisa uses her intelligence to save her husband from imprisonment.

Small, Ernest. *Baba Yaga*. Illustrated by Blair Lent. Boston: Houghton Mifflin, 1966. Grades 1 and up.
   Marusia and her hedgehog friend take on Baba Yaga, a traditional Russian folk character.

Tate, Carole. *Pancakes and Pies*. New York: Peter Bedrick Books, 1989. Grades kindergarten and up.
   An old man and his wife acquire a magic handmill that produces pancakes and pies. When a rich man steals the handmill, their cockerel rescues it.

Tompert, Ann. *The Tzar's Bird*. Illustrated by Robert Rayevsky. New York: Macmillan, 1990. Grades 1 and up.
   When Baba Yaga is not invited to the Tzar's coronation, she comes anyway and commands him to care for her firebird. The lesson he learns is important for all readers to share.

Vernon, Adele, reteller. *The Riddle*. Illustrated by Robert Rayevsky and Vladimir Radunsky. New York: Dodd, Mead, 1987. Grades 1 and up.
   A king is intrigued by a charcoal maker's riddle: How can he make enough to pay back a debt, survive, save for his old age, and have money to throw out the window?

Voight, Erna. *Peter and the Wolf*. Boston: David R. Godine, 1979. Grades kindergarten and up.
   Musical phrases highlight the illustrations of Sergei Prokofiev's musical tale of Peter's capture of a wolf.

Weiss, Pola. *Russian Legends*. Translated by Alice Sachs. New York: Crescent Books, 1980. Grades 4 and up.
   Photographs of Russian art, people, and country enhance this collection of 19 tales.

Winthrop, Elizabeth, adapter. *Vasilissa the Beautiful*. Illustrated by Alexander Koshkin. New York: Harper-Collins, 1991. Grades 2 and up.
   In this Cinderella variant, Vasilissa is protected from her evil stepmother and stepsisters by a magic doll.

Zemach, Harve, reteller. *Salt*. Illustrated by Margot Zemach. New York: Farrar, Straus & Giroux, 1965. Grades kindergarten and up.
   Ivan the Fool finds an island of salt and shows his true abilities.

VIDEOS

The Fool and the Flying Ship. We All Have Tales Series. Rabbit Ears. 30 minutes. Grades 2 and up.
   The fool is aided by eccentrics and a flying ship in his quest to win the czar's daughter.

Rechenka's Eggs. Spoken Arts, 1992. Grades preschool and up.
   Based on Patricia Polacco's book, Old Babushka befriends an injured goose who breaks all her beautiful eggs.

Student Life in the Soviet Union. Society for Visual Education. 25 minutes. Grades 4 and up.
   Learn how school life in the former Soviet Union differs from that in the United States.

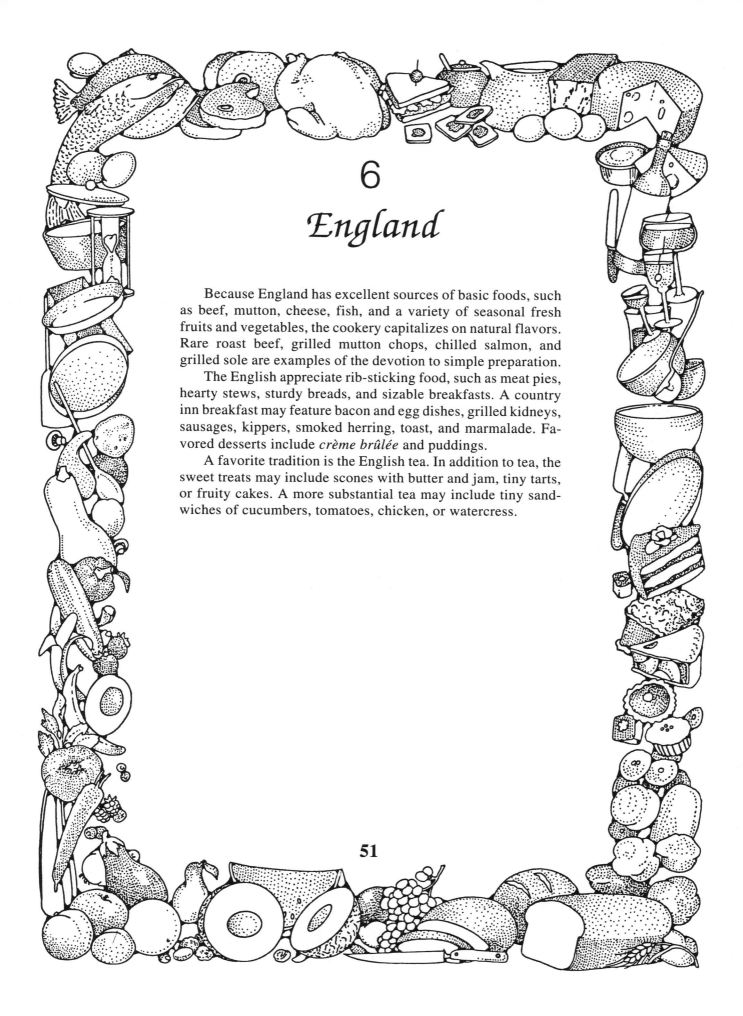

6

England

Because England has excellent sources of basic foods, such as beef, mutton, cheese, fish, and a variety of seasonal fresh fruits and vegetables, the cookery capitalizes on natural flavors. Rare roast beef, grilled mutton chops, chilled salmon, and grilled sole are examples of the devotion to simple preparation.

The English appreciate rib-sticking food, such as meat pies, hearty stews, sturdy breads, and sizable breakfasts. A country inn breakfast may feature bacon and egg dishes, grilled kidneys, sausages, kippers, smoked herring, toast, and marmalade. Favored desserts include *crème brûlée* and puddings.

A favorite tradition is the English tea. In addition to tea, the sweet treats may include scones with butter and jam, tiny tarts, or fruity cakes. A more substantial tea may include tiny sandwiches of cucumbers, tomatoes, chicken, or watercress.

51

FISH AND CHIPS

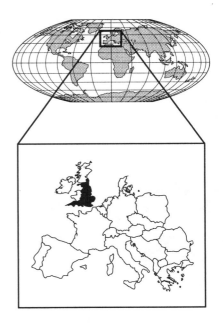

England

INGREDIENTS

4 potatoes, peeled and cut into sticks 3 inches long
    and ⅛ inch wide

Vegetable oil for frying

Salt and pepper

6 fillets of flounder

¾ cup flour

½ teaspoon baking powder

1 teaspoon salt

¼ teaspoon pepper

⅔ cup milk

Cooking thermometer

STEPS

1. Rinse potatoes. Drain and dry thoroughly.
2. Heat oil in deep fat fryer to 360 degrees.
3. Cook potato sticks in oil until brown. Salt and pepper to taste.
4. Wash and dry fillets.
5. Make batter by mixing flour, baking powder, salt, and pepper in a bowl. Stir in milk.
6. Dip fillets in batter. Cook in hot oil until brown.
7. Serve hot.

Serves 6.

📖 **Library Link 1:** What species of flounder is found in the English Channel?

LANCASHIRE STEW

INGREDIENTS

2 pounds lamb

5 large potatoes, peeled

4 medium onions

½ pound mushrooms

1 small head cabbage

4 carrots, peeled

4 tablespoons butter

Salt and pepper

2¼ cups water

1 tablespoon parsley, chopped

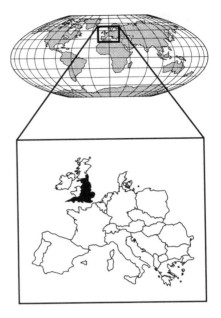

England

STEPS

1. Chop lamb, potatoes, onions, mushrooms, cabbage, and carrots into small cubes.
2. Preheat oven to 325 degrees.
3. Spread 2 tablespoons butter over the bottom and sides of a 4-quart casserole dish.
4. Put ⅓ of the potatoes in the bottom of the casserole dish.
5. Add ½ of the meat and other vegetables.
6. Put ⅓ more of the potatoes on top of this mixture.
7. Add the rest of the meat and vegetables.
8. Put the rest of the potatoes on top of the mixture.
9. Sprinkle with salt and pepper.
10. Pour water over the mixture.
11. Drop 2 tablespoons butter on top.
12. Cover the casserole dish and cook 2½ hours.
13. Check after 2 hours to make sure the water has not evaporated. Add water if necessary.
14. Remove cover from casserole dish during the last half hour to brown the potatoes.
15. Sprinkle with parsley. Serve hot.

Serves 4.

📖 **Library Link 2:** When and how did cabbage come to England?

YORKSHIRE PUDDING

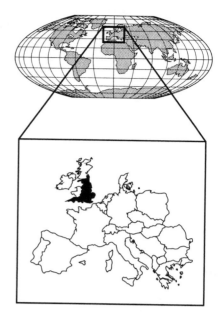

England

INGREDIENTS

1 cup flour

2 teaspoons baking powder

½ teaspoon salt

¼ teaspoon pepper

1 large egg, beaten well

2 cups milk

4 tablespoons hot beef fat

STEPS

1. Preheat oven to 425 degrees.
2. Mix flour, baking powder, salt, and pepper in a bowl.
3. Stir in egg and milk. Mix until well blended.
4. Remove 4 tablespoons of hot fat from a roast beef or use melted lard. Put into a 9-x-13-inch pan.
5. Pour pudding mixture into the pan.
6. Bake for 20 minutes or until browned and cooked through.
7. Cut pudding into squares. Serve hot with roast beef.

Serves 6-8.

📖 **Library Link 3:** What is the origin of the word "pudding"?

SHORTBREAD

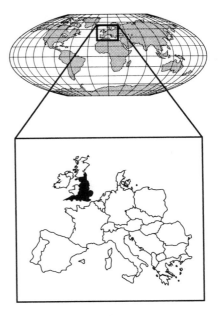

England

INGREDIENTS

1 cup softened butter (2 sticks)

½ cup powdered sugar

2 cups flour

Pinch of salt

STEPS

1. Preheat oven to 325 degrees.

2. Beat butter and sugar together in a large bowl.

3. Stir in flour and salt. Mix with hands until smooth.

4. Press dough onto a cookie sheet. Prick all over with a fork.

5. Bake shortbread in middle of oven 25 minutes or until slightly brown around the edges.

6. Remove from oven. Immediately cut into squares with a sharp knife.

7. Let cool and serve.

Serves 10.

📖 **Library Link 4:** What is the origin of shortbread?

SCONES

INGREDIENTS

2 cups flour

2 teaspoons baking powder

½ teaspoon salt

4 tablespoons softened butter

⅓ cup sugar

⅓ cup currants

¼ cup buttermilk

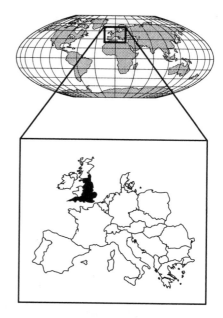

England

STEPS

1. Preheat oven to 425 degrees.
2. Mix flour, baking powder, and salt in a large bowl.
3. Mix in butter with your fingers.
4. Mix in sugar and currants.
5. Stir in enough milk to make a soft dough.
6. Flour a surface. Roll dough out to ¾ inches thick.
7. Use a round cookie cutter to cut dough into circles.
8. Place circles on a greased and floured cookie sheet.
9. Bake for 10 minutes or until lightly browned.
10. Serve hot with jam.

Serves 6.

📖 **Library Link 5:** When and where were currants first cultivated commercially?

TRIFLE

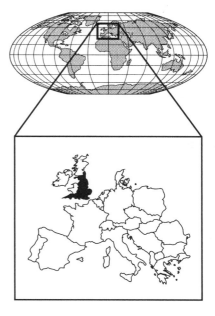

England

INGREDIENTS

16 ladyfingers

⅔ cup raspberry jam

2 teaspoons cornstarch

2 cups milk

5 tablespoons sugar

2 eggs, beaten well

1 teaspoon vanilla

2 cups whipped cream

STEPS

1. Line the bottom of a deep, flat-bottomed dish with ladyfingers.

2. Spread jam on top of ladyfingers.

3. Mix cornstarch with a small amount of milk to make a thin paste.

4. Cook rest of milk over medium heat until it boils.

5. Remove from heat and stir in cornstarch paste and sugar.

6. Return to low heat, stirring constantly until sauce thickens.

7. Remove from heat. Stir in eggs and vanilla.

8. Pour hot custard over ladyfingers and jam.

9. Refrigerate for 2 hours.

10. Spread whipped cream over mixture and serve.

Serves 4.

📖 **Library Link 6:** What does "ladiesfingers" refer to in England?

ANNOTATED BIBLIOGRAPHY

Aliki. *A Medieval Feast*. New York: Harper & Row, 1983. Grades kindergarten and up.
The preparations for a fictional English feast are described.

Avery, Gillian. *Maria Escapes*. Illustrated by Scott Snow. New York: Simon & Schuster, 1992. Grades 4 and up.
Maria, a young orphan, escapes a boarding school and lives with her uncle, where she has wonderful adventures with neighbor boys.

Bawden, Nina. *The Finding*. New York: Lothrop, Lee & Shepard, 1985. Grades 4 and up.
In London, adopted 11-year-old Alex struggles to understand his family relationships.

Calhoun, Mary. *Jack the Wise and the Cornish Cuckoos*. Illustrated by Lady McCrady. New York: William Morrow, 1978. Grades 1 and up.
In this comic tale from West Cornwall, Jack is so wise the people depend on him to solve their silly dilemmas.

Cooper, Susan. *Dawn of Fear*. New York: Macmillan, 1970. Grades 4 and up.
During World War II, Derek and his friends play in bomb craters and build a secret camp. Trouble with a rival gang and a devastating night of bombing bring home the realities of war.

de Angeli, Marguerite. *The Door in the Wall*. New York: Scholastic, 1949. Grades 4 and up.
The plague and war have devastated London, and Robin must make his way to his father near the dangerous Welsh border.

Frost, Abigail. *Myths and Legends of the Age of Chivalry*. Illustrated by Francis Phillipps. New York: Marshall Cavendish, 1990. Grades 3 and up.
Legends of Arthur and Charlemagne, background information, large color illustrations, and an index provide a strong introduction to English literature.

Garner, Alan. *Book of British Fairy Tales*. New York: Delacorte Press, 1984. Grades 2 and up.
Familiar tales such as "Tom Tit Tot" and "Mally Whuppy" are included with lesser-known stories.

Hastings, Selina, reteller. *Sir Gawain and the Loathly Lady*. Illustrated by Juan Wijngaard. New York: Lothrop, Lee & Shepard, 1985. Grades 4 and up.
In this tale from Great Britain, a loathly lady helps King Arthur, and in return he must give her a knight as a husband. Sir Gawain breaks her spell by marrying her and giving her freedom of choice. Preread for suitability for your students.

Hodges, Margaret, reteller. *The Kitchen Knight: A Tale of King Arthur*. Illustrated by Trina Schart Hyman. New York: Holiday House, 1990. Grades 4 and up.
Gareth volunteers to rescue Linette's imprisoned sister and is rewarded by knighthood and marriage to Linette.

Ish-Kishor, Sulamith. *Our Eddie*. New York: Alfred A. Knopf, 1969. Grades 4 and up.
In London and New York, a Jewish family struggles with mother's and Eddie's multiple sclerosis.

Majorian, Michelle. *Good Night, Mr. Tom*. New York: Harper & Row, 1981. Grades 4 and up.
In this powerful novel, crusty Tom Oakley adopts an abused boy during World War II.

Middleton, Haydn. *Island of the Mighty: Stories of Old Britain*. Illustrated by Anthea Toorchen. Oxford, England: Oxford University Press, 1987. Grades 2 and up.
Merlin, Old King Cole, giant King Bran, and Prince Maxen people this collection of Welsh legends.

Roop, Peter, and Connie Roop. *Stonehenge: Opposing Viewpoints*. San Diego, CA: Greenhaven Press, 1983. Grades 3 and up.
A bibliography for further reading, an index, black-and-white photographs, and straightforward text provide possible explanations for Stonehenge.

Turner, Dorothy. *William Shakespeare*. Illustrated by Richard Hook. New York: Bookwright Press, 1985. Grades 3 and up.
Photographs, drawings, a glossary, and a booklist add to the text about Shakespeare's life and environment.

Walsh, Jill Paton. *A Chance Child*. New York: Farrar, Straus & Giroux, 1978. Grades 5 and up.
In this compelling novel, Creep escapes abuse by traveling through time to nineteenth-century England.

Wiesner, David, and Kim Kahng, retellers. *The Loathsome Dragon*. Illustrated by David Wiesner. New York: G.P. Putnam's Sons, 1987. Grades kindergarten and up.
The English countryside is troubled by a loathsome dragon that is really an enchanted princess.

Zemach, Harve, reteller. *Duffy and the Devil*. Illustrated by Margot Zemach. New York: Farrar, Straus & Giroux, 1973. Grades kindergarten and up.
Duffy struggles with the devil in this amusing Cornish tale.

VIDEOS

Boy and Girl of Britain. Coronet, 1976. 11 minutes. Grades kindergarten and up.
Children show different lifestyles in rural and urban England.

Christmas Time in Europe. Coronet, 1971. 21 minutes. Grades kindergarten and up.
Visit families in Holland, Belgium, Luxembourg, France, and Great Britain at Christmas time.

Touring England. Society for Visual Education. 60 minutes. Grades 4 and up.
This extensive tour of England includes Buckingham Palace, Windsor Castle, Stonehenge, and other historic sites.

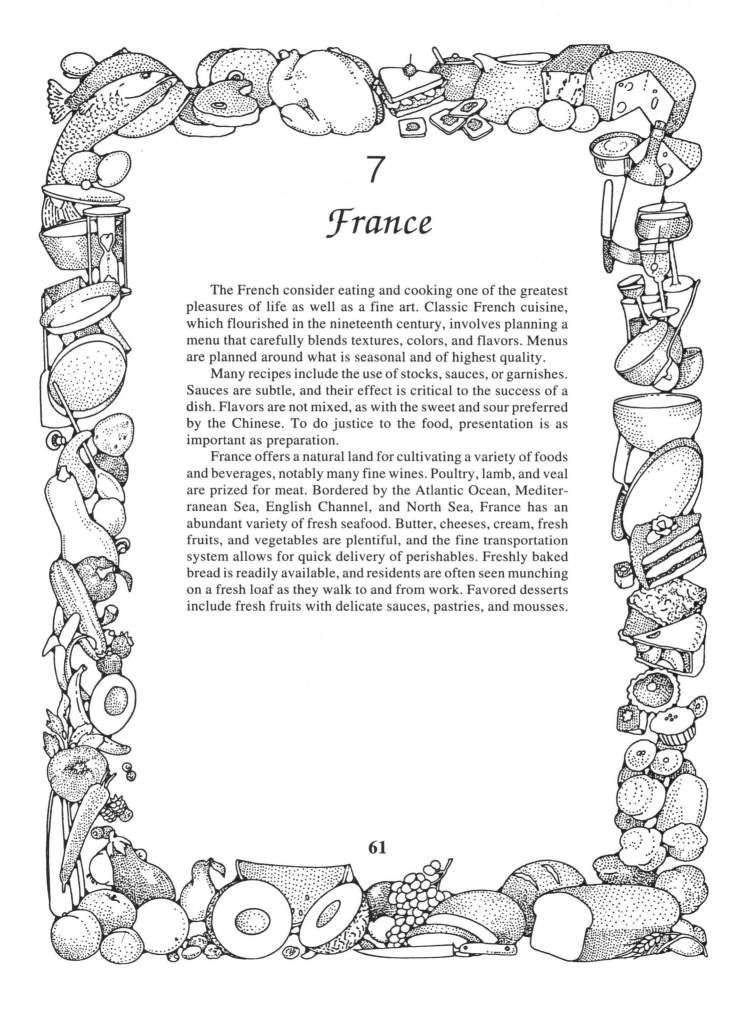

7

France

The French consider eating and cooking one of the greatest pleasures of life as well as a fine art. Classic French cuisine, which flourished in the nineteenth century, involves planning a menu that carefully blends textures, colors, and flavors. Menus are planned around what is seasonal and of highest quality.

Many recipes include the use of stocks, sauces, or garnishes. Sauces are subtle, and their effect is critical to the success of a dish. Flavors are not mixed, as with the sweet and sour preferred by the Chinese. To do justice to the food, presentation is as important as preparation.

France offers a natural land for cultivating a variety of foods and beverages, notably many fine wines. Poultry, lamb, and veal are prized for meat. Bordered by the Atlantic Ocean, Mediterranean Sea, English Channel, and North Sea, France has an abundant variety of fresh seafood. Butter, cheeses, cream, fresh fruits, and vegetables are plentiful, and the fine transportation system allows for quick delivery of perishables. Freshly baked bread is readily available, and residents are often seen munching on a fresh loaf as they walk to and from work. Favored desserts include fresh fruits with delicate sauces, pastries, and mousses.

STRAWBERRY CREPES

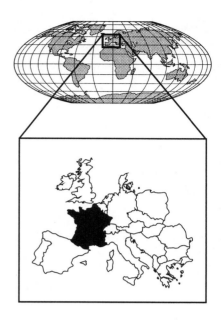

France

INGREDIENTS

4 eggs

1 cup flour

3 tablespoons sugar

1 cup milk

⅓ cup water

1 tablespoon melted butter

4 cups sliced strawberries

⅔ cup sugar

1 cup cottage cheese

1 cup sour cream

½ cup powdered sugar

½ cup powdered sugar, optional

STEPS

1. Beat eggs in a large bowl.

2. Add ½ of the flour and 2 tablespoons sugar. Stir well.

3. Stir in milk and water.

4. Stir in the rest of the flour and other tablespoon of sugar.

5. Stir in the melted butter.

6. Chill batter while making the strawberry filling.

7. Mix strawberries and ⅔ cup sugar in a large bowl.

8. Beat cottage cheese, sour cream, and ½ cup powdered sugar in a medium bowl with an electric mixer until smooth.

9. To make crepes, pour a small amount of batter into a greased, heated crepe pan or small frying pan. Swirl around until the bottom of the pan is coated. Cook until browned on both sides. Repeat until all the batter is used.

10. Fill the crepes with a small amount of the strawberry and cheese mixtures. Roll up.

11. Crepes may be reheated in a warm (300 degree) oven.

12. Sprinkle with extra powdered sugar to serve.

Serves 6-8.

📖 **Library Link 1:** What was the origin of strawberries in France?

From *Cooking Up World History*. Copyright © 1994. Teacher Ideas Press, P.O. Box 6633, Englewood, CO 80155-6633.

SAUTÉ DE POULET
(Sautéed Chicken)

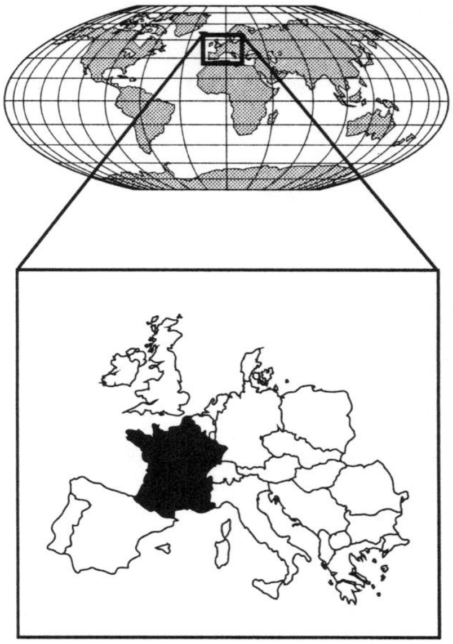

INGREDIENTS

3 pounds of chicken pieces

⅓ cup flour

½ teaspoon salt

½ teaspoon thyme

¼ teaspoon pepper

2 tablespoons butter

1 tablespoon olive oil

1 bay leaf, crumpled

2 cloves garlic, finely chopped

1¾ cups chicken broth

1 3-ounce can sliced mushrooms

France

STEPS

1. Rinse and pat dry the chicken.
2. Put flour, salt, thyme, and pepper in a large plastic bag.
3. Shake chicken pieces, one at a time, in the bag.
4. Heat butter and oil in a large pot over medium-high heat.
5. Add chicken. Brown on all sides.
6. Reduce heat to low. Cover pot. Cook 20 minutes, turning chicken twice.
7. Sprinkle chicken with bay leaf and garlic.
8. Pour broth and mushrooms over the chicken.
9. Cover and cook for 30 minutes or until ½ the liquid has cooked away. The chicken should be tender.
10. Pour sauce over chicken. Serve.

Serves 4-6.

📖 **Library Link 2:** How does the French term "sauté" relate to frying?

SOUFFLÉ AU FROMAGE

(Cheese Soufflé)

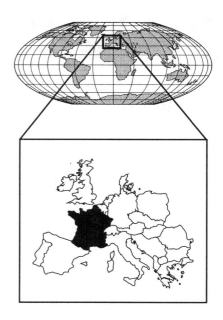

France

INGREDIENTS

1 tablespoon butter

3 tablespoons butter

3 tablespoons flour

1 cup hot milk

½ teaspoon salt

¼ teaspoon pepper

4 egg yolks

6 egg whites, room temperature

Pinch of salt

1 cup grated Swiss cheese

¼ cup grated Parmesan cheese

STEPS

1. Preheat oven to 400 degrees.
2. Grease well a 2-quart soufflé dish with 1 tablespoon butter.
3. Melt 3 tablespoons butter over medium heat in a large saucepan.
4. Remove pan from stove. Stir in flour.
5. Slowly stir in milk, salt, and pepper.
6. Return pan to the stove. Stir until mixture boils and thickens.
7. Remove pan from heat. Use a wire whisk to stir in the egg yolks, one at a time.
8. Put egg whites and salt in a medium bowl.
9. Beat egg whites with an electric mixer until they form very stiff peaks.
10. Stir a large spoonful of the egg whites into the milk mixture.
11. Stir in the cheeses.
12. Carefully fold the rest of the egg whites into the milk mixture.
13. Spoon mixture into the soufflé dish.
14. Put the dish on the middle shelf of the oven. Lower heat to 375 degrees.
15. Do not open the oven until the soufflé is nearly done.
16. Bake for 25-30 minutes until top is lightly browned.
17. Serve immediately.

Serves 4-6.

📖 **Library Link 3:** What is the meaning of the word "soufflé"? How does it relate to the process of making a soufflé?

CAROTTES VICHY

(Glazed Carrots)

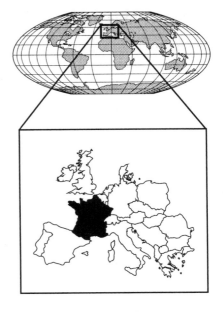

France

INGREDIENTS

1 pound carrots, peeled and sliced thinly

¼ cup water

¼ teaspoon salt

3 tablespoons butter

2 teaspoons sugar

STEPS

1. Put all ingredients in a medium saucepan.
2. Cook over low heat for 10 minutes or until carrots are tender.
3. Stir well. Continue cooking until most of the liquid is gone.
4. Stir before serving.

Serves 4.

📖 **Library Link 4:** What is the name of the wild carrot? (Hint: Think of royalty.)

POIRE HÉLÈNE
(Pears Helen)

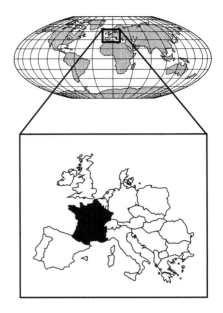

France

INGREDIENTS

1 cup chocolate syrup

8 large scoops vanilla ice cream

8 canned pear halves

1 cup raspberry jam

2 tablespoons hot water

STEPS

1. First, put 2 tablespoons chocolate syrup in each of 8 ice cream bowls.

2. Put a scoop of ice cream in each bowl.

3. Put a pear half on top of each scoop of ice cream.

4. Mix jam and water in small bowl.

5. Spoon jam mixture over pears. Serve.

Serves 8.

📖 **Library Link 5:** France is regarded as the leading producer of pears. What other region claims pears as a native fruit?

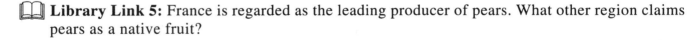

MOUSSE AU CHOCOLAT
(Chocolate Mousse)

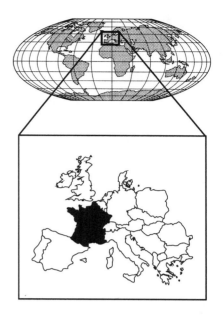

France

INGREDIENTS

2 cups milk

⅓ cup sugar

3 ounces grated sweet chocolate

4 beaten egg yolks

¾ cup whipping cream

1 teaspoon vanilla

STEPS

1. Scald milk in medium saucepan over medium heat.

2. Stir in sugar and chocolate.

3. Pour 4 tablespoons of chocolate mixture into egg yolks. Stir well.

4. Pour egg yolks into chocolate mixture. Stir well.

5. Cook over low heat until mixture thickens. Stir constantly.

6. Cool mixture by placing pan in a large bowl of cold water.

7. Whip cream until stiff. Stir in vanilla.

8. Fold cream carefully into the cooled chocolate mixture.

9. Pour mixture into custard cups. Chill.

Serves 6.

📖 **Library Link 6:** What is the meaning of the French word *mousse*?

CHOCOLAT

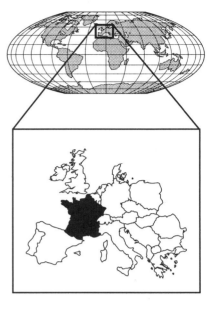

France

INGREDIENTS

6 ounces milk chocolate chips (1 cup)

5 tablespoons water

6½ cups whole milk

STEPS

1. Put chocolate chips in a small, heavy saucepan. Add the water.

2. Cook over low heat until chocolate melts. Stir constantly.

3. Remove from heat. Stir well.

4. Heat milk over medium heat in a large saucepan until milk boils.

5. Remove milk from heat.

6. Add about ½ cup of milk to the chocolate. Stir well.

7. Stir chocolate mixture into rest of the milk.

8. Heat to desired temperature.

9. Serve in mugs.

Serves 6.

📖 **Library Link 7:** What controversy was associated with chocolate during the 1600s?

ANNOTATED BIBLIOGRAPHY

Aliki. *The King's Day: Louis XIV of France.* New York: Thomas Y. Crowell, 1989. Grades kindergarten and up.
Aliki describes a day in the life of the Sun King, the glamorous ruler of seventeenth-century France.

Björk, Christina. *Linnea in Monet's Garden.* Illustrated by Lena Anderson. New York: Farrar, Straus & Giroux, 1987. Grades 3 and up.
Linnea learns about Monet from seeing his paintings and visiting his home and garden.

Brown, Marcia, translator. *Puss in Boots.* New York: Charles Scribner's Sons, 1952. Grades 1 and up.
The Marquis of Carabas and his clever cat outwit the king.

Burkert, Nancy Ekholm. *Valentine & Orson.* New York: Farrar, Straus and Giroux, 1989. Grades 4 and up.
Two brothers, separated at birth, are reunited as adults in search of their identities. This sixteenth-century tale is told in the form of a folk play.

Carter, Angela, translator. *Sleeping Beauty and Other Favourite Fairy Tales.* Illustrated by Michael Foreman. New York: Schocken Books, 1984. Grades 2 and up.
Carter and Foreman bring humor and drama to these tales by Charles Perrault and Madame Le Prince de Beaumont.

Goffstein, M. B. *Artists' Helpers Enjoy the Evenings.* New York: Harper & Row, 1987. Grades preschool and up.
When work is done, the artists' helpers enjoy an evening in Paris.

Knight, Joan. *Bon Appétit, Bertie!* Illustrated by Penny Dann. New York: Dorling Kindersley Children's Books, 1993. Grades preschool and up.
Children can learn basic French words in this charming bilingual story of Bertie and his family's visit to Paris.

McCully, Emily Arnold. *Mirette on the High Wire.* New York: G. P. Putnam's Sons, 1992. Grades kindergarten and up.
Mirette learns tightrope walking, not realizing her teacher is the once famous, but now fearful, Great Bellini. Their work together leads to him conquering his fears.

Milton, Nancy *The Giraffe That Walked to Paris.* Illustrated by Roger Roth. New York: Crown, 1992. Grades 2 and up.
Based on a true event, this is the story of a giraffe given to France by the pasha of Egypt, Muhammad Ali, in 1826.

Meyers, Odette. *The Enchanted Umbrella.* Illustrated by Margot Zemach. San Diego, CA: Harcourt Brace Jovanovich, 1988. Grades kindergarten and up.
A magic umbrella helps Patou find his fortune.

Monro, Roxie. *The Inside-Outside Book of Paris.* New York: Dutton Children's Books, 1992. Grades kindergarten and up.
Brilliant color illustrations and simple text introduce the reader to the wonders of Paris.

Montresor, Beni. *Little Red Riding Hood*. Garden City, NY: Doubleday, 1991. Grades 6 and up.
    Montresor's illustrations are disturbing in this traditional version in which Little Red's rescue is only implied. This book, appropriate for mature students interested in comparing folktales, is a fascinating, though provocative interpretation.

Munthe, Nelly. *Meet Matisse*. Boston: Little, Brown, 1983. Grades 3 and up.
    Readers are introduced to Matisse's method of cutouts and given instruction for trying several techniques.

Perrault, Charles. *Cinderella*. Retold by Amy Ehrlich. Illustrated by Susan Jeffers. New York: Dial Books for Young Readers, 1985. Grades 1 and up.
    Jeffers's illustrations make this retelling a treasure.

Skira-Venturi, Rosabianca. *A Weekend with Renoir*. New York: Rizzoli International, 1990. Grades 3 and up.
    Readers will enjoy nineteenth-century France through this imaginary visit with Pierre-Auguste Renoir.

Skurzynski, Gloria. *The Minstrel in the Tower*. Illustrated by Julek Heller. New York: Random House, 1988. Grades 3 and up.
    During 1195, two children search for their invalid mother's brother.

Wilkes, Angela. *Mon Premier Livre de Mots en Français*. Translated by Annie Frankland. New York: Dorling Kindersley Children's Books, 1993. Grades kindergarten and up.
    My First Word Book gives clear, colorful photographs and corresponding words for the 1,000 most commonly used words. This colorful reference book is fascinating for browsing and introducing French.

VIDEOS

Christmas in France. Educational Video, 1987. 10 minutes. Grades kindergarten and up.
    This video includes a look at the decorations and customs of Christmas in France.

Christmas Time in Europe. Coronet, 1971. 21 minutes. Grades kindergarten and up.
    Visit families in Holland, Belgium, Luxembourg, France, and Great Britain at Christmas time.

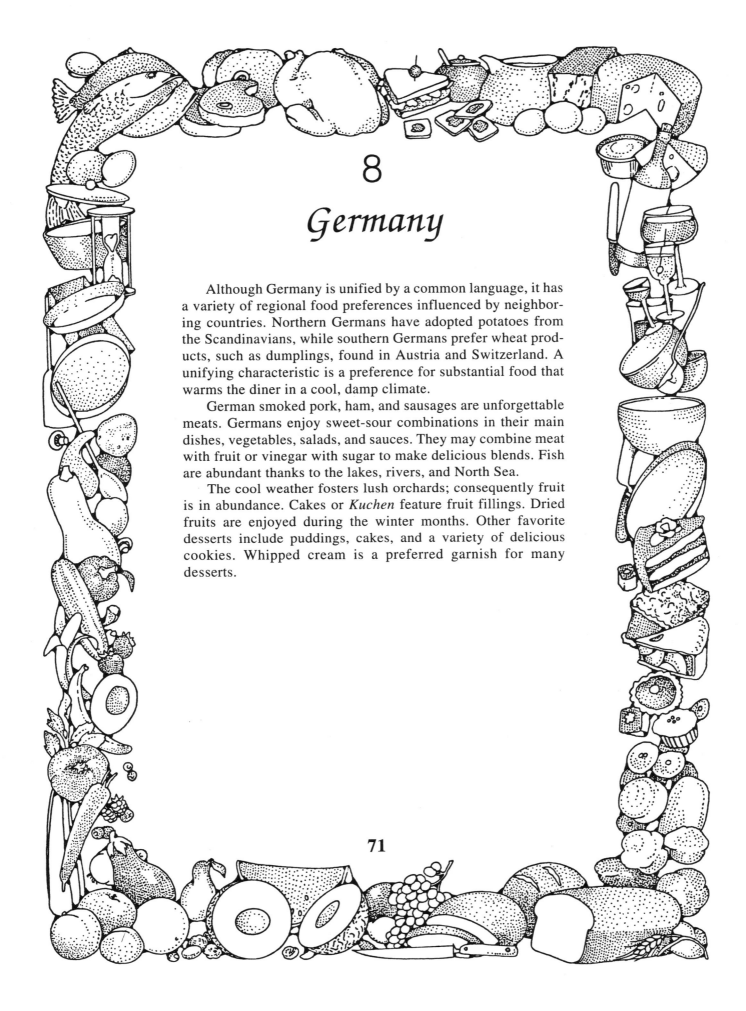

8

Germany

Although Germany is unified by a common language, it has a variety of regional food preferences influenced by neighboring countries. Northern Germans have adopted potatoes from the Scandinavians, while southern Germans prefer wheat products, such as dumplings, found in Austria and Switzerland. A unifying characteristic is a preference for substantial food that warms the diner in a cool, damp climate.

German smoked pork, ham, and sausages are unforgettable meats. Germans enjoy sweet-sour combinations in their main dishes, vegetables, salads, and sauces. They may combine meat with fruit or vinegar with sugar to make delicious blends. Fish are abundant thanks to the lakes, rivers, and North Sea.

The cool weather fosters lush orchards; consequently fruit is in abundance. Cakes or *Kuchen* feature fruit fillings. Dried fruits are enjoyed during the winter months. Other favorite desserts include puddings, cakes, and a variety of delicious cookies. Whipped cream is a preferred garnish for many desserts.

71

BERLINER PFANNKÜCHEN
(Berlin Doughnuts)

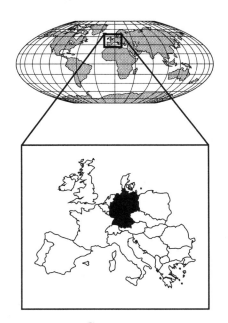

Germany

INGREDIENTS

1 pound flour	1 tablespoon vanilla
½ teaspoon salt	4 tablespoons butter, melted
1¼ cups warm milk	Jam
1 package dry yeast	Oil for frying
3 egg yolks	Powdered sugar
¼ cup sugar	Cooking thermometer

STEPS

1. Put flour and salt in a large bowl.
2. Put ¾ cup of the warm milk in a small bowl. Sprinkle yeast over top of milk.
3. Let sit in a warm place about 15 minutes or until it gets foamy.
4. In another small bowl, whip egg yolks with sugar until thick.
5. Add egg mixture, yeast mixture, and vanilla to flour and salt. Add more of the milk, as needed, to make a firm dough.
6. Knead dough on a floured board until smooth.
7. Gradually knead in the butter. Keep kneading until shiny and stretchy.
8. Put dough in a bowl. Cover and put in a warm place for 1-2 hours or until double in size.
9. Remove dough from bowl. Knead until smooth. Roll out on a floured board into a rectangle ¼-inch thick.
10. Cut dough into rounds using a 2- to 3-inch round cookie cutter.
11. Put small amount of jam in center of ½ of the rounds.
12. Put a plain round on top of each. Seal well.
13. Put doughnuts on a floured board.
14. Let rise until puffy.
15. Put oil for frying in a deep-fat fryer or large pan.
16. Heat to 375 degrees.
17. Fry until browned on both sides.
18. Drain on paper towels.
19. Sprinkle with powdered sugar.
20. Serve warm.

Serves 6-8.

📖 **Library Link 1:** Research various breakfasts in Germany.

RINDERGULASCH

(Beef Goulash)

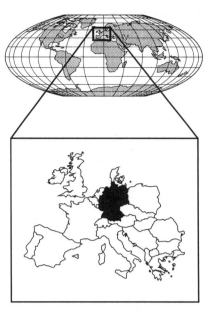

Germany

INGREDIENTS

3 tablespoons butter

2 onions, chopped

2 cloves garlic, minced finely

1 pound beef, cubed

1 teaspoon salt

½ teaspoon pepper

1 teaspoon paprika

1 cup water

2 tablespoons flour

1 cup beef stock

3 tomatoes, sliced

STEPS

1. Put butter in a large skillet over medium-high heat.

2. Add onion and garlic. Cook until soft.

3. Add meat, salt, pepper, and paprika. Cook until meat is browned.

4. Stir in water and cover. Reduce heat and simmer for 1 hour.

5. When juice has evaporated, sprinkle with flour. Stir until bubbly.

6. Add beef stock and tomatoes. Cook together for 10 minutes.

7. Add more salt and pepper to taste.

8. Serve hot.

Serves 4.

📖 **Library Link 2:** Research German ratskellers.

PAPRIKA SCHNITZEL
(Veal with Paprika Sauce)

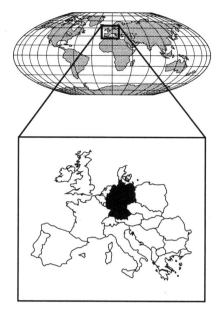

Germany

INGREDIENTS

2 pounds veal steaks, ½-inch thick

1 teaspoon salt

½ teaspoon pepper

3 tablespoons butter

2 tablespoons butter

2 shallots, chopped

1 clove garlic, minced finely

2 tablespoons flour

1½ tablespoons paprika

2 cups beef stock or bouillon

⅓ cup water

2 tablespoons vinegar

¼ cup sour cream

STEPS

1. Pound veal steaks until thin.
2. Sprinkle salt and pepper on both sides.
3. Melt 3 tablespoons butter in large skillet over medium-high heat.
4. Add veal steaks. Fry on both sides until browned and cooked through.
5. Put veal on an oven-proof serving dish. Keep warm in a 250-degree oven.
6. Put 2 tablespoons butter in skillet over medium-high heat.
7. Add shallots and garlic. Cook until soft.
8. Stir in flour and paprika.
9. Slowly stir in bouillon, water, and vinegar.
10. Cook over low heat 10-15 minutes or until thickened.
11. Stir in sour cream.
12. Remove veal steaks from oven. Pour paprika sauce over them.
13. Serve hot.

Serves 4.

📖 **Library Link 3:** Research the Schnitzel.

BOCKWURST
(Veal Sausage)

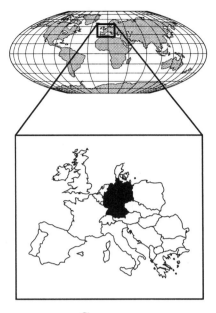

Germany

INGREDIENTS

2 pounds veal

1½ pounds pork shoulder

Water

1 pound pork suet

1 pint heavy cream

3 tablespoons chives, chopped

1 onion, minced finely

1½ teaspoons salt

½ teaspoon pepper

½ teaspoon allspice

1 teaspoon nutmeg

¼ teaspoon cloves

Sheep casings, washed and dried

STEPS

1. Boil veal and pork shoulder in water in a large saucepan for ¾ hour.
2. Drain water. Grind veal and pork three times.
3. Add suet to meats.
4. Stir rest of ingredients except casings into meat. Mix well.
5. Stuff meat mixture into casings. Tie into 4-inch lengths.
6. Put into large saucepan. Cover with water.
7. Bring to boil over medium-high heat.
8. Reduce heat and simmer ½ hour.
9. Refrigerate.

Serves 8-10.

📖 **Library Link 4:** Research Bockwurst.

HIMMEL UND ERDE

(Heaven and Earth Potatoes,
Apple, and Bacon)

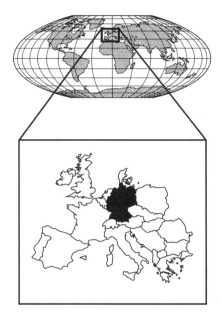

Germany

INGREDIENTS

$\frac{1}{2}$ pound potatoes, peeled and cubed

Water

$\frac{1}{2}$ teaspoon salt

1 apple, peeled, cored, and sliced

1 teaspoon butter

$\frac{1}{4}$ cup chopped onion

4 slices bacon, cut into 2-inch pieces

STEPS

1. Put potatoes in a medium saucepan.
2. Add water to $1\frac{1}{2}$ inches in pan.
3. Add salt.
4. Bring to boil over medium-high heat.
5. Reduce heat. Cover pan and cook for 10-15 minutes or until potatoes are tender.
6. Stir in apple slices. Continue cooking until apple is tender.
7. Put butter in small saucepan over medium heat.
8. Stir in onion. Cook until soft.
9. Add bacon. Cook until done.
10. Using a large spoon or fork, mash potatoes and apple slices until blended but lumpy.
11. Stir in bacon mixture.
12. Serve hot.

Serves 4.

📖 **Library Link 5:** Research the varying terrain of Germany.

KARTOFFELKLÖSSE
(Potato Dumplings)

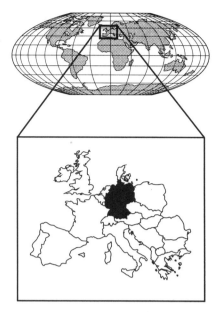

Germany

INGREDIENTS

3 tablespoons butter

2 slices white bread, cut into small cubes

1⅓ cups flour

1¾ pounds potatoes, peeled and cooked

2 eggs

1 teaspoon salt

¼ teaspoon pepper

¼ teaspoon nutmeg

Water

STEPS

1. Put butter in medium skillet over medium heat.
2. Add bread and cook until browned. Set aside.
3. Put flour in large bowl. Take out 2 tablespoons and set aside.
4. Grate potatoes. Add to flour in large bowl.
5. Stir in eggs, salt, pepper, and nutmeg.
6. Use 2 tablespoons flour to flour hands.
7. Knead mixture and shape into 24 balls.
8. Press a few of the cooked bread cubes into the center of each ball. Seal well.
9. Fill a large pot (4-5 quarts) with water to within 2 inches from top.
10. Bring water to a boil over medium-high heat.
11. Gently lower dumpling balls into water.
12. After dumplings rise to the top, cook 3-5 more minutes or until cooked through.
13. Remove dumplings from water. Keep on a warmed platter.
14. Repeat with rest of dumplings.
15. Serve as a side dish to meats.

Serves 10-12.

📖 **Library Link 6:** Research special foods for the Easter season.

APFEL STRUDEL
(Apple Strudel)

INGREDIENTS

2 eggs
6 tablespoons butter, softened
1 cup flour
¼ teaspoon salt
4 medium apples, peeled, cored, and chopped
½ cup blanched almonds, chopped
2 tablespoons citron, minced finely
¼ cup currants
⅔ cup sugar
1½ teaspoons cinnamon
½ teaspoon nutmeg
Whipped cream, optional

Germany

STEPS

1. Put eggs in a medium bowl. Beat well.
2. Beat in ½ of the butter.
3. Beat in flour and salt.
4. Knead dough 15 minutes.
5. Stretch dough out to a very thin rectangle.
6. Sprinkle apples along one side of the dough.
7. Sprinkle almonds, citron, currants, sugar, cinnamon, and nutmeg on top of apples.
8. Dot with 1 tablespoon butter.
9. Fold pastry over filling. Shape in long roll.
10. Place on greased baking pan.
11. Spread rest of butter over top.
12. Bake in 375-degree oven for 35-45 minutes or until browned.
13. Serve warm with or without whipped cream.

Serves 6.

📖 **Library Link 7:** Research favorite cakes and cookies of Germany.

ANNOTATED BIBLIOGRAPHY

Bell, Anthea. *The Wise Queen*. Illustrated by Chihiro Iwasaki. Natick, MA: Picture Book Studio, 1984. Grades 1 and up.
When a king banishes his queen, she outwits him.

Chaikin, Miriam. *A Nightmare in History: The Holocaust 1933-1945*. New York: Clarion Books, 1987. Grades 5 and up.
Diary excerpts, illustrations, photographs, and text describe the history of anti-Semitism, the wartime ghettos, and the death camps.

Chmielarz, Sharon. *End of Winter*. Illustrated by Annette Cable. New York: Crown, 1992. Grades kindergarten and up.
Based on German customs, this is the story of townspeople who try to scare winter away.

Corrin, Sara, and Stephen Corrin, retellers. *The Pied Piper of Hamelin*. Illustrated by Errol Le Cain. San Diego, CA: Harcourt Brace Jovanovich, 1988. Grades 1 and up.
Rich illustrations enliven this traditional tale.

Gauch, Patricia. *Once upon a Dinkelsbühl*. Illustrated by Tomie de Paola. New York: G.P. Putnam's Sons, 1977. Grades 2 and up.
Based on a legend celebrated in Germany, the children help save their town of Dinkelsbühl when it is invaded.

Grimm, Jacob, and Wilhelm Grimm. *The Golden Goose*. Retold and illustrated by Dorothée Duntze. New York: North-South Books, 1988. Grades 1 and up.
Three brothers are tested, and Simpleton proves to be the most successful.

_____. *Snow White and Rose Red*. Retold and illustrated by Bernadette Watts. New York: North-South Books, 1988. Grades 1 and up.
Two sisters are visited and befriended by an enchanted bear.

Latimer, Jim. *The Irish Piper*. Illustrated by John O'Brien. New York: Charles Scribner's Sons, 1991. Grades 2 and up.
The town of Hamelin, Germany, is overrun with rats, and only the Pied Piper from County Clare in Ireland can lure the rats away with his tune about cheese and bacon. In this telling, the mayor and alderman challenge the piper to take their children as well, and he does.

Manheim, Ralph, selector and translator. *Rare Treasures from Grimm: Fifteen Little-Known Tales*. Illustrated by Erik Blegvad. Garden City, NY: Doubleday, 1977. Grades 3 and up.
Selections include "Thousandfurs," "Darling Roland," "The Three Spinners," "Iron Hans," and others.

Mayer, Mercer. *Favorite Tales from Grimm*. New York: Four Winds Press, 1982. Grades 3 and up.
Mercer has illustrated a striking collection of Grimm tales.

Skurzynski, Gloria. *What Happened in Hamelin*. New York: Four Winds Press, 1979. Grades 5 and up.
This is a novelized version of the Pied Piper of Hamelin story. Pair with the picture book version by Jim Latimer.

Zelinsky, Paul O., reteller. *Rumpelstiltskin*. New York: Dutton Children's Books, 1986. Grades kindergarten and up.
   This traditional Grimm folktale shimmers with Zelinsky's oil paintings.

VIDEO

Pied Piper of Hamelin. Coronet, 1980. 11 minutes. Grades kindergarten and up.
   The tale of a minstrel who helps rid a town of rats and teaches the townspeople a lesson.

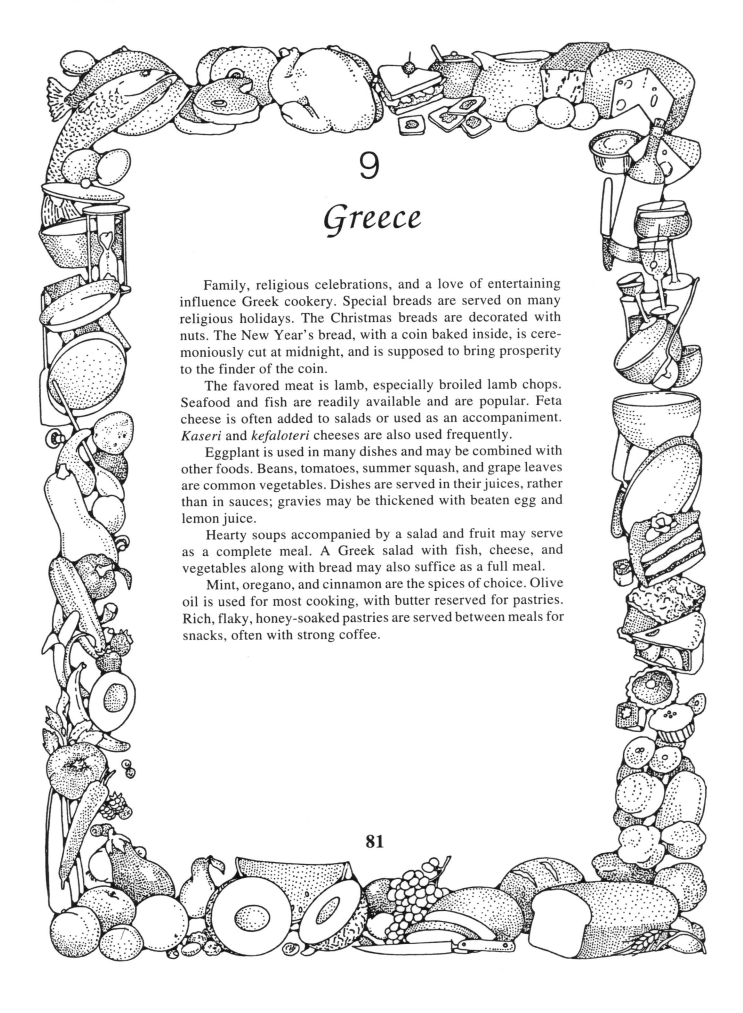

9

Greece

Family, religious celebrations, and a love of entertaining influence Greek cookery. Special breads are served on many religious holidays. The Christmas breads are decorated with nuts. The New Year's bread, with a coin baked inside, is ceremoniously cut at midnight, and is supposed to bring prosperity to the finder of the coin.

The favored meat is lamb, especially broiled lamb chops. Seafood and fish are readily available and are popular. Feta cheese is often added to salads or used as an accompaniment. *Kaseri* and *kefaloteri* cheeses are also used frequently.

Eggplant is used in many dishes and may be combined with other foods. Beans, tomatoes, summer squash, and grape leaves are common vegetables. Dishes are served in their juices, rather than in sauces; gravies may be thickened with beaten egg and lemon juice.

Hearty soups accompanied by a salad and fruit may serve as a complete meal. A Greek salad with fish, cheese, and vegetables along with bread may also suffice as a full meal.

Mint, oregano, and cinnamon are the spices of choice. Olive oil is used for most cooking, with butter reserved for pastries. Rich, flaky, honey-soaked pastries are served between meals for snacks, often with strong coffee.

GREEK SALAD

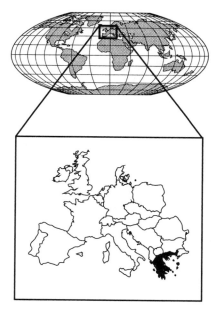

Greece

INGREDIENTS

1 head romaine lettuce

1 tomato, cut into chunks

½ cucumber, peeled and sliced

½ green pepper, seeded and chopped

1 scallion, chopped

1 small can black olives

⅔ cup feta cheese

⅓ cup lemon juice

1 cup olive oil

Salt, pepper, oregano to taste

STEPS

1. Wash and dry lettuce.
2. Tear lettuce into bite-sized pieces.
3. Add tomato, cucumber, pepper, scallion, olives, and feta. Toss lightly.
4. Mix lemon juice, oil, salt, pepper, and oregano in a jar.
5. Put lid on jar. Shake well.
6. Add desired amount of oil mixture to salad.

Serves 6-8.

📖 **Library Link 1:** What is the source of feta cheese?

PSARI PLAKI
(Fish Plaki)

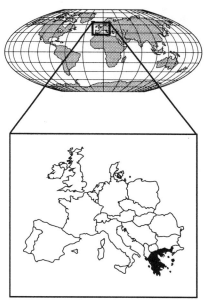

Greece

INGREDIENTS

3 pounds fish (bass, halibut, cod, or haddock fillets)

Salt and pepper

½ cup olive oil

3 tomatoes, sliced

2 scallions, chopped

¾ cup parsley, chopped

2 cloves garlic, minced

15 saltine crackers, ground into crumbs

2 tablespoons butter

2 onions, sliced into rings

1 lemon, sliced

1 cup water

STEPS

1. Put fish in a large, greased baking pan.
2. Sprinkle fish with salt, pepper, and olive oil.
3. Add tomato slices, scallions, parsley, and garlic.
4. Sprinkle cracker crumbs over mixture and dot with butter.
5. Place onion and lemon rings over mixture.
6. Add water.
7. Bake in a 350-degree oven for 45 minutes.

Serves 6.

📖 **Library Link 2:** Research the olive, including nonfood uses.

ARNI PSITO
(Leg of Lamb)

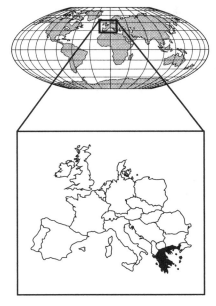

Greece

INGREDIENTS

1 leg of lamb

3 cloves garlic

Salt and pepper

5 tablespoons melted butter

1 lemon

2 cups hot water

STEPS

1. Wash leg of lamb. Pat dry.
2. Cut slits in several places on leg of lamb.
3. Slice garlic and place in slits.
4. Sprinkle lamb all over with salt and pepper.
5. Brush butter all over lamb.
6. Put lamb in roasting pan.
7. Cut lemon in half. Squeeze juice from both halves over lamb.
8. Roast lamb in a 450-degree oven for $\frac{1}{2}$ hour.
9. Lower heat to 350 degrees. Add water. Roast for 3 hours.
10. Add more water if needed.
11. Baste lamb with juices. Serve.

Serves 6-8.

📖 **Library Link 3:** Research the age of lamb at slaughter. Compare to other ages of meat at slaughter.

MOUSSAKA

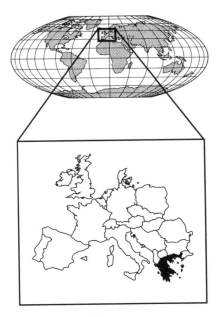

Greece

INGREDIENTS

4 eggplants, peeled and cut
    into thick slices
Salt
4 tablespoons butter
2 pounds ground beef
2 onions, chopped
2 tablespoons tomato paste
⅓ cup parsley, chopped
½ cup beef broth
Salt and pepper
½ cup water

¼ teaspoon cinnamon
3 eggs, beaten
⅓ cup grated cheese
½ cup bread crumbs
6 tablespoons butter
6 tablespoons flour
3 cups scalded milk
¼ teaspoon nutmeg
4 egg yolks, beaten
Cooking oil
Grated cheese

STEPS

1. Put eggplant slices on a plate. Sprinkle with salt. Set aside.
2. Melt 4 tablespoons butter in a large frying pan over medium heat.
3. Add ground beef and onions. Fry until meat is browned.
4. Add tomato paste, parsley, beef broth, salt, pepper, and water.
5. Simmer until liquid is absorbed.
6. Remove from heat.
7. Stir in cinnamon, eggs, cheese, and ½ of the bread crumbs.
8. Melt 6 tablespoons butter in a saucepan over low heat.
9. Stir in the flour.
10. Slowly stir in milk.
11. Continue to cook until sauce is thick.
12. Add salt and pepper to taste.
13. Add nutmeg.
14. Stir a small amount of the sauce into the egg yolks.
15. Stir egg yolks into sauce.
16. Cook for 2 minutes, stirring constantly.
17. Remove from heat.
18. Brown eggplant in cooking oil over medium-high heat.
19. Grease a large casserole dish.
20. Sprinkle rest of bread crumbs in bottom of dish.
21. Add a layer of eggplant slices. Add some of the ground beef mixture. Continue making layers.
22. Cover with sauce and grated cheese.
23. Bake in a 350-degree oven for 1 hour.

Serves 10-12.

📖 **Library Link 4:** What botanical family does eggplant belong to? What are other members of the family?

FAVA

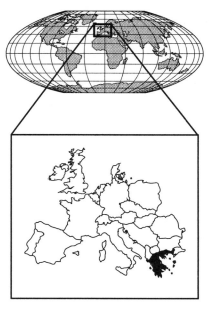

Greece

INGREDIENTS

1 cup yellow dried split peas

Water

3 tablespoons butter

1 onion, minced

2 cloves garlic, minced

1 teaspoon salt

⅛ teaspoon oregano

Olive oil

STEPS

1. Wash peas.
2. Put peas in a saucepan. Cover with water.
3. Bring to a boil over medium-high heat. Remove scum.
4. Melt butter in frying pan over medium heat.
5. Stir in onion and garlic. Cook until browned.
6. Add onion mixture to beans.
7. Stir in salt and oregano.
8. Cover pan. Reduce to simmer.
9. Simmer until water is absorbed, stirring occasionally.
10. Remove from heat. Sprinkle with olive oil.
11. May be served hot or cold.

Serves 4-6.

📖 **Library Link 5:** Research Pythagoras's belief about fava, also called the broad bean.

BAKLAVA

INGREDIENTS

1 pound phyllo pastry sheets

1½ cups butter, melted

1 pound walnuts, chopped finely

6 tablespoons sugar

1 teaspoon cinnamon

¼ teaspoon nutmeg

3 cups sugar

2½ cups water

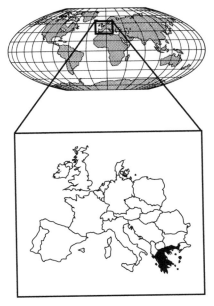

Greece

STEPS

1. Place 10 sheets of phyllo pastry in a 13-x-9-x-2 inch pan.
    Brush each sheet with butter.

2. Mix walnuts, 6 tablespoons sugar, cinnamon, and nutmeg in a small bowl.

3. Sprinkle ⅓ of mixture over top phyllo sheet.

4. Place another 6 sheets of phyllo pastry on top. Brush each with butter.

5. Sprinkle another ⅓ of walnut mixture over these sheets.

6. Place remaining phyllo sheets on top, brushing them with butter.

7. Sprinkle with last ⅓ of walnut mixture.

8. Use a sharp knife to cut the baklava into diamond shapes.

9. Pour remaining butter over baklava. Bake in 350-degree oven for 30 minutes.

10. Reduce heat to 300 degrees. Bake for 1 hour longer.

11. Remove from oven. Let cool.

12. While baklava is cooling, put 3 cups sugar and 2½ cups water in a saucepan.

13. Bring to a boil over medium-high heat.

14. Reduce heat. Simmer for 15 minutes.

15. Pour hot syrup over cooked baklava.

16. Let sit for 30 minutes before serving.

Serves 30.

📖 **Library Link 6:** How were the first Greek breads and cakes baked?

ANNOTATED BIBLIOGRAPHY

Aliki. *Three Gold Pieces*. New York: Pantheon Books, 1967. Grades kindergarten and up.
    Yannis leaves his family to work as a servant to a rich man. When he is paid for his hard work with only advice he is disappointed, but he follows the advice and is amply rewarded.

_____. *The Twelve Months*. New York: Greenwillow Books, 1978. Grades kindergarten and up.
    A widow with five children is rewarded for her diligence, good cheer, and wisdom, but a jealous neighbor fails in her attempts to earn an equal reward.

D'Aulaire, Ingri, and Edgar Parin D'Aulaire. *Book of Greek Myths*. Garden City, NY: Doubleday, 1962. Grades 4 and up.
    This oversize collection provides a wide variety of myths.

Delton, Juli. *My Uncle Nikos*. Illustrated by Marc Simont. New York: Thomas Y. Crowell, 1983. Grades 1 and up.
    Helen spends her summer gardening with her uncle in a village in the mountains of Greece.

Fox, Paula. *Lily and the Lost Boy*. New York: Orchard Books, 1987. Grades 5 and up.
    Lily and Paul spend a summer on the Greek island of Thasos with an unpredictable American boy.

Hutton, Warwick, reteller. *The Trojan Horse*. New York: Margaret K. McElderry Books, 1992. Grades 2 and up.
    King Menelaus uses an enormous wooden horse to sneak his soldiers into and conquer Troy.

Lasker, Joe. *The Great Alexander the Great*. New York: Viking, 1983. Grades 2 and up.
    Alexander's exploits with his great horse, Bucephalus, are described with vivid paintings and narrative.

Powell, Anton. *The Greek World*. New York: Warwick Press, 1987. Grades 4 and up.
    Rich photographs and drawings highlight this overview of Greek history.

VIDEOS

Aesop's Fables. Society for Visual Education, 1985. 29:40 minutes. Grades preschool and up.
    Fables include "The Boy Who Cried Wolf," "The Country Mouse and the Town Mouse," "The Fox and the Grapes," "The Tortoise and the Hare," and "The Wolf in Sheep's Clothing."

Athens and the Greek Spirit. Society for Visual Education. 30 minutes. Grades 4 and up.
    Visit the birthplace of Western civilization.

Greece: The Land and the People. Coronet, 1977. 11 minutes. Grades 4 and up.
    A Greek man and woman describe the people, geography, industry, agriculture, arts, and sciences of Greece.

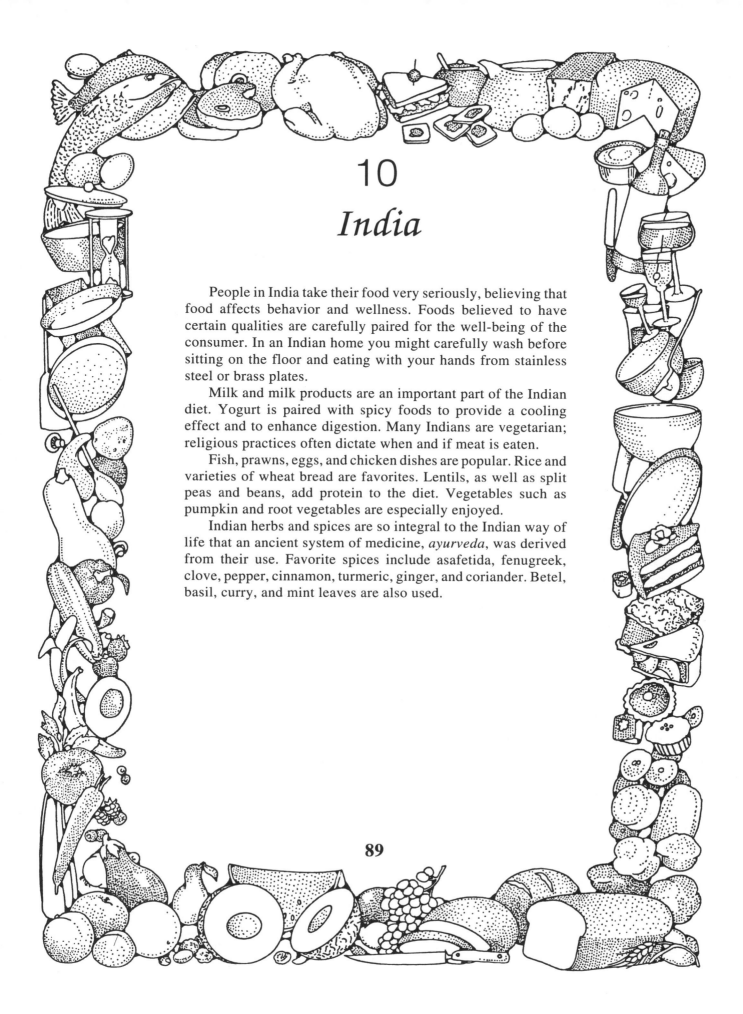

10

India

People in India take their food very seriously, believing that food affects behavior and wellness. Foods believed to have certain qualities are carefully paired for the well-being of the consumer. In an Indian home you might carefully wash before sitting on the floor and eating with your hands from stainless steel or brass plates.

Milk and milk products are an important part of the Indian diet. Yogurt is paired with spicy foods to provide a cooling effect and to enhance digestion. Many Indians are vegetarian; religious practices often dictate when and if meat is eaten.

Fish, prawns, eggs, and chicken dishes are popular. Rice and varieties of wheat bread are favorites. Lentils, as well as split peas and beans, add protein to the diet. Vegetables such as pumpkin and root vegetables are especially enjoyed.

Indian herbs and spices are so integral to the Indian way of life that an ancient system of medicine, *ayurveda*, was derived from their use. Favorite spices include asafetida, fenugreek, clove, pepper, cinnamon, turmeric, ginger, and coriander. Betel, basil, curry, and mint leaves are also used.

CHANNA DAL

(Curried Chickpeas)

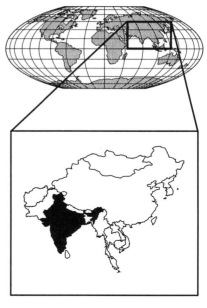

India

INGREDIENTS

1½ cups chickpeas, washed and drained

Water to soak

5 cups water

1 teaspoon ground turmeric

¼ teaspoon ground cumin

½ teaspoon ground coriander

¼ teaspoon pepper

3 tablespoons butter

1 teaspoon cumin seed

1 small onion, chopped finely

1 clove garlic, chopped finely

1 teaspoon ground ginger

STEPS

1. Put chickpeas in a large bowl. Cover with water and soak overnight.

2. Drain water off chickpeas. Put chickpeas in a heavy saucepan.

3. Add 5 cups water, turmeric, cumin, coriander, and pepper.

4. Bring to boil over medium-high heat.

5. Reduce heat to low. Cover pan. Simmer for 1 hour.

6. Melt butter over medium heat in a saucepan. Add the cumin seed and cook one minute.

7. Stir the chopped onion, chopped garlic, and ginger into the butter. Cook for 3-5 minutes or until the onion turns brown.

8. Stir butter mixture into chickpea mixture.

9. Bring to a boil.

10. Reduce heat to low. Cover pan. Simmer for 30 minutes.

Serves 6-9.

📖 **Library Link 1:** What are Asian nonfood uses of turmeric?

SHEB KI CHATNI

(Apple Chutney)

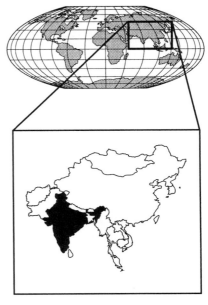

India

INGREDIENTS

3 medium sour apples

½ cup dried peaches

½ cup dried pears

½ cup raisins

2 cloves garlic, chopped finely

2 teaspoons fresh ginger, chopped finely

1 teaspoon salt

¼ teaspoon cayenne pepper

1 cup vinegar

1⅔ cups sugar

STEPS

1. Peel and core the apples. Chop finely.
2. Put all ingredients in a heavy saucepan. Bring to a boil over medium-high heat. Stir well.
3. Reduce heat to low. Simmer for 45 minutes. Stir every 10 minutes. Mixture will become thick.
4. Remove from heat. Let mixture cool.
5. Store chutney in a covered plastic or glass container in the refrigerator.

Serves 6.

📖 **Library Link 2:** What is the purpose of a chutney in an Indian meal?

CHEPATIS
(Flat Wheat Bread)

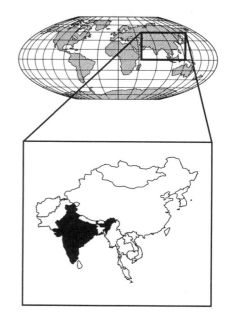

India

INGREDIENTS

2 cups whole wheat flour

2½ tablespoons butter, softened

1 teaspoon salt

1 cup water

½ cup white flour

STEPS

1. Put whole wheat flour in a large bowl.
2. Add softened butter to flour. Cut in with two knives until mixture is crumbly.
3. Add salt to water. Stir well.
4. Add water mixture to flour, a little at a time, until it makes a firm dough. You may not need all of the water.
5. Sprinkle some of the white flour on a pastry board. Knead the dough for 5 minutes.
6. Put the dough back in the bowl. Cover with a damp cloth. Let stand for one hour.
7. Divide the dough into small balls about the size of a walnut.
8. Use the rest of the white flour on the pastry board. Roll out each ball until it is flattened to about ⅛-inch thick.
9. Lightly grease griddle and heat over medium-high heat.
10. Put 1 flat piece of dough in the griddle. Cook 1-2 minutes on each side or until brown spots appear.
11. Wrap cooked pieces in a towel to keep them warm while cooking the rest.
12. Serve warm with butter.

Serves 8.

📖 **Library Link 3:** Wheat is eaten more than rice in northern India. How many years has wheat been cultivated in Eurasia?

DAHI MURGHI
(Chicken Cooked with Yogurt)

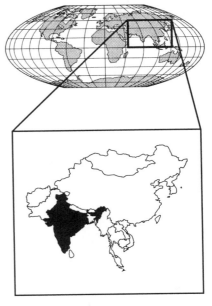

India

INGREDIENTS

3½ to 4 pounds chicken pieces

2 small cups plain yogurt (12 ounces)

1 teaspoon salt

1 piece ginger root (½ to 1 inch long), peeled and grated

1 green chili, seeded and chopped fine

5 cloves garlic, crushed

2 ounces (2 tablespoons) clarified butter

3 chives, chopped

STEPS

1. Remove the skin from the chicken pieces. Prick them all over with a fork.

2. Put chicken pieces in a deep bowl.

3. Mix the yogurt, salt, ginger, chili, and garlic in a small bowl.

4. Pour mixture over chicken. Stir well.

5. Cover the bowl with plastic wrap. Store in the refrigerator for 4-5 hours.

6. Heat half the butter in a large saucepan over medium-high heat.

7. Put the chicken and yogurt mixture in the pan. Cook, stirring constantly, until the chicken is cooked through and most of the yogurt mixture has evaporated.

8. Heat the rest of the butter over medium heat in a small frying pan.

9. Add the chives to the butter and cook for 3 minutes.

10. Sprinkle chives over the chicken mixture. Serve hot.

Serves 4.

📖 **Library Link 4:** Research the origins of yogurt.

SAFFRON RICE

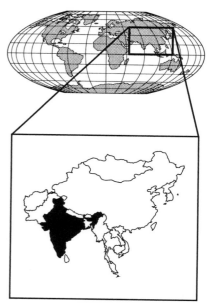

India

INGREDIENTS

4 ounces uncooked, long-grain rice

1 cup water

1½ teaspoons salt

½ teaspoon ground saffron

STEPS

1. Put all ingredients in a 1½-quart saucepan. Stir well.
2. Cook on high heat until mixture boils.
3. Reduce heat to low. Cover pan. Let simmer for 15-20 minutes until rice is tender and liquid has been absorbed.
4. Serve hot.

Serves 4.

📖 **Library Link 5:** Research how saffron is made.

GAJAR HALVA
(Carrot Halva)

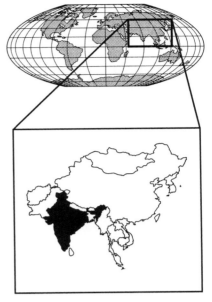

India

INGREDIENTS

1 cup whole milk

2 cups shredded carrots

5 tablespoons raisins

3 teaspoons honey

4 teaspoons margarine

¼ teaspoon cardamom

⅛ teaspoon ground saffron

1 ounce slivered almonds

STEPS

1. Put milk in a medium saucepan. Bring to boil over medium heat.

2. Reduce heat to low. Add carrots, raisins, and honey.

3. Cook 30-40 minutes, stirring every 5 minutes. Mixture should be thick.

4. Stir in margarine, cardamom, and saffron. Cook 1 minute.

5. Put mixture in food processor. Process until smooth.

6. Pour mixture in a serving dish. Sprinkle with almonds.

7. May be served hot or cold.

Serves 4.

📖 **Library Link 6:** What climatic conditions are necessary to grow cardamom? What role did cardamom play in trade?

ANNOTATED BIBLIOGRAPHY

Birch, David. *The King's Chessboard*. Illustrated by Devis Grebu. New York: Dial Books for Young Readers, 1988. Grades 1 and up.

A king insists on rewarding a wise man for his service. The wise man reluctantly tells the king he will take one grain of rice for one square of the chessboard, doubling it each day. The wise man gives the rice to the poor, but soon the king realizes he has promised 549,755,830,887 tons of rice. They resolve the dilemma in a most satisfying, and wise, manner.

Brown, Marcia. *The Blue Jackal*. New York: Charles Scribner's Sons, 1977. Grades 1 and up.

When a jackal jumps into a vat of indigo to escape a pack of dogs, he must face other animals' reactions. Taken from the *Panchatantra*.

Cowcher, Helen. *Tigress*. New York: Farrar, Straus & Giroux, 1991. Grades kindergarten and up.

When a tigress kills a bullock in a sanctuary, the people find a humane way to drive away the tigress.

Demi, adapter. *The Hallowed Horse*. New York: Dodd, Mead, 1987. Grades 1 and up.

A beautiful white horse saves the kingdom from 500 hissing snakes.

Duff, Maggie, reteller. *Rum Pum Pum*. Illustrated by Jose Aruego and Ariane Dewey. New York: Macmillan, 1978. Grades preschool and up.

When the king steals Blackbird's wife, Blackbird and other wronged animals make war on the king.

Jaffrey, Madhur. *Seasons of Splendour: Tales, Myths and Legends of India*. Illustrated by Michael Foreman. New York: Atheneum, 1985. Grades 2 and up.

Jaffrey has provided information not only about the tales but also about her childhood, bringing India alive. The tales are arranged to correspond with religious festivals throughout the Hindu year.

Myers, Walter Dean. *The Golden Serpent*. Illustrated by Alice and Martin Provensen. New York: Viking, 1980. Grades 1 and up.

The king demands that the wise man Pundabi and a young boy named Ali solve a mystery, but the king insists they must discover the mystery. Pundabi and Ali outwit the king and help the people.

Newton, Pam. *The Stonecutter*. New York: G.P. Putnam's Sons, 1990. Grades kindergarten and up.

A poor stonecutter is dissatisfied with his life until his wishes are repeatedly granted. Finally he learns that being a poor stonecutter is best.

Ram, Govinder. *Rama and Sita*. London: Blackie and Son, 1987. Grades 2 and up.

In this tale taken from *The Ramayana*, King Dasaratha's wife has her stepson Rama, his wife, and his brother banished to the forest so her son can become king.

Rodanas, Kristina. *The Story of Wali Dâd*. New York: Lothrop, Lee & Shepard, 1988. Grades 1 and up.

An old grass cutter in India has his generosity repaid many fold.

Siberell, Anne. *A Journey to Paradise*. New York: Henry Holt, 1990. Grades 1 and up.

A magic elephant takes Guba and his friends to paradise, where they learn that what they already have in their garden is quite enough.

Tagore, Rabindranath. *Paper Boats*. Illustrated by Grayce Bochak. Honesdale, PA: Caroline House, 1992. Grades preschool and up.

Paper illustrations and simple text tell of a young boy who sends paper boats with his and the village's name down the river.

Towle, Faith M. *The Magic Cooking Pot*. Boston: Houghton Mifflin, 1975. Grades 1 and up.

A goddess gives a poor man a magic pot that provides rice. But when an innkeeper trades the magic pot for an ordinary one, the poor man returns to the goddess and receives an even more powerful pot.

VIDEOS

Boy of India: Rana and His Elephant. Coronet, 1985. 12 minutes. Grades kindergarten and up.

Rana is learning to be an elephant handler like his father.

Deepa and Rupa. Barr Films, 1991. 30 minutes. Grades kindergarten and up.

Animation and live action are used to tell an Indian folktale of two stepsisters, one kind and caring, the other unkind.

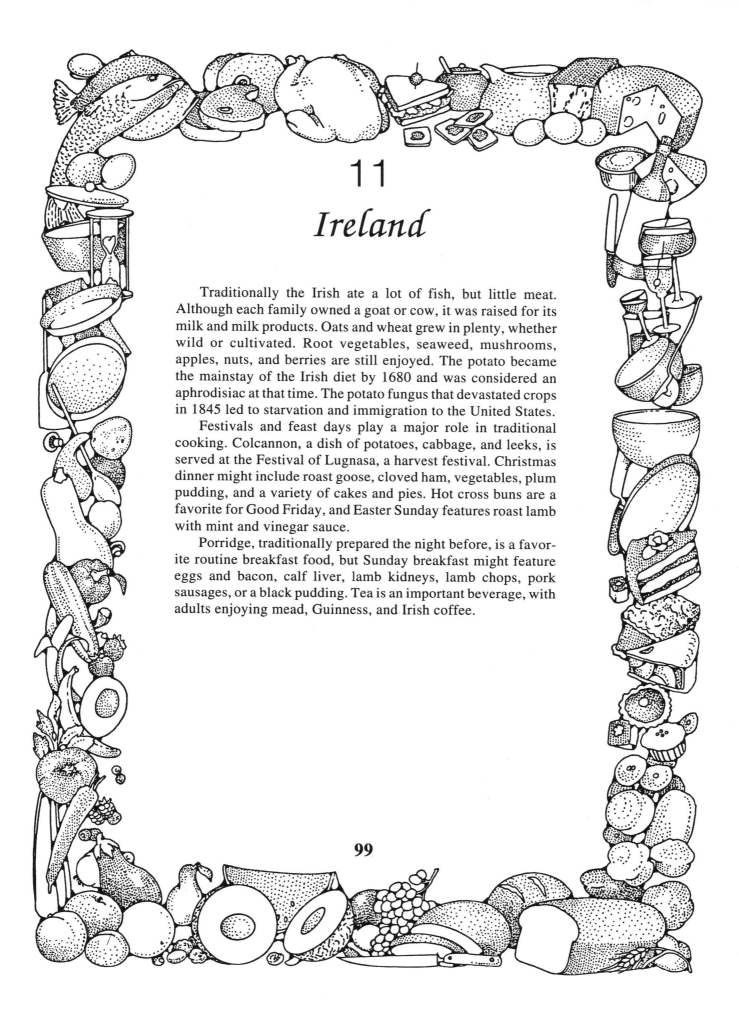

11

Ireland

Traditionally the Irish ate a lot of fish, but little meat. Although each family owned a goat or cow, it was raised for its milk and milk products. Oats and wheat grew in plenty, whether wild or cultivated. Root vegetables, seaweed, mushrooms, apples, nuts, and berries are still enjoyed. The potato became the mainstay of the Irish diet by 1680 and was considered an aphrodisiac at that time. The potato fungus that devastated crops in 1845 led to starvation and immigration to the United States.

Festivals and feast days play a major role in traditional cooking. Colcannon, a dish of potatoes, cabbage, and leeks, is served at the Festival of Lugnasa, a harvest festival. Christmas dinner might include roast goose, cloved ham, vegetables, plum pudding, and a variety of cakes and pies. Hot cross buns are a favorite for Good Friday, and Easter Sunday features roast lamb with mint and vinegar sauce.

Porridge, traditionally prepared the night before, is a favorite routine breakfast food, but Sunday breakfast might feature eggs and bacon, calf liver, lamb kidneys, lamb chops, pork sausages, or a black pudding. Tea is an important beverage, with adults enjoying mead, Guinness, and Irish coffee.

99

CORNED BEEF AND CABBAGE

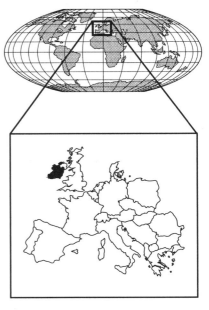

Ireland

INGREDIENTS

2 pounds corned beef

Cold water

2 onions, sliced

1 head of cabbage, shredded

Salt and pepper

STEPS

1. Put corned beef in a large pot. Cover with water.

2. Bring to a boil over high heat. Skim off grease.

3. Cover pan with a lid. Reduce heat to a simmer.

4. Simmer for 1½ hours.

5. Add onions and cabbage. Cover and simmer for another 30 minutes.

6. Drain liquid off. Season meat and vegetables with salt and pepper to taste.

7. Serve meat on a platter with onions and cabbage around it.

Serves 6.

Library Link 1: Research how hot stones were used for cooking.

IRISH STEW

INGREDIENTS

3 pounds neck of mutton, cut into pieces

1½ pounds of potatoes, peeled and cut into large chunks

3 onions, sliced

4 carrots, sliced

Salt and pepper to taste

1 teaspoon thyme

⅓ cup chopped parsley

3 cups cold water

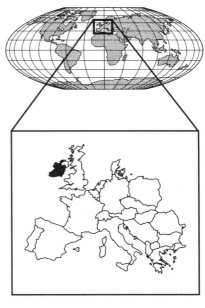

Ireland

STEPS

1. Put mutton, potatoes, onions, and carrots in a large casserole dish.

2. Sprinkle salt, pepper, thyme, and parsley over meat and vegetables.

3. Cover with water.

4. Cover dish.

5. Bake in a 275-degree oven for about 2½ hours or until meat is tender. Add more water if necessary.

6. Serve hot from the casserole dish, adding more salt and pepper if desired.

Serves 6.

📖 **Library Link 2:** Research the benefits of the potato.

POTATO CAKES

INGREDIENTS

1 pound potatoes, peeled

Water

⅓ cup butter, melted

¾ teaspoon salt

¼ teaspoon nutmeg

½ cup flour

Bacon fat or oil for frying

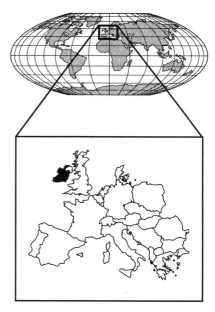

Ireland

STEPS

1. Put potatoes in a saucepan. Cover with water and boil until soft.

2. Mash potatoes and spread them onto a pastry board.

3. Spread butter, salt, nutmeg, and flour over potatoes. Knead until well mixed. Use extra flour if needed.

4. Roll out to ¼-inch thickness.

5. Cut into squares or wedges.

6. Put bacon fat or oil in a large skillet over medium-high heat.

7. Fry potato cakes until browned on both sides.

Serves 6.

📖 **Library Link 3:** Research the potato famine of 1845-49.

CHRISTMAS PUDDING

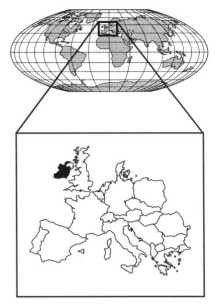

Ireland

INGREDIENTS

1½ cups plus 2 tablespoons flour

6½ cups fresh bread crumbs

1¼ cups brown sugar

1 cup currants

1⅔ cups raisins

1 cup mixed candied fruit

10 ounces chopped suet

½ teaspoon salt

¾ teaspoon nutmeg

¾ teaspoon allspice

Grated rind of 1 lemon

2 large eggs, beaten

⅔ cup milk

1¼ cups apple cider

STEPS

1. Put all ingredients in a large bowl. Mix well.

2. Pour mixture into 2 greased pudding dishes about ¾ full. There should be room to rise.

3. Cover pudding dishes with waxed paper and then with foil.

4. Tie string around foil.

5. Put pudding dishes into a large pot. Put water into the pot to within 1 inch from the top of the pudding dishes.

6. Bring water to a boil over medium-high heat.

7. Cover pan. Reduce heat to simmer.

8. Steam pudding in the pot for 7 hours. Check and add water every hour or so.

9. Remove pudding from dishes and eat warm.

10. May serve with Irish coffee sauce following (see recipe on page 104).

Serves 8-10.

📖 **Library Link 4:** What is the symbolism of the candle in the window on Christmas Eve?

IRISH COFFEE SAUCE

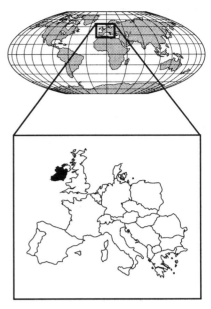

Ireland

INGREDIENTS

1 cup sugar

5 tablespoons water

1 cup black coffee

1 teaspoon vanilla

Candy thermometer

STEPS

1. Put sugar and water into a saucepan. Cook over medium-high heat. Stir well.

2. When mixture boils, stop stirring. Cook to the caramel stage on a candy thermometer.

3. Remove from heat.

4. Have an adult put potholders on both hands and very slowly stir coffee into the caramel mixture.

5. Put mixture back on heat. Stir until smooth.

6. Remove from heat.

7. When mixture cools, stir in vanilla.

8. May be served over puddings or ice cream.

Serves 4-5.

📖 **Library Link 5:** Coffee contains caffeine. What are the effects of caffeine?

ANNOTATED BIBLIOGRAPHY

Boden, Alice, reteller. *The Field of Buttercups*. New York: Henry Z. Walck, 1974. Grades kindergarten and up.
   In this Irish tale, Michael O'Grady is certain he will be able to retrieve a leprechaun's pot of gold, only to discover the leprechaun has outwitted him.

Cooper, Susan, reteller. *The Selkie Girl*. Illustrated by Warwick Hutton. New York: Margaret K. McElderry Books, 1986. Grades 2 and up.
   Donallan falls in love with a seal girl and marries her, only to eventually lose her to her life in the sea off the coasts of Ireland and Scotland.

Delaney, Frank. *Legends of the Celts*. New York: Sterling, 1992. Grades 5 and up.
   Drawn from the earliest Celtic literature, this is for the mature reader.

de Paola, Tomie. *Fin M'Coul: The Giant of Knockmany Hill*. New York: Holiday House, 1981. Grades preschool and up.
   Cucullin is the strongest giant in Ireland, but Fin M'Coul's wife outwits the giant.

_____. *Patrick: Patron Saint of Ireland*. New York: Holiday House, 1992. Grades kindergarten and up.
   The life of Patrick is described with simple text and bold illustrations.

Fritz, Jean. *Brendan the Navigator*. Illustrated by Enrico Arno. New York: Coward, McCann & Geoghegan, 1979. Grades 3 and up.
   Children in Ireland believe that St. Brendan discovered America long before Columbus. Fritz explores what she describes as a "history mystery."

Haugaard, Erik Christian. *Prince Boghole*. Illustrated by Julie Downing. New York: Macmillan, 1987. Grades 1 and up.
   When the princess and her father can't decide who she will marry, they have a contest that no one expects the shabby Prince Brian (Boghole) to win.

Jacobs, Joseph. *Celtic Fairy Tales*. Illustrated by John D. Batten. New York: Dover Publications, 1968. Grades 3 and up.
   This collection of 26 tales provides a good introduction to Celtic stories.

Kessel, Joyce K. *St. Patrick's Day*. Illustrated by Cathy Gilchrist. Minneapolis, MN: Carolrhoda Books, 1982. Grades preschool and up.
   This easy-to-read book is a fine introduction to the history and customs of St. Patrick's Day.

Langford, Sondra Gordon. *Red Bird of Ireland*. New York: Atheneum, 1983. Grades 4 and up.
   When Aderyn's father flees Ireland in 1846, she must face famine, fever, and cruelty.

Latimer, Jim. *The Irish Piper*. Illustrated by John O'Brien. New York: Charles Scribner's Sons, 1991. Grades 2 and up.
   The town of Hamelin, Germany, is overrun with rats and only the Pied Piper from County Clare in Ireland can lure the rats away with his tune about cheese and bacon. In this telling, the mayor and alderman challenge the piper to take their children as well, and he does.

Mayer, Marianna. *The Black Horse*. Illustrated by Katie Thamer. New York: Dial Books for Young Readers, 1984. Grades 2 and up.
   In this Celtic tale, Tim and his black horse demonstrate devotion to the Princess of the Mountain.

McDermott, Gerald, reteller. *Daniel O'Rourke*. New York: Viking Kestrel, 1986. Grades preschool and up.
    Daniel is led on a strange adventure after resting under the pooka spirit's wall.

_____. *Tim O'Toole and the Wee Folk*. New York: Viking, 1990. Grades 1 and up.
    Tim and his family are so poor that he sets out in search of a job. Instead he discovers some little people who bring him prosperity.

Shute, Linda. *Clever Tom and the Leprechaun*. New York: Lothrop, Lee & Shepard, 1988. Grades preschool and up.
    When Tom finds a leprechaun, he is determined to get the creature's pot of gold.

FILM

P Is for Potato. Handel Film, 1988. 14 minutes. Grades kindergarten and up.
    From the *Food from A to Z* series, this film discusses the importance of the potato to the Irish.

VIDEO

The Tale of the Wonderful Potato. Phoenix/PBA Films and Video. 24 minutes. Grades 1 and up.
    This video about the journey of the potato from South America to Ireland introduces viewers to the history and politics of the potato.

12

Italy

Climate, geography, and government have combined to provide a variety of Italian cookery. For example, climate is a factor in the availability of two important ingredients of Italian food: butter and oil. The cool climes of northern Italy provide for excellent butter. Oil and pork fats are staples of central and southern Italy.

The independent tribes, cities, duchies, and kingdoms before unification in 1870 fostered local traditions and loyalties. Food may be distinctly different in two cities that are only 100 miles apart. Certain dishes are prepared on a strictly seasonal basis, based entirely on what is available locally.

One unifying feature is the country's creativity with pasta. No other country has used flour and water to such advantage, stretching expensive meats or enhancing seasonal vegetables. Tomatoes, oil, cheese, and a few herbs may be transformed with bread or pasta into a variety of flavorful textures.

A final noteworthy feature of Italian cookery is the abundance of excellent wine. Vineyards, prolific throughout the country, provide regional wines, but the most famous remains the red Chianti.

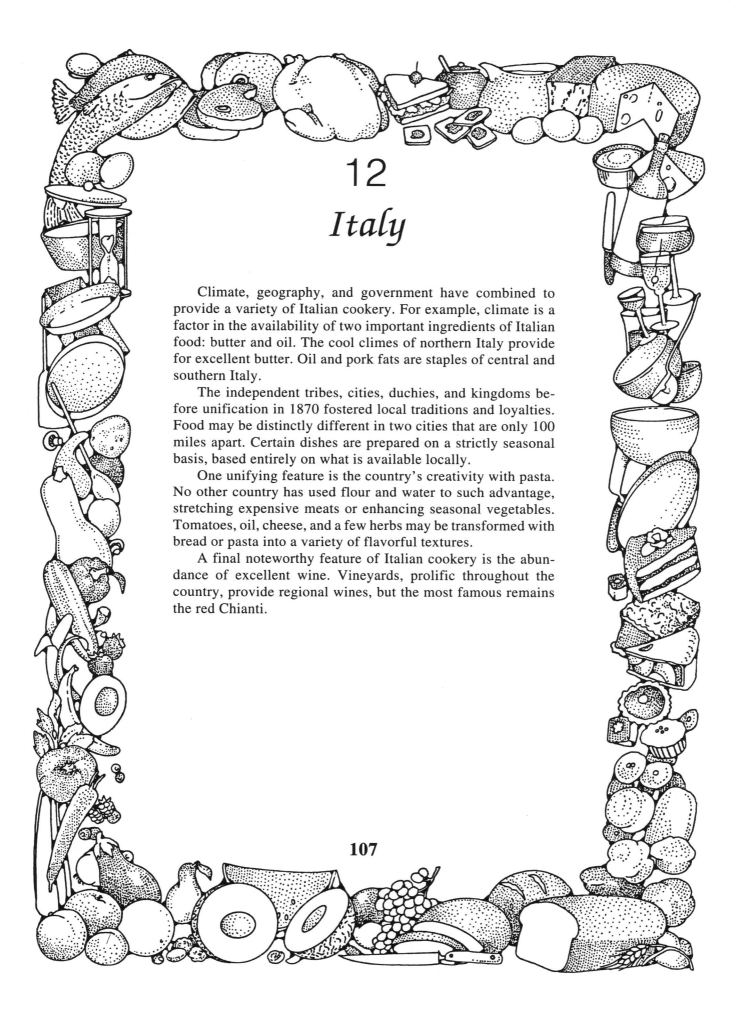

POLLO ALLA CACCIATORE
(Chicken Cacciatore)

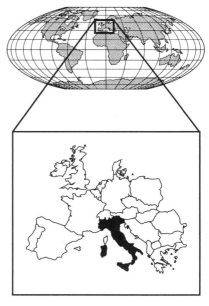

Italy

INGREDIENTS

1 4-pound chicken, cut into pieces

¼ cup flour

¼ cup olive oil

2 tablespoons chopped onion

1 clove garlic, finely chopped

¼ cup tomato paste

1¼ teaspoons salt

¼ teaspoon pepper

1 cup chicken stock

1 bay leaf

⅛ teaspoon thyme

½ teaspoon basil

1 cup sliced mushrooms

STEPS

1. Rinse and pat dry chicken pieces.
2. Cover chicken pieces with flour.
3. Heat oil in large pan over medium-high heat.
4. Stir in onions and garlic.
5. Add chicken pieces. Brown on both sides.
6. Add rest of ingredients.
7. Cover and cook over low heat for 1 hour. Stir frequently until chicken is tender.

Serves 4-6.

📖 **Library Link 1:** Research the history of domesticated chickens.

SPINACI, OLIO E LIMONE
(Spinach with Oil and Lemon)

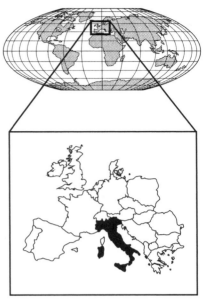

Italy

INGREDIENTS

1¼ pounds fresh spinach

Water

3 tablespoons olive oil

Juice of half a lemon

Salt and freshly ground pepper to taste

STEPS

1. Wash spinach and leave whole.
2. Put 2 inches water in a large saucepan. Bring to a boil over high heat.
3. Add spinach. Cook for 2 minutes.
4. Drain immediately.
5. Put spinach in large bowl.
6. Mix oil and lemon in a small bowl. Pour it over the spinach.
7. Season with salt and pepper.

Serves 4.

📖 **Library Link 2:** Research the origin and relatives of spinach.

FETTUCCINE ALFREDO

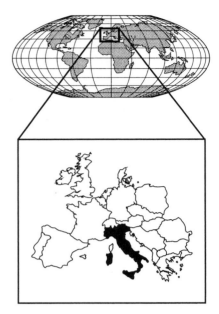

Italy

INGREDIENTS

8 tablespoons butter

½ pound sliced mushrooms

½ teaspoon salt

¼ teaspoon pepper

¼ teaspoon oregano

1 teaspoon finely chopped garlic cloves

1 pound fettuccine noodles, cooked

¼ cup grated Romano cheese

¼ cup shredded mozzarella cheese

STEPS

1. Preheat oven to 375 degrees.
2. Melt butter in a skillet over medium heat.
3. Add mushrooms, salt, pepper, oregano, and garlic.
4. Cook over low heat until mushrooms are heated through.
5. Drain cooked noodles and put in shallow dish.
6. Stir in Romano cheese and butter mixture.
7. Sprinkle with mozzarella cheese.
8. Bake about 5 minutes in oven until cheese is melted, but not browned.

Serves 6.

📖 **Library Link 3:** What is the earliest evidence of pasta in Italy?

ANISE COOKIES

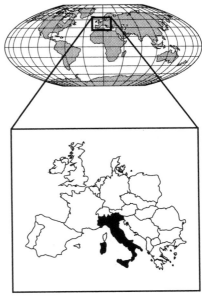

Italy

INGREDIENTS

4 eggs

1 cup sugar

1 teaspoon vanilla

⅓ cup milk

2 tablespoons anise seed

3 cups flour

4 teaspoons baking powder

1 cup margarine, softened

STEPS

1. Preheat oven to 375 degrees.
2. Beat eggs well in a large bowl.
3. Add sugar, vanilla, milk, and anise. Stir well.
4. In another bowl, mix flour and baking powder. Cut in margarine.
5. Combine 2 mixtures.
6. Roll dough out onto floured board. Cut into shapes.
7. Bake on greased cookie sheet 12 minutes or until lightly browned.

Makes 6-8 dozen cookies.

📖 **Library Link 4:** How did the Romans use anise?

LEMON ICE

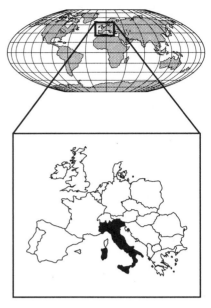

Italy

INGREDIENTS

2 cups water

1 cup sugar

1 cup lemon juice

STEPS

1. Bring the water and sugar to a boil over medium-high heat in a 2-quart pan.

2. Cook and stir until sugar dissolves.

3. Boil 5 more minutes.

4. Remove the pan from heat. Cool mixture.

5. Stir in lemon juice.

6. Pour mixture into a freezer tray. Freeze, stirring occasionally, about 4 hours. Mixture should be the texture of snow.

Serves 4.

📖 **Library Link 5:** How were lemons introduced to Europe?

BLUEBERRY SPUMONI

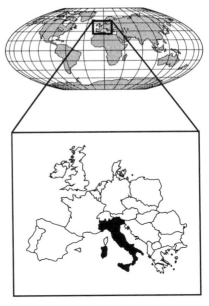

Italy

INGREDIENTS

1 quart blueberries

1 tablespoon lemon juice

⅓ cup sugar

1 pint heavy cream

⅔ cup powdered sugar

STEPS

1. Crush blueberries in a large bowl.

2. Add lemon juice and sugar. Stir well.

3. Whip heavy cream in a medium bowl until it forms stiff peaks.

4. Fold powdered sugar into whipped cream.

5. Combine blueberry and cream mixtures.

6. Place in a 1-quart mold. Freeze for at least 2 hours.

Serves 4.

📖 **Library Link 6:** Research the history of ice cream.

ANNOTATED BIBLIOGRAPHY

Calvino, Italo, reteller. *Italian Folktales*. Translated by George Martin. New York: Pantheon Books, 1956. Grades 4 and up.
Notes and a bibliography accompany 200 tales.

Connolly, Peter. *Pompeii*. Oxford, England: Oxford University Press, 1990. Grades 4 and up.
Detailed drawings and color photographs explore a myriad of details of life in Pompeii. Although the focus is on life before the eruption of Vesuvius, the information about the excavations is fascinating.

Cossi, Olga. *Orlanda and the Contest of Thieves*. Illustrated by Tom Sarmo. Lakewood, CO: Bookmakers Guild, 1989. Grades 2 and up.
Orlanda is a master pickpocket and thief, but the mayor's wife's contest changes her forever.

de Paola, Tomie, reteller. *The Clown of God*. San Diego, CA: Harcourt Brace Jovanovich, 1978. Grades 2 and up.
Giovanni is a wonderful juggler, but as he grows older he faces poverty and ridicule. He juggles for the Holy Child in a church and causes a miracle.

_____. *The Legend of Old Befana*. San Diego, CA: Harcourt Brace Jovanovich, 1980. Grades kindergarten and up.
On Twelfth Night, Old Befana sweeps across the sky, bringing cakes to children as she continues her search for the Christ Child.

_____. *The Mysterious Giant of Barletta*. San Diego, CA: Harcourt Brace Jovanovich, 1984. Grades kindergarten and up.
When an army threatens the town of Barletta, a giant statue cleverly intimidates the enemy.

Humphrey, Kathryn Long. *Pompeii: Nightmare at Midday*. New York: Franklin Watts, 1990. Grades 2 and up.
Color photographs, drawings, and simple text explore the tragedy of the eruption of Vesuvius.

Manson, Christopher, reteller. *The Crab Prince*. New York: Henry Holt, 1991. Grades 2 and up.
Rosella befriends a giant crab, breaks its spell, and marries the prince.

Plume, Ilse. *The Story of Befana*. Boston: David R. Godine, 1981. Grades 1 and up.
See above entry, *The Legend of Old Befana*, by Tomie de Paola.

Sis, Peter. *Follow the Dream: The Story of Christopher Columbus*. New York: Alfred A. Knopf, 1991. Grades kindergarten and up.
Several illustrations about Columbus's youth in Genoa, Italy, provide an interesting backdrop for his voyages to the New World.

VIDEOS

Ancient Empire. Society for Visual Education, 1985. 25:20 minutes. Grades 7 and up.
  Visit Rome and discover the reasons for the rise and fall of the Roman Empire.

Five Secrets in a Box. Spoken Arts. Grades 1 and up.
  Galileo's daughter Virginia explores her father's observatory by day, learning about his important work by night. By Catherine Brighton.

Rembrandt's Beret or The Painter's Crown. Spoken Arts, 1992. Grades 1 and up.
  In this story by Johnny Alcorn, a young boy describes how the paintings and artists of a secret hall came alive and spoke to him.

Strega Nona and Other Stories. Children's Circle. 30 minutes. Grades preschool and up.
  Additional tales include "Tikki Tikki Tembo," "A Story—A Story," and "The Foolish Frog."

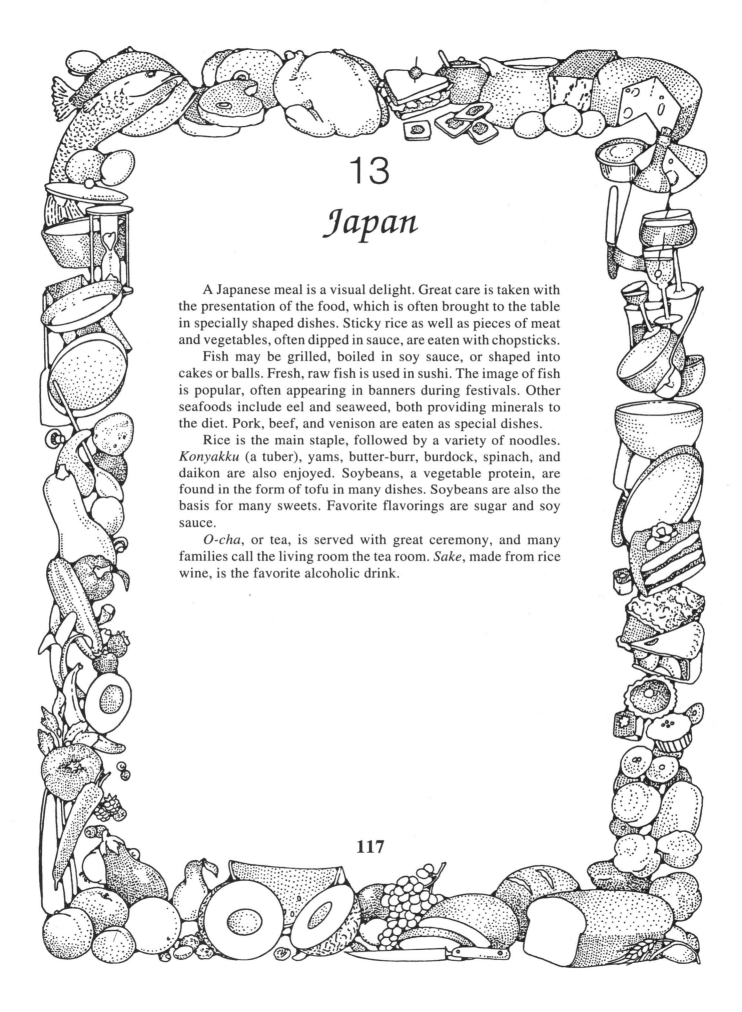

13

Japan

A Japanese meal is a visual delight. Great care is taken with the presentation of the food, which is often brought to the table in specially shaped dishes. Sticky rice as well as pieces of meat and vegetables, often dipped in sauce, are eaten with chopsticks.

Fish may be grilled, boiled in soy sauce, or shaped into cakes or balls. Fresh, raw fish is used in sushi. The image of fish is popular, often appearing in banners during festivals. Other seafoods include eel and seaweed, both providing minerals to the diet. Pork, beef, and venison are eaten as special dishes.

Rice is the main staple, followed by a variety of noodles. *Konyakku* (a tuber), yams, butter-burr, burdock, spinach, and daikon are also enjoyed. Soybeans, a vegetable protein, are found in the form of tofu in many dishes. Soybeans are also the basis for many sweets. Favorite flavorings are sugar and soy sauce.

O-cha, or tea, is served with great ceremony, and many families call the living room the tea room. *Sake*, made from rice wine, is the favorite alcoholic drink.

CHAWAN MUSHI
(Eggs Steamed in Cups)

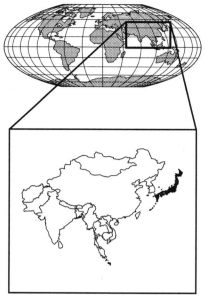

Japan

INGREDIENTS

4 eggs

3 cups chicken broth

2 teaspoons soy sauce

⅔ cup chicken, cooked and cut into cubes

6 mushrooms

1 tablespoon chopped scallions

6 small pieces lemon peel

STEPS

1. Beat eggs in a medium bowl.
2. Stir in chicken broth and soy sauce.
3. Skim foam off the top with a spoon.
4. Divide chicken and mushrooms among 6 small heat-resistant bowls.
5. Pour egg mixture into the 6 bowls over chicken and mushrooms.
6. Sprinkle scallions over top of egg mixture.
7. Put 1 piece of lemon peel on top of mixture in each bowl.
8. Set the bowls in a large cake pan in 1 inch of water.
9. Put pan with bowls into oven. Bake at 350 degrees for 25-30 minutes.
10. Serve hot.

Serves 6.

📖 **Library Link 1:** What are the *okonomiya*?

KUSHIYAKI
(Shrimp and Vegetables on Skewers)

INGREDIENTS

¼ cup soy sauce

2½ tablespoons sugar

1 tablespoon grated gingerroot

1 pound large shrimp, peeled and deveined

1 green pepper, cut into 1-inch pieces

1 large onion, cut into 1-inch chunks

1 pound whole mushrooms

Cooked rice, optional

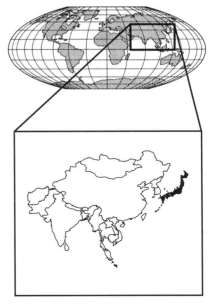

Japan

STEPS

1. Put soy sauce, sugar, and gingerroot in a small bowl.
2. Preheat oven to broil. (You may use an outdoor grill.)
3. Alternate shrimp, peppers, onion chunks, and mushrooms on skewers.
4. Brush soy sauce mixture on shrimp and vegetables.
5. Broil shrimp and vegetables for 6-10 minutes or until cooked through.
6. Brush sauce over skewers several times during cooking.
7. Serve hot over rice if desired. May pour rest of soy sauce mixture over all.

Serves 6.

📖 **Library Link 2:** Find photographs of presentations of Japanese food to share with the class.

SUKIYAKI

(Simmered Beef and Vegetables)

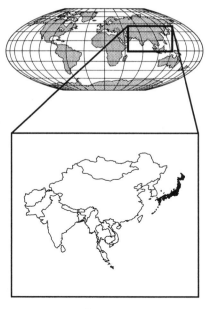

Japan

INGREDIENTS

2 pounds rib eye of beef

1 12-ounce block of tofu,
    cut into 1-inch cubes

½ tablespoon oil

6 scallions, cut into 1-inch pieces

1 can shirataki noodles

16 ounces bamboo shoots

½ cup sliced mushrooms

¼ cup soy sauce

2 cups water

3½ tablespoons sugar

Cooked rice, optional

STEPS

1. Slice beef into thin slices.
2. Slice tofu into thin slices.
3. Heat oil in skillet over medium heat.
4. Sauté beef in skillet.
5. Add scallions, shirataki noodles, bamboo shoots, mushrooms, and tofu to beef in skillet.
6. Mix soy sauce, water, and sugar in bowl.
7. Pour soy sauce mixture over the meat and vegetables in the skillet.
8. Simmer in skillet about 10 minutes or until meat is cooked through.
9. Serve hot over rice if desired.

Serves 6.

📖 **Library Link 3:** Research why tofu became popular in Japan.

SUSHI

INGREDIENTS

3 tablespoons white vinegar

4 tablespoons sugar

2½ teaspoons salt

1 tablespoon lemon juice

1 tablespoon shoyu (Japanese soy sauce)

2 cups white rice

2½ cups cold water

6 sheets *nori* (dried seaweed)

1 cucumber, peeled, halved, and cut into six ¼-inch strips

½ pound shrimp, peeled, deveined, and cooked

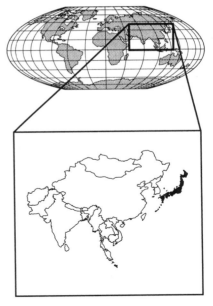

Japan

STEPS

1. Put vinegar, sugar, salt, and lemon juice in a medium saucepan.
2. Bring to a boil over medium-high heat.
3. Stir in shoyu. Let cool.
4. Put rice and cold water in a 2-quart saucepan.
5. Let rice soak for 30 minutes.
6. Bring rice and water to boil over medium-high heat. Cook for 10 minutes or until all water is absorbed.
7. Remove rice from heat. Let sit for 10 minutes.
8. Stir vinegar mixture into rice. Mix thoroughly.
9. Cool to room temperature.
10. Put *nori* on baking sheet. Put under broiler 4 seconds.
11. Place a sheet of *nori* on a bamboo mat or heavy cloth napkin.
12. Spread ⅙th of the vinegared rice over the *nori* sheet.
13. Place ⅙th of the cucumber and shrimp in the middle of the rice in a row.
14. Use the mat or napkin to roll the *nori* up tightly.
15. Squeeze gently to make the roll firm.
16. Unroll mat or napkin. Slice sushi into 1-inch rounds. Repeat with the remaining sheets of *nori*.
17. May be served with pickled ginger.

Serves 10-12.

📖 **Library Link 4:** Research the varieties of fish eaten in Japan.

GREEN TEA BAVARIAN CREAM

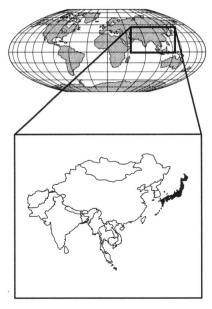

Japan

INGREDIENTS

2½ tablespoons gelatin powder

½ cup water

2 tablespoons green tea powder (*matcha*)

6 tablespoons hot tap water

⅔ cup sugar

3 egg yolks, well beaten

2 cups milk

1½ cups whipping cream

1 tablespoon sugar

STEPS

1. Dissolve gelatin powder in ½ cup water.
2. Put green tea powder, 6 tablespoons hot water, and 1 teaspoon of the sugar in another bowl.
3. Stir well.
4. Strain well to remove any lumps.
5. Beat the rest of the sugar into the egg yolks in a third bowl.
6. Put the milk into a saucepan. Heat over very low heat until milk is warm.
7. Stir ¼ cup of the warm milk into the egg yolks.
8. Stir the egg yolk mixture very slowly into the saucepan of milk.
9. Continue to heat, stirring constantly, until mixture begins to thicken.
10. Slowly stir in the gelatin and the green tea mixtures.
11. Whip 1 cup of the whipping cream until thick, but not stiff.
12. Slowly stir the egg and milk mixture into the whipped cream.
13. Rinse out a large serving bowl.
14. Pour mixture into the serving bowl and chill in refrigerator until set, about 2-3 hours.
15. Whip rest of whipping cream. Stir in 1 tablespoon sugar.
16. Put into a pastry tube. Pipe designs onto the chilled Bavarian cream.

Serves 6.

📖 **Library Link 5:** Find the Japanese name for a family's tea room.

ANNOTATED BIBLIOGRAPHY

Bang, Garrett, translator. *Men from the Village Deep in the Mountains and Other Japanese Folktales*. New York: Macmillan, 1973. Grades 2 and up.
Bang's translations and illustrations of these 12 traditional tales include familiar themes of lessons, tricks, and rewards.

Birdseye, Tom, adapter. *A Song of Stars*. Illustrated by Ju-Hong Chen. New York: Holiday House, 1990. Grades 2 and up.
When Princess Chauchau, a weaver, and Newlang, a herdsman, fall in love, they neglect their work. The Emperor of the Heavens decrees that they will be allowed to meet only on the seventh night of the seventh moon. This Asian legend is the inspiration for the Festival of the Milky Way in China and the Weaving Loom Festival in Japan.

Bryan, Ashley, reteller. *SH-KO and His Eight Wicked Brothers*. Illustrated by Fumio Yoshimura. New York: Atheneum, 1988. Grades 1 and up.
Sh-ko, the youngest and ugliest of nine brothers, is rewarded for his kindness with a princess's admiration.

Clément, Claude. *The Painter and the Wild Swans*. Illustrated by Frédéric Clément. New York: Dial Books for Young Readers, 1986. Grades 1 and up.
Telling the story through Japanese, English, and exquisite paintings, the Cléments tell of Teiji, a painter who goes in search of his beloved swans.

Coerr, Eleanor. *Sadako and the Thousand Paper Cranes*. New York: Dell, 1977. Grades 4 and up.
When Sadako was two, the atomic bomb was dropped on Hiroshima. At 12 she tries to fold a thousand paper cranes so she can be granted her wish for health. She dies with 644 folded, and her classmates finish for her.

Compton, Patricia, reteller. *The Terrible EEK*. Illustrated by Sheila Hamanaka. New York: Simon & Schuster, 1991. Grades kindergarten and up.
When a father shares his fears with his family, a lurking wolf and a thief hear "eek" instead of "leak." The comical chain reaction is illustrated with zest and humor.

Demi. *In the Eyes of the Cat: Japanese Poetry for All Seasons*. Translated by Tze-si Huang. New York: Henry Holt, 1992. Grades 1 and up.
Poems from nature are illustrated with rich color paintings.

Hughes, Monica, reteller. *Little Fingerling*. Illustrated by Brenda Clark. Toronto: Kids Can Press, 1989. Grades 1 and up.
When Issuun Boshi, the size of one finger, defeats evil demons he is granted one wish.

Ishii, Momoko. *The Tongue-Cut Sparrow*. Illustrated by Suekichi Akaba. Translated by Katherine Paterson. New York: Lodestar Books, 1982. Grades kindergarten and up.
An old man goes in search of his beloved sparrow after his wife cuts its tongue. While searching, he is rewarded for his kindness, but the wife must learn to overcome her greediness.

Johnston, Tony, adapter. *The Badger and the Magic Fan*. Illustrated by Tomie de Paola. New York: G.P. Putnam's Sons, 1990. Grades kindergarten and up.
When a badger tricks the *tengu* children (goblins) out of their magic fan, the goblins develop an amusing revenge.

Kimmel, Eric A., reteller. *The Greatest of All*. Illustrated by Giora Carmi. New York: Holiday House, 1991. Grades kindergarten and up.

Father Mouse does not want his daughter to marry a field mouse and sets out to discover the greatest spouse of all.

Maruki, Toshi. *Hiroshima No Pika*. New York: Lothrop, Lee & Shepard, 1980. Grades 3 and up.

This is a strikingly illustrated telling of the U.S. bombing of Hiroshima.

Morimoto, Junko. *The Inch Boy*. New York: Viking Kestrel, 1984. Grades kindergarten and up.

An inch-high boy defeats a demon, wins normal size, and marries a princess.

_____. *My Hiroshima*. Translated by Isao Morimoto. New York: Viking, 1987. Grades 3 and up.

Morimoto illustrates and tells the story of her experience when the United States dropped an atomic bomb on Hiroshima.

Paterson, Katherine. *The Tale of the Mandarin Ducks*. Illustrated by Leo and Diane Dillon. New York: Lodestar Books, 1990. Grades 2 and up.

When a kitchen maid and servant release an imprisoned mandarin duck, the greedy lord sentences them to death. The duck and its mate outsmart the lord, and the couple live happily together until they are old.

San Souci, Robert D. *The Samurai's Daughter*. Illustrated by Stephen T. Johnson. New York: Dial Books for Young Readers, 1992. Grades 2 and up.

In this haunting Japanese tale, a young girl must brave many terrors to save her father exiled on an island.

Say, Allen. *The Bicycle Man*. Oakland, CA: Parnassus Press, 1982. Grades kindergarten and up.

It is Sportsday at a small mountain school in Japan when two American soldiers arrive and one entrances the students with his bicycle riding.

Shute, Linda, reteller. *Momotaro the Peach Boy*. New York: Lothrop, Lee & Shepard, 1986. Grades kindergarten and up.

An old woodcutter and his wife find a baby boy who grows up to save an island from *oni* (ogres).

Snyder, Dianne. *The Boy of the Three-Year Nap*. Illustrated by Allen Say. Boston: Houghton Mifflin, 1988. Grades 1 and up.

Taro, the laziest boy in a Japanese village, uses his wit to gain a better home and a wife, but he cannot stay lazy after his marriage.

Takeshita, Fumiko. *The Park Bench*. Illustrated by Mamoru Suzuki. Translated by Ruth A. Kanagy. Brooklyn, NY: Kane/Miller, 1985. Grades kindergarten and up.

In this book with text in English and Japanese, life in a park is explored from the perspective of a park bench.

Tejima. *Ho-Limlim: A Rabbit Tale from Japan*. New York: Philomel, 1990. Grades kindergarten and up.

An old rabbit sets out on a spring adventure, only to learn that home is best.

Uchida, Yoshiko. *The Two Foolish Cats*. Illustrated by Margot Zemach. New York: Margaret K. McElderry Books, 1987. Grades 1 and up.

When two cats go to the monkey to settle a dispute over rice cakes, the monkey surprises them with his resolution.

Wells, Ruth. *A to Zen: A Book of Japanese Culture*. Illustrated by Yoshi. Saxonville, MA: Picture Book Studio, 1992. Grades kindergarten and up.
Each letter of the Japanese alphabet is enhanced by discussion of a related word and a lush illustration. Of particular interest is the layout of the book, which proceeds from right to left.

Winthrop, Elizabeth. *Journey to the Bright Kingdom*. Illustrated by Charles Mikolaycak. New York: Holiday House, 1979. Grades 3 and up.
A blind woman sees the world through her daughter's eyes until they bravely take a journey to a kingdom ruled by mice.

Wisniewski, David. *The Warrior and the Wise Man*. New York: Lothrop, Lee & Shepard, 1989. Grades 3 and up.
Striking illustrations of cut paper combine with text for this tale of twin brothers who compete to become emperor.

VIDEOS

The Children of Japan: Learning the New, Remembering the Old. Walt Disney, 1987. 21 minutes. Grades 4 and up.
An 11-year-old boy describes life in Japan.

Japan. Society for Visual Education. 50 minutes. Grades 4 and up.
This video introduces viewers to the history, culture, and peoples of Japan.

The Rolling Rice Ball: A Japanese Fairy Tale. Coronet, 1967. 11 minutes. Grades kindergarten and up.
A Japanese woodcutter drops his luncheon balls in a mouse hole and then follows them down.

Sadako and the Thousand Paper Cranes. Informed Democracy. 30 minutes. Grades 5 and up.
The film version of the story by Eleanor Coerr (see above).

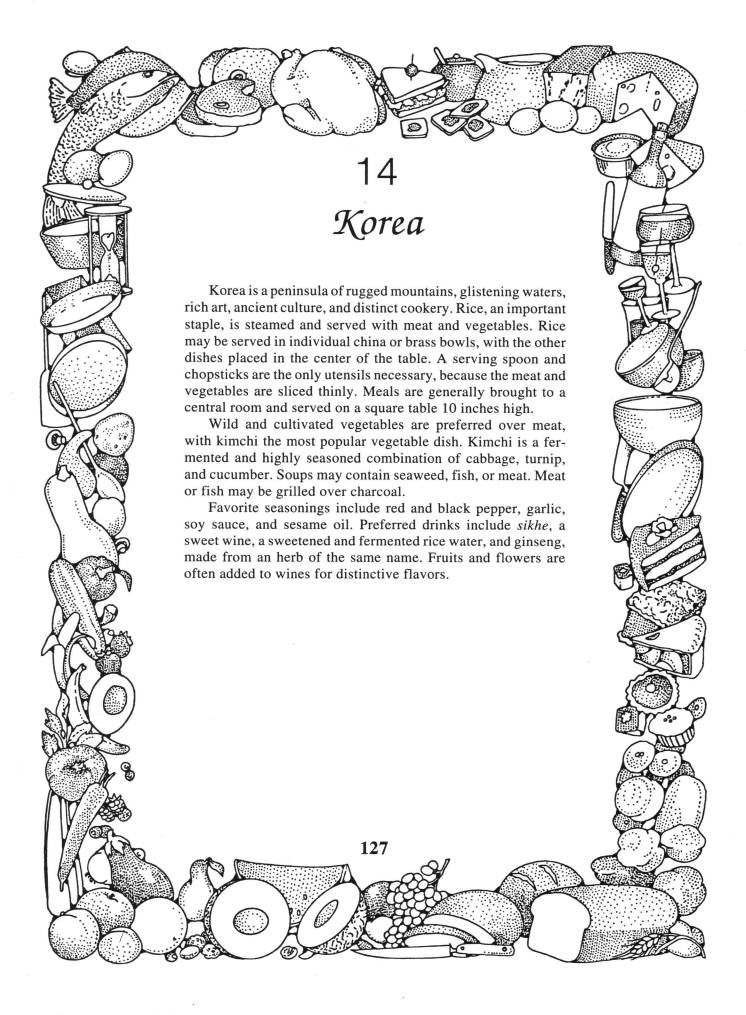

14

Korea

Korea is a peninsula of rugged mountains, glistening waters, rich art, ancient culture, and distinct cookery. Rice, an important staple, is steamed and served with meat and vegetables. Rice may be served in individual china or brass bowls, with the other dishes placed in the center of the table. A serving spoon and chopsticks are the only utensils necessary, because the meat and vegetables are sliced thinly. Meals are generally brought to a central room and served on a square table 10 inches high.

Wild and cultivated vegetables are preferred over meat, with kimchi the most popular vegetable dish. Kimchi is a fermented and highly seasoned combination of cabbage, turnip, and cucumber. Soups may contain seaweed, fish, or meat. Meat or fish may be grilled over charcoal.

Favorite seasonings include red and black pepper, garlic, soy sauce, and sesame oil. Preferred drinks include *sikhe*, a sweet wine, a sweetened and fermented rice water, and ginseng, made from an herb of the same name. Fruits and flowers are often added to wines for distinctive flavors.

127

BEEF-SPINACH SOUP

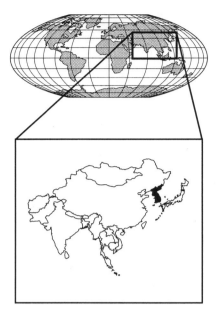

Korea

INGREDIENTS

8 ounces boneless round steak

1 tablespoon oil

¼ cup scallions, chopped

2 tablespoons sesame seeds

1 clove garlic, minced finely

1 quart water

2 tablespoons soy sauce

1 tablespoon cornstarch dissolved in 2 tablespoons water

2½ cups spinach leaves

¼ teaspoon salt

½ teaspoon pepper

STEPS

1. Put steak on broiling pan.
2. Broil under broiler in oven for 3 minutes on each side or until cooked through.
3. Cut steak into thin strips. Set aside.
4. Put oil in large saucepan over medium heat.
5. Add scallions, sesame seeds, and garlic. Cook until seeds are lightly browned.
6. Add steak strips and cook 1 minute.
7. Add water and soy sauce. Bring to a boil.
8. Reduce heat. Cover pan and simmer for 25 minutes.
9. Stir in dissolved cornstarch. Continue to stir until soup begins to thicken.
10. Stir in spinach, salt, and pepper. Cook for 5 more minutes. Serve hot.

Serves 4.

📖 **Library Link 1:** Research the traditional consumption of soup.

BINTAETOK
(Filled Mung Bean Pancakes)

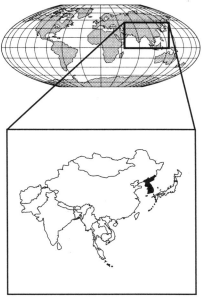

Korea

INGREDIENTS

1 cup split, skinned mung beans

½ cup long-grain rice

Water

2 cloves garlic, minced finely

1 onion, peeled and chopped

2 scallions, chopped

1 carrot, peeled and grated

1 teaspoon salt

1½-inch piece gingerroot, peeled and minced finely

2 eggs, beaten

3 teaspoons sesame oil

4 tablespoons peanut oil

⅓ cup chicken, cooked and chopped

⅓ cup bean sprouts, chopped

1 sweet red pepper, chopped

½ sweet green pepper, chopped

STEPS

1. Put mung beans and rice in a bowl. Cover with water and soak overnight.
2. The next day drain beans and rice.
3. Put beans and rice in a blender and blend until smooth.
4. Add garlic, onion, scallions, carrot, salt, gingerroot, eggs, and sesame oil. Blend until smooth. If batter is thicker than pancake batter, add some water.
5. Put 1 tablespoon peanut oil in a skillet over medium-high heat. Heat until oil is hot, but not smoking.
6. Pour ¼ of the batter into the pan. Swirl pan until batter forms a thin pancake.
7. Sprinkle ¼ of the chicken, bean sprouts, and red and green peppers over half of the pancake. Fold the pancake in half.
8. Fry pancake for 3 minutes or until pancake is slightly browned.
9. Turn pancake and fry for another 3 minutes.
10. Repeat process for other 3 pancakes.
11. Serve warm or cold, with or without Korean dipping sauce (see recipe on p. 130).

Serves 4.

📖 **Library Link 2:** How do political differences affect Korean food?

CHO KANJANG
(Korean Dipping Sauce)

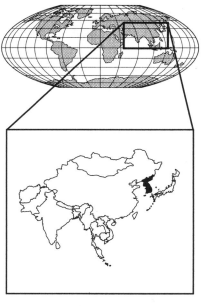

Korea

INGREDIENTS

1 tablespoon peanut oil

3 tablespoons sesame seeds

3 scallions, chopped

2 teaspoons sugar

2 tablespoons vinegar

1 tablespoon sesame oil

1 cup soy sauce

STEPS

1. Put peanut oil in a small frying pan over medium-high heat.
2. Add sesame seeds. Cook until seeds are lightly browned.
3. Remove from heat. Put seeds in a blender.
4. Blend to a paste.
5. Add scallions. Blend well.
6. Add rest of ingredients. Blend until smooth.
7. Serve immediately in small bowls or refrigerate. Use within 1 week.

 **Library Link 3:** Research holiday feasts.

KIMCHI
(Vegetable Pickle)

INGREDIENTS

1 cup sliced carrots

1 cup Chinese cabbage, cut into chunks

1 cup cauliflower, separated in florets

2½ teaspoons salt

3 scallions, minced finely

1 thin slice gingerroot, minced finely

2 teaspoons salt

½ teaspoon garlic salt

½ teaspoon sugar

¼ teaspoon crushed red pepper

Korea

STEPS

1. Put carrots, cabbage, and cauliflower in a medium bowl.

2. Sprinkle with 2½ teaspoons salt. Toss well.

3. Let stand 30 minutes.

4. Rinse with cold water. Drain well.

5. Toss well with rest of ingredients.

6. Cover tightly. Refrigerate for 48 hours.

7. Toss well. Serve cold.

Serves 4.

📖 **Library Link 4:** What colors will a Korean cook include in a meal?

BUL KO KEE
(Barbecued Beef)

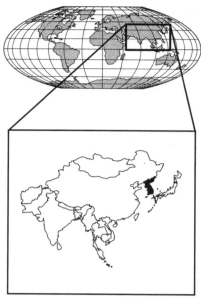

Korea

INGREDIENTS

1 pound boneless sirloin steak

¼ cup soy sauce

3½ tablespoons sugar

2½ tablespoons sesame oil

¼ teaspoon pepper

3 scallions, minced finely

3 cloves garlic, minced finely

STEPS

1. Trim fat from steak. Cut diagonally across the grain into thin strips.

2. Put rest of ingredients in a bowl. Mix well.

3. Add steak strips. Stir until steak is well coated.

4. Cover and refrigerate for 1 hour.

5. Drain steak.

6. Stir-fry in a heated skillet or wok over medium-high heat for 3 minutes or until browned.

7. May be served with rice.

Serves 4.

📖 **Library Link 5:** Beef is scarce and expensive in Korea. Research alternatives.

CHICKEN, PEAR, AND PINE NUT SALAD WITH SESAME DRESSING

Korea

INGREDIENTS

3 tablespoons oil

1 onion, peeled and chopped

3 stalks celery, sliced

8 mushrooms, washed and sliced

1½ cups cooked chicken, cut into cubes

1 1-inch piece of gingerroot, peeled and minced finely

1 clove garlic, minced finely

1 slightly underripe pear, peeled, cored, and sliced

1½ tablespoons soy sauce

1½ tablespoons vinegar

1½ tablespoons sesame oil

1½ tablespoons sugar

¾ teaspoon pepper

1½ teaspoons salt

2 tablespoons pine nuts

STEPS

1. Heat oil in frying pan or wok over medium-high heat.
2. Fry onion until soft. Remove onion.
3. Put celery in hot frying pan. Fry until tender. Remove celery from pan.
4. Fry mushrooms in hot frying pan for 2 minutes. Remove from pan.
5. Remove pan from heat.
6. Put chicken, gingerroot, and garlic in a large bowl. Stir.
7. Add cooked onions, celery, and mushrooms.
8. Stir in pear slices.
9. In a small bowl stir together soy sauce, vinegar, sesame oil, sugar, pepper, and salt. Stir well until sugar and salt are dissolved.
10. Pour the soy sauce mixture over the chicken and vegetables. Toss well.
11. Sprinkle with pine nuts. Serve.

Serves 4-6.

Library Link 6: Research the war in 1950.

ANNOTATED BIBLIOGRAPHY

Choi, Sook Nyul. *Echoes of the White Giraffe*. Boston: Houghton Mifflin, 1993. Grades 5 and up.
   In this sequel to *Year of Impossible Goodbyes*, Sookan is fifteen, living in Pusan in South Korea. Through a forbidden friendship with a young boy, she challenges tradition.

———. *Year of Impossible Goodbyes*. Boston: Houghton Mifflin, 1991. Grades 5 and up.
   Ten-year-old Sookan's family lives in northern Korea during the Japanese occupation of World War II. The end of the war brings only more challenges as northern Korea is taken over by the Soviet Union.

Ginsburg, Mirra, adapter. *The Chinese Mirror*. Illustrated by Margot Zemach. San Diego, CA: Harcourt Brace Jovanovich, 1988. Grades preschool and up.
   A Korean villager brings a Chinese mirror back to the village, creating havoc until the mirror is broken.

Han, Oki S., and Stephanie H. Plunkett, adapters. *Sir Whong and the Golden Pig*. New York: Dial Books for Young Readers, 1993. Grades kindergarten and up.
   A stranger uses a golden pig as security for the loan of a large sum of money from Sir Whong. When the pig turns out to be worthless, Sir Whong outwits the stranger.

Koh, Frances M. *Korean Holidays and Festivals*. Illustrated by Liz B. Dodson. Minneapolis, MN: EastWest Press, 1990. Grades 2 and up.
   Color illustrations accompany a year of important observations such as the Cherry Blossom Festival, Children's Day, Buddha's Birthday, and Winter Solstice Day.

Kwon, Holly H., reteller. *The Moles and the Mireuk: A Korean Folktale*. Illustrated by Woodleigh Hubbard. Boston: Houghton Mifflin, 1993. Grades preschool and up.
   Papa Mole searches above and below ground for a perfect husband for his daughter and learns from the wise Mireuk that the best husband is close at hand.

Paek, Min. *Aekyung's Dream*. San Francisco: Children's Book Press, 1988. Grades 1 and up.
   After a special dream, Aekyung tries harder to master English. This simple story is presented in English and Korean.

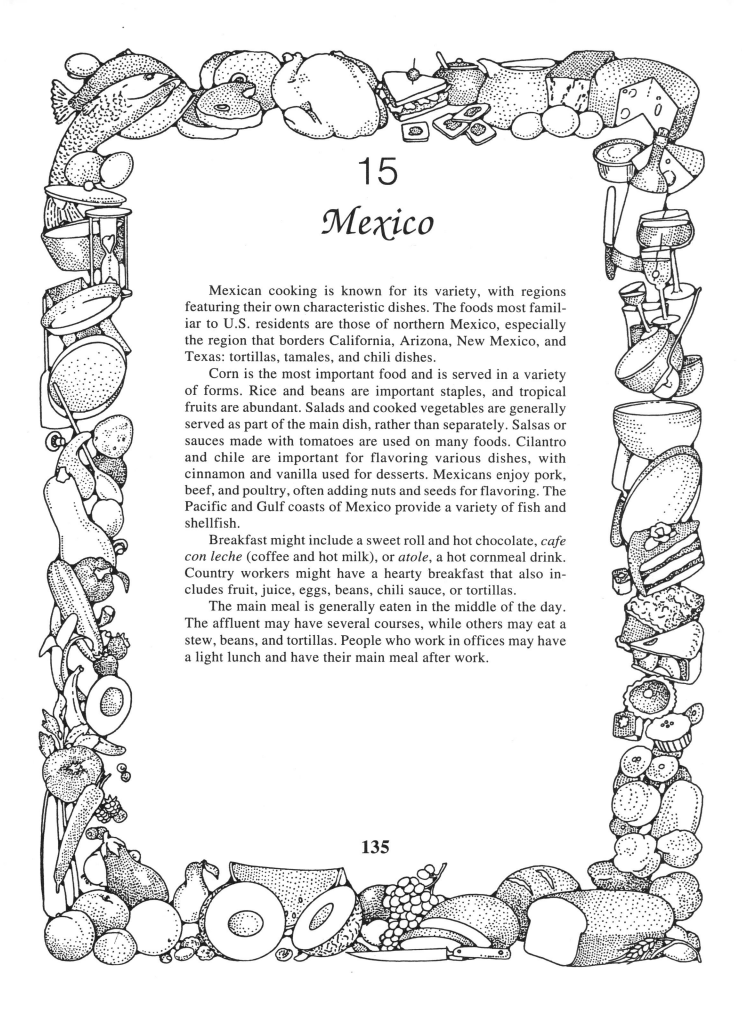

15

Mexico

Mexican cooking is known for its variety, with regions featuring their own characteristic dishes. The foods most familiar to U.S. residents are those of northern Mexico, especially the region that borders California, Arizona, New Mexico, and Texas: tortillas, tamales, and chili dishes.

Corn is the most important food and is served in a variety of forms. Rice and beans are important staples, and tropical fruits are abundant. Salads and cooked vegetables are generally served as part of the main dish, rather than separately. Salsas or sauces made with tomatoes are used on many foods. Cilantro and chile are important for flavoring various dishes, with cinnamon and vanilla used for desserts. Mexicans enjoy pork, beef, and poultry, often adding nuts and seeds for flavoring. The Pacific and Gulf coasts of Mexico provide a variety of fish and shellfish.

Breakfast might include a sweet roll and hot chocolate, *cafe con leche* (coffee and hot milk), or *atole*, a hot cornmeal drink. Country workers might have a hearty breakfast that also includes fruit, juice, eggs, beans, chili sauce, or tortillas.

The main meal is generally eaten in the middle of the day. The affluent may have several courses, while others may eat a stew, beans, and tortillas. People who work in offices may have a light lunch and have their main meal after work.

135

AVOCADO SOUP

INGREDIENTS

2 tablespoons olive oil

½ cup onion, minced finely

2 cloves garlic, minced finely

1 teaspoon flour

½ cup chicken broth

¼ teaspoon Tabasco

1 cup light cream

½ avocado, peeled and cut into large chunks

¼ teaspoon pepper

¼ cup sour cream

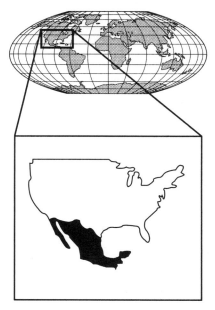

Mexico

STEPS

1. Heat oil in medium saucepan over medium heat.
2. Add onion and garlic. Cook until onion is clear.
3. Add flour. Cook and stir well for 1 minute.
4. Slowly stir in chicken broth and Tabasco. Bring to a boil.
5. Reduce heat. Simmer for 2 minutes.
6. Put cream, avocado, and pepper in a blender. Process until smooth.
7. Stir avocado mixture into broth mixture. Heat through.
8. Pour soup into bowls. Top with sour cream.

Serves 4.

📖 **Library Link 1:** Avocado soup is *sopa aquada* or wet soup. Research other kinds of soups.

TORTILLAS

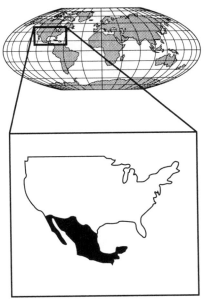

Mexico

INGREDIENTS

1 cup masa harina (tortilla flour)

1¼ cups warm water

STEPS

1. Put masa harina in a medium bowl.

2. Mix in the water to form a soft dough.

3. Shape dough into balls the size of an egg.

4. Flatten on a tortilla press or floured board to thin pancakes, about 4 inches wide.

5. Heat an ungreased griddle over medium heat. Cook tortillas about 1 minute per side or until browned.

6. Tortillas may be filled or served plain. Serve hot.

Serves 6-8.

📖 **Library Link 2:** Research Mayan beliefs about corn.

BEEF-FILLED TORTILLAS

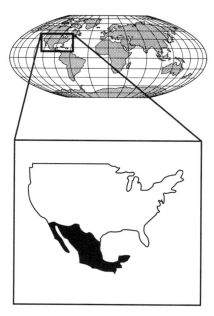

Mexico

INGREDIENTS

12 flour tortillas

2 tablespoons olive oil

5 cloves garlic, minced finely

2 small onions, minced finely

2 pounds ground beef

1 teaspoon oregano

¾ teaspoon chili powder

½ teaspoon salt

1 cup beef bouillon

¼ cup salsa

2 cups chopped tomatoes

3 cups shredded lettuce

2 cups sour cream

1½ cups shredded cheese

STEPS

1. Warm tortillas in a 400-degree oven for 3 minutes or for 30-60 seconds in a microwave oven.

2. Heat oil in a skillet over medium heat.

3. Add garlic and onions. Cook until onions are clear.

4. Add ground beef. Cook until browned.

5. Stir in oregano, chili powder, salt, bouillon, and salsa. Cook for 5 minutes or until most of the liquid evaporates.

6. Spread meat mixture on the center of each tortilla. Roll each up and top with tomatoes, lettuce, sour cream, and cheddar cheese.

7. Serve hot.

Serves 6.

📖 **Library Link 3:** Tortillas are considered the national bread of Mexico. What other Mexican foods use tortillas?

CHAYOTES RELLENOS

INGREDIENTS

4 chayotes (mango squash)

2 tablespoons olive oil

½ cup onion, minced finely

6 tablespoons green pepper, minced finely

3 teaspoons jalapeño pepper, minced finely

1 cup chopped, canned tomatoes

3 cloves garlic, minced finely

⅔ cup shredded cheddar cheese

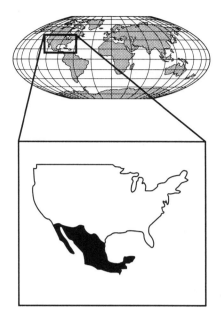

Mexico

STEPS

1. Put chayotes in a large saucepan and fill pan with 1 inch of water.

2. Bring water to a boil over medium-high heat.

3. Cover pan and reduce heat. Simmer for 30 minutes or until chayotes are tender.

4. Remove chayotes from pan. Rinse with cold water and set aside.

5. Heat oil in a skillet over medium heat.

6. Add onion and green peppers. Cook until onions are clear.

7. Stir in jalapeño pepper, tomatoes, and garlic. Cook for 3 more minutes.

8. Remove saucepan from heat.

9. Slice chayotes in half, lengthwise. Remove pits and core.

10. Scoop out pulp, being careful not to break through the skin.

11. Chop pulp. Add to tomato mixture and stir well.

12. Stir in ⅓ cup of the cheese.

13. Put chayote shells on a baking sheet. Fill with tomato mixture.

14. Sprinkle rest of cheese on top.

15. Bake in 375-degree oven for about 15 minutes or until cheese melts.

16. Serve hot.

Serves 4-8.

📖 **Library Link 4:** Research the chayote.

FRIJOLES

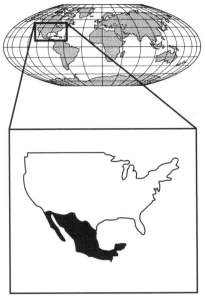

Mexico

INGREDIENTS

1¼ pounds beans (red, pinto, or black)

1 onion, minced finely

2 cloves garlic, minced finely

Water

2 tablespoons lard

1 teaspoon salt

STEPS

1. Wash beans and put in a large pot.

2. Add onion and garlic and enough water to cover the beans.

3. Bring to a boil over high heat.

4. Reduce heat to low. Cover pot and simmer for 20 minutes.

5. Stir in the lard. Cover pot and continue cooking until beans are tender. Add more water if needed.

6. Stir in salt. Cover and cook for 30 more minutes.

7. Remove 4 tablespoons of beans and a little of the liquid. Mash them together.

8. Stir this into the beans. Cook a few minutes more to thicken the liquid.

9. Serve beans warm.

Serves 6.

📖 **Library Link 5:** Research the common bean.

POLVORÓNES
(Tea Cakes)

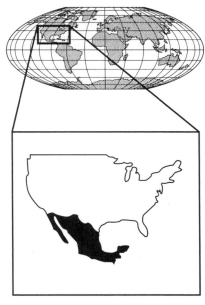

Mexico

INGREDIENTS

1¾ cups flour
½ teaspoon baking soda
½ teaspoon cream of tartar
¼ teaspoon salt
1 stick margarine, softened
½ cup powdered sugar
1 egg
¼ cup sour cream
1 teaspoon vanilla
¾ teaspoon almond flavoring
2 tablespoons flour
½ teaspoon cinnamon

STEPS

1. Put 1¾ cups flour, baking soda, cream of tartar, and salt in a small bowl. Stir well and set aside.

2. Put margarine and half of powdered sugar in a large bowl. Mix well.

3. Add egg, sour cream, vanilla, and almond flavoring to margarine and sugar. Use an electric mixer to mix well.

4. Beat in flour mixture a little at a time.

5. Wrap dough in plastic wrap. Put in refrigerator for 15 minutes.

6. Remove dough from refrigerator. Cut into 20 pieces.

7. Use hands to form each piece of dough into a ball. Use 2 tablespoons of flour to sprinkle over hands so dough doesn't stick.

8. Put balls of dough onto a greased baking sheet.

9. Bake at 400 degrees 8 minutes or until lightly browned.

10. Mix cinnamon with rest of powdered sugar.

11. Roll cakes in cinnamon mixture while warm.

12. Serve warm or cool.

Serves 10.

📖 **Library Link 6:** Research favorite desserts in Mexico.

ANNOTATED BIBLIOGRAPHY

Aardema, Verna. *Pedro and the Padre*. Illustrated by Friso Henstra. New York: Dial Books for Young Readers, 1991. Grades kindergarten and up.
In this tale from Jalisco, Mexico, Pedro lives by wit and lies until he finally learns his lesson.

____. *The Riddle of the Drum: A Tale from Tizapán, Mexico*. Illustrated by Tony Chen. New York: Four Winds Press, 1979. Grades 1 and up.
A king announces that no man may marry his daughter unless he can guess the kind of leather used in a drum.

Bierhorst, John, translator. *Spirit Child: A Story of the Nativity*. Illustrated by Barbara Cooney. New York: William Morrow, 1984. Grades 3 and up.
Recited in Mexico City, this is an Aztec version of the birth of Jesus.

Blackmore, Vivien, adapter. *Why Corn Is Golden: Stories About Plants*. Illustrated by Susana Martínez-Ostos. Boston: Little, Brown, 1984. Grades 2 and up.
Mexican tales are told of corn, sunflowers, chocolate, and other foods in this richly illustrated collection.

Campos, Anthony John, translator and editor. *Mexican Folk Tales*. Illustrated by Mark Sanders. Tucson, AZ: University of Arizona Press, 1977. Grades 4 and up.
This collection includes legends of the devil, saints, and man and beast.

de Paola, Tomie. *The Lady of Guadalupe*. New York: Holiday House, 1980. Grades 3 and up.
Juan Diego, a poor Indian, carries a miraculous sign from the Lady of Guadalupe to the bishop.

Ets, Marie Hall, and Aurora Labastida. *Nine Days to Christmas: A Story of Mexico*. New York: Viking, 1959. Grades kindergarten and up.
Ceci helps her mother choose a piñata for a posada (inn) in Mexico City.

George, Jean Craighead. *Shark Beneath the Reef*. New York: HarperCollins, 1989. Grades 5 and up.
Tomás struggles between dropping out of school to help his family or staying in school and eventually becoming a marine biologist. His encounter with a great shark prompts his decision.

Lattimore, Deborah Nourse. *The Flame of Peace: A Tale of the Aztecs*. New York: HarperTrophy, 1991. Grades 1 and up.
A brave Aztec boy must outwit the gods to prevent war.

Lewis, Richard. *All of You Was Singing*. Illustrated by Ed Young. New York: Atheneum, 1991. Grades kindergarten and up.
This is a richly illustrated retelling of an Aztec myth of how music came to the earth.

Martinez, Alejandro Cruz. *The Woman Who Outshone the Sun: The Legend of Lucia Zenteno*. Illustrated by Fernando Olivera. Translated by Rosalma Zubizarreta. Adapted by Harriet Rohmer and David Schecter. San Francisco: Children's Book Press, 1991. Grades kindergarten and up.
When beautiful Lucia is taunted, she leaves the village and takes the river with her. The villagers realize their error and Lucia graciously returns the river. Based on a poem and presented in English and Spanish.

McKissack, Patricia. *Aztec Indians*. Chicago: Childrens Press, 1985. Grades kindergarten and up.
Color photographs enhance this simple nonfiction treatment of the Aztec Indians.

Merino, José María. *The Gold of Dreams*. Translated by Helen Lane. New York: Farrar, Straus & Giroux, 1986. Grades 6 and up.
   Miguel joins a search party to find a temple of gold in southern Mexico. The expedition struggles to survive, and Miguel faces many personal challenges.

Piggott, Juliet, reteller. *Mexican Folk Tales*. Illustrated by John Spencer. New York: Crane Russak, 1976. Grades 4 and up.
   The author retells 11 tales, drawn from the traditions of ancient Mexico and the Spanish conquest.

Rhoads, Dorothy. *The Corn Grows Ripe*. Illustrated by Jean Charlot. New York: Puffin Books, 1993. Grades 4 and up.
   Tigre's father is injured, and the family struggles to plant and harvest the corn necessary for their survival and the pleasure of the Mayan gods.

Rohmer, Harriet, and Mary Anchondo, adapters. *How We Came to the Fifth World: A Creation Story from Ancient Mexico*. Illustrated by Graciela Carrillo. San Francisco: Children's Book Press, 1988. Grades 2 and up.
   A couple moves through each of the four worlds, or historical ages, leading to the fifth world, the sun of movement. Presented in English and Spanish.

Schon, Isabel, collector and translator. *Doña Blanca and Other Hispanic Nursery Rhymes and Games*. Minneapolis, MN: T. S. Denison, 1983. Grades preschool and up.
   Nursery rhymes and games are presented in English and Spanish.

Winter, Jonah. *Diego*. Illustrated by Jeanette Winter. Translated by Amy Prince. New York: Alfred A. Knopf, 1991. Grades kindergarten and up.
   Presented in English and Spanish, this is a simple telling of the early years of Mexico's most famous artist, Diego Rivera.

Wisniewski, David. *Rain Player*. New York: Clarion Books, 1991. Grades 1 and up.
   Stunning cut paper illustrations integrate with the story of Pik, who strives to save the people from a terrible drought.

VIDEOS

Children of Mexico. Disney Educational Productions, Coronet/MIT, 1989. 26 minutes. Grades 4 and up.
   Gloria Garcia writes to her American pen pal about Mexican life.

Feliz Navidad. Walt Disney, 1975. 6 minutes. Grades kindergarten and up.
   Donald Duck's Mexican friends teach him about the Mexican celebration of Las Posadas.

Kids Explore Mexico. Children's International Network, Encounter Video. 1989. 40 minutes. Grades 1 and up.
   Children explore Aztec and Mayan ruins, and Mexican art, music, dance, food, and festivals.

Mexico. Gessler. 1988. 36 minutes. Grades 1 and up.
   Explores bullfights, *charros*, dance, and history.

Touring Mexico. Society for Visual Education. 60 minutes. Grades 4 and up.
   Viewers enjoy the historical and cultural sites of Mexico.

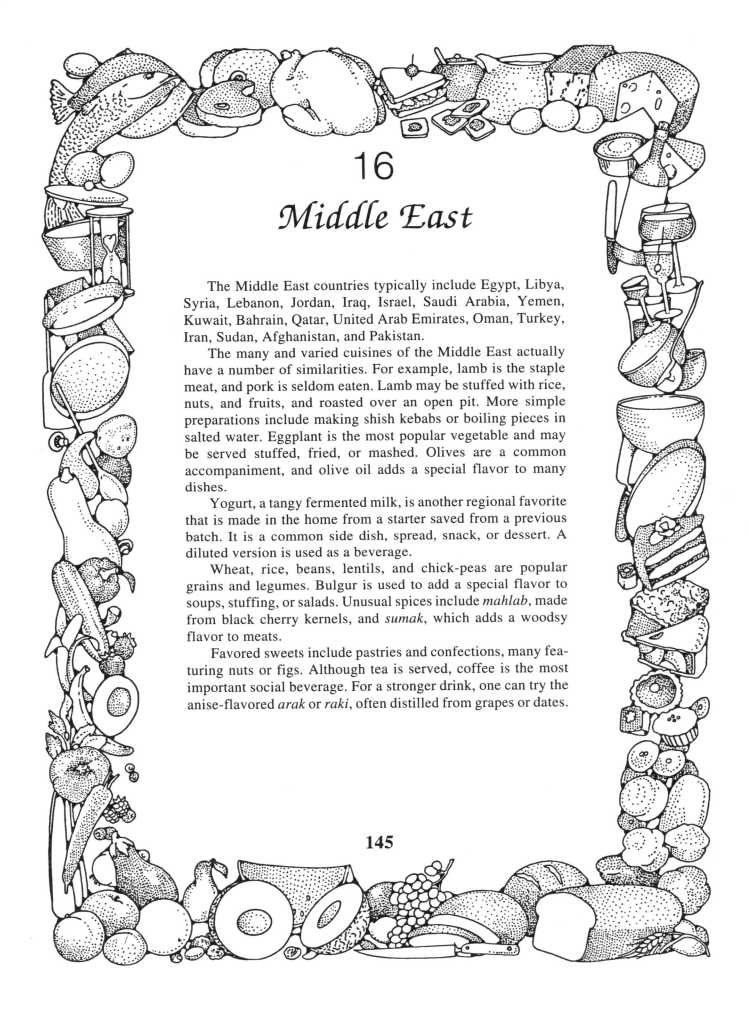

16
Middle East

The Middle East countries typically include Egypt, Libya, Syria, Lebanon, Jordan, Iraq, Israel, Saudi Arabia, Yemen, Kuwait, Bahrain, Qatar, United Arab Emirates, Oman, Turkey, Iran, Sudan, Afghanistan, and Pakistan.

The many and varied cuisines of the Middle East actually have a number of similarities. For example, lamb is the staple meat, and pork is seldom eaten. Lamb may be stuffed with rice, nuts, and fruits, and roasted over an open pit. More simple preparations include making shish kebabs or boiling pieces in salted water. Eggplant is the most popular vegetable and may be served stuffed, fried, or mashed. Olives are a common accompaniment, and olive oil adds a special flavor to many dishes.

Yogurt, a tangy fermented milk, is another regional favorite that is made in the home from a starter saved from a previous batch. It is a common side dish, spread, snack, or dessert. A diluted version is used as a beverage.

Wheat, rice, beans, lentils, and chick-peas are popular grains and legumes. Bulgur is used to add a special flavor to soups, stuffing, or salads. Unusual spices include *mahlab*, made from black cherry kernels, and *sumak*, which adds a woodsy flavor to meats.

Favored sweets include pastries and confections, many featuring nuts or figs. Although tea is served, coffee is the most important social beverage. For a stronger drink, one can try the anise-flavored *arak* or *raki*, often distilled from grapes or dates.

ALMOND SOUP

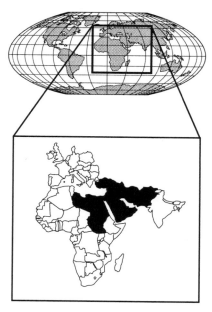

Middle East

INGREDIENTS

3 tablespoons butter

1 medium onion, chopped

3 tablespoons flour

1½ quarts chicken bouillon

⅔ cup ground almonds

¾ cup heavy cream

Salt and pepper to taste

STEPS

1. Melt butter in large saucepan over medium-high heat.
2. Add onions. Cook until soft and clear.
3. Stir in flour.
4. Pour in the bouillon slowly, stirring constantly.
5. Simmer over low heat 5 minutes.
6. Stir in almonds. Simmer for 15 minutes.
7. Add cream. Heat through, but do not boil.
8. Add salt and pepper to taste.
9. Serve hot.

Serves 6.

📖 **Library Link 1:** Almonds are not nuts. Research their origin.

LAMB STEW

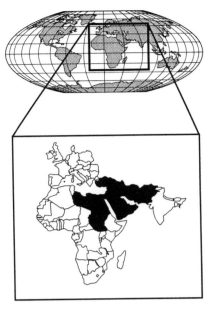

Middle East

INGREDIENTS

1½ tablespoons butter

1 medium onion, chopped

1 garlic clove, chopped finely

2½ cups diced lamb

½ teaspoon allspice

¼ teaspoon nutmeg

½ teaspoon paprika

Salt and pepper to taste

2¼ cups water

1 pound fresh, clean spinach

STEPS

1. Melt butter over medium-high heat in large skillet.

2. Add onions and garlic. Cook until soft and clear.

3. Add lamb, allspice, nutmeg, paprika, salt, pepper, and water.

4. Simmer over low heat until lamb is tender, about 1 hour.

5. Add spinach leaves. Simmer another 20 minutes.

6. Serve hot.

Serves 5.

📖 **Library Link 2:** Research the use of the white lotus or water lily in Egypt.

MATZO BALLS

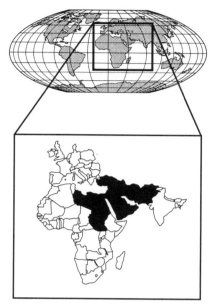

Middle East

INGREDIENTS

2 cups matzo meal

1 cup chicken stock

¼ teaspoon ginger

Dash nutmeg

2 large eggs, well beaten

4 tablespoons oil

2 quarts soup broth

STEPS

1. Put meal, stock, ginger, nutmeg, eggs, and oil in large bowl. Mix well.

2. Refrigerate mixture for 4 hours or until all moisture is absorbed.

3. Take dough out of bowl 1 tablespoon at a time. Roll dough into balls using wet hands.

4. Heat soup broth to a boil over medium heat.

5. Reduce heat so broth simmers.

6. Drop matzo balls into broth. Cook for 30 minutes.

Serves 12.

📖 **Library Link 3:** When are matzo balls traditionally eaten?

Note: Although matzo balls originated in Eastern Europe, matzo meal's first historical use was in an unleavened bread that the Jews hastily baked before their exodus from Egypt. As a symbol, the matzo is known as the "bread of affliction" and is used during the Jewish festival of Passover.

CURRIED CHICKEN

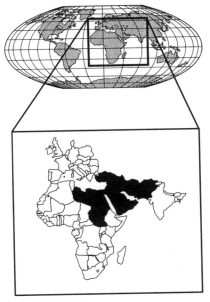

Middle East

INGREDIENTS

2 tablespoons butter

2 tablespoons flour

2 teaspoons curry

½ teaspoon salt

Dash pepper

1 cup milk

2 cooked chicken breasts, boned and cut in cubes

½ teaspoon paprika

Cooked rice, optional

STEPS

1. Melt butter in large saucepan over medium-high heat.
2. Stir in flour, curry, salt, and pepper.
3. Slowly stir in milk. Keep stirring over medium heat until mixture boils and thickens.
4. Stir in chicken. Heat thoroughly.
5. Sprinkle with paprika.
6. May be served with rice.

Serves 4.

📖 **Library Link 4:** Research the source of paprika.

BURGHUL

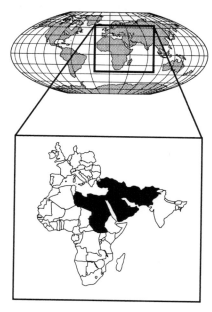

Middle East

INGREDIENTS

6 tablespoons oil

2 cups bulgur (cracked wheat)

4 cups soup stock

Salt and pepper to taste

STEPS

1. Put oil in a large skillet over medium-high heat.

2. Sauté bulgur in oil.

3. Add soup stock and salt and pepper. Cook over medium-low heat until all the liquid is absorbed, about 1½ to 2 hours.

4. Add extra salt and pepper to taste.

5. Serve immediately.

Serves 6-8.

📖 **Library Link 5:** How is bulgur made?

RICE PILAF

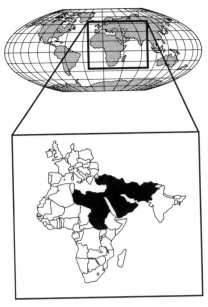

Middle East

INGREDIENTS

4 tablespoons butter

1 cup long-grain rice

2 cups chicken broth

1 teaspoon salt

¼ teaspoon pepper

STEPS

1. Melt butter in a large skillet over medium-high heat.
2. Sauté rice in butter until clear.
3. Stir in broth, salt, and pepper.
4. Bring to a boil. Cover.
5. Reduce heat to simmer. Cook for 20 minutes.
6. Remove from heat. Do not uncover for 15 more minutes.
7. Stir. Serve hot.

Serves 4-6.

📖 **Library Link 6:** What is *shekar polo*?

PITA

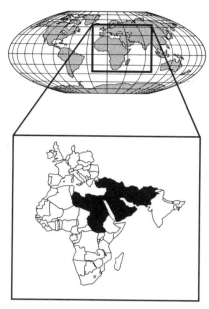

Middle East

INGREDIENTS

2 packages yeast

1½ teaspoons sugar

1¼ cups very warm water

4 cups flour

1 teaspoon salt

STEPS

1. Put yeast and sugar in large bowl.
2. Add warm water. Stir until yeast and sugar are dissolved.
3. Stir in flour and salt.
4. Knead the dough for 5 minutes on a floured board.
5. Divide dough into 20 balls.
6. Roll each ball out onto a floured board to about ¼-inch thick.
7. Let dough rise in a warm place about 30-40 minutes or until puffy.
8. Bake in a 500-degree oven for 3-5 minutes or until puffy and slightly browned.
9. May be served with dip or split open and filled.

Serves 10-20, depending on use.

📖 **Library Link 7:** Research the word "yeast."

SWEET FIGS

INGREDIENTS

4 cups water

1⅔ cups sugar

¼ teaspoon ginger

¼ teaspoon cinnamon

1 pound dried figs

Juice of 1 orange

1 tablespoon lemon juice

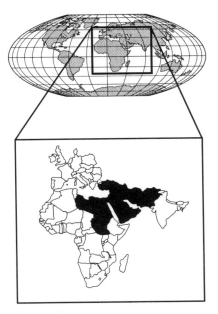

Middle East

STEPS

1. Put water, sugar, ginger, and cinnamon in a large saucepan. Stir well.

2. Add figs. Cook 10-15 minutes over medium-high heat until syrup has thickened. Stir frequently.

3. Add fruit juices. Stir well.

4. Remove from heat. Chill.

5. Serve cold.

Serves 6.

📖 **Library Link 8:** How are figs pollinated?

ANNOTATED BIBLIOGRAPHY

Abodaher, David J. *Youth in the Middle East: Voices of Despair*. New York: Franklin Watts, 1990. Grades 4 and up.
Black-and-white photographs of people in Lebanon, Israel, and Egypt enhance the essays about life in these war-torn areas.

Banks, Lynne Reid. *One More River*. New York: Morrow Junior Books, 1973, 1992. Grades 5 and up.
Lesley has the perfect teenage life until her parents announce they will be moving from Canada to Israel. Lesley not only survives the war in 1967 but also becomes a self-reliant young woman.

Bergman, Tamar. *The Boy from Over There*. Translated by Hillel Halkin. Boston: Houghton Mifflin, 1988. Grades 4 and up.
Avramik and Rina struggle to adjust to a kibbutz after World War II.

Carrick, Carol. *Aladdin and the Wonderful Lamp*. Illustrated by Donald Carrick. New York: Scholastic, 1989. Grades 1 and up.
Aladdin learns to use the power of the lamp and its genie wisely as he matures in the Carricks' boldly illustrated version of the traditional tale.

Climo, Shirley. *The Egyptian Cinderella*. Illustrated by Ruth Heller. New York: HarperTrophy, 1989. Grades kindergarten and up.
Rhodopis, a slave girl, eventually becomes the pharaoh's queen.

Dewey, Ariane, reteller. *The Fish Peri*. New York: Macmillan, 1979. Grades 1 and up.
Ahmed catches a fish that turns into a young woman who helps him achieve impossible feats.

Edwards, Michelle. *Chicken Man*. New York: Lothrop, Lee & Shepard, 1991. Grades kindergarten and up.
Chicken Man loves working in the chicken coop at the kibbutz, but he must rotate through other jobs until the chickens ensure his permanent return.

Giblin, James Cross. *The Riddle of the Rosetta Stone: Key to Ancient Egypt*. New York: Thomas Y. Crowell, 1990. Grades 3 and up.
Giblin discusses how the Rosetta Stone led to an understanding of the Egyptian hieroglyphs.

Gold, Sharlya, and Mishael Maswari Caspi. *The Answered Prayer and Other Yemenite Folktales*. Illustrated by Marjory Wunsch. Philadelphia: Jewish Publication Society, 1990. Grades 4 and up.
In addition to the 12 folktales, the authors provide background information, a glossary, and a pronunciation guide to the Yemenite names.

Harris, Geraldine. *Gods and Pharaohs from Egyptian Mythology*. Illustrated by David O'Connor. New York: Schocken Books, 1982. Grades 4 and up.
Stories of Egypt, line drawings, colorful illustrations, maps, and background information make this a useful resource.

Heide, Florence Parry, and Judith Heide Gilliland. *The Day of Ahmed's Secret*. Illustrated by Ted Lewin. New York: Lothrop, Lee & Shepard, 1990. Grades kindergarten and up.
Ahmed treasures his secret as he works in the fascinating city of Cairo.

Hiçyilmaz, Gaye. *Against the Storm*. Boston: Little, Brown, 1990. Grades 5 and up.
Mehmet expects their move from a Turkish village to Ankara to bring the family comfort and abundance, but he finds only misery.

Hort, Lenny, reteller. *The Tale of Caliph Stork*. From the tale by Wilhelm Hauf. Illustrated by Friso Henstra. New York: Dial Books for Young Readers, 1989. Grades 1 and up.
In this tale of Arabia, when the caliph of Baghdad and his grand vizier are tricked into becoming storks, they have trouble undoing the spell.

Ludwig, Warren, adapter. *Old Noah's Elephants*. New York: G.P. Putnam's Sons, 1991. Grades preschool and up.
In this amusing tale, Noah has to convince the elephants that they can't eat all the food on the ark.

MacQuitty, William. *Tutankhamun: The Last Journey*. New York: Crown, 1978. Grades 5 and up.
Photographs and text tell the story of Tutankhamun, from ancient history to excavation.

Mayers, Florence Cassen. *ABC: The Alef-Bet Book: The Israel Museum, Jerusalem*. New York: Harry N. Abrams, 1989. Grades preschool and up.
The Hebrew alphabet is illustrated with art photographed in the Israel Museum, Jerusalem.

Travers, P.L., reteller. *Two Pairs of Shoes*. Illustrated by Leo and Diane Dillon. New York: Viking, 1980. Grades 2 and up.
In "Abu Kassem's Slippers," a rich but miserly merchant in Baghdad struggles to rid himself of old slippers. In "The Sandals of Ayaz," the king's trusted treasurer uses his tattered sandals to prove his loyalty.

Walker, Barbara K., reteller. *A Treasury of Turkish Folktales for Children*. Hamden, CT: Linnet Books, 1988. Grades 2 and up.
Thirty-four tales are accompanied by a Turkish pronunciation guide, a glossary, notes, and riddles.

Walker, Barbara K., and Ahmet E. Uysal. *New Patches for Old*. Illustrated by Harold Berson. New York: Parents' Magazine Press, 1974. Grades kindergarten and up.
In honor of a holiday, Hasan buys presents for his family and new trousers for himself. The trousers are in need of hemming, which leads to an amusing sequence of events.

Zemach, Margot. *It Could Always Be Worse*. New York: Scholastic, 1976. Grades kindergarten and up.
In this Yiddish tale, a rabbi helps a man appreciate his crowded hut.

VIDEOS

The Middle East: A Closer Look. Society for Visual Education, 1992. 17 minutes. Grades 4 and up.
Discover how the Middle East got its name, the countries included, and the impact of Islam. Skill sheets available.

Touring Egypt. Society for Visual Education. 60 minutes. Grades 4 and up.
Visit the Nile, Cairo, the pyramids, Suez, the Red Sea, and other features of Egypt.

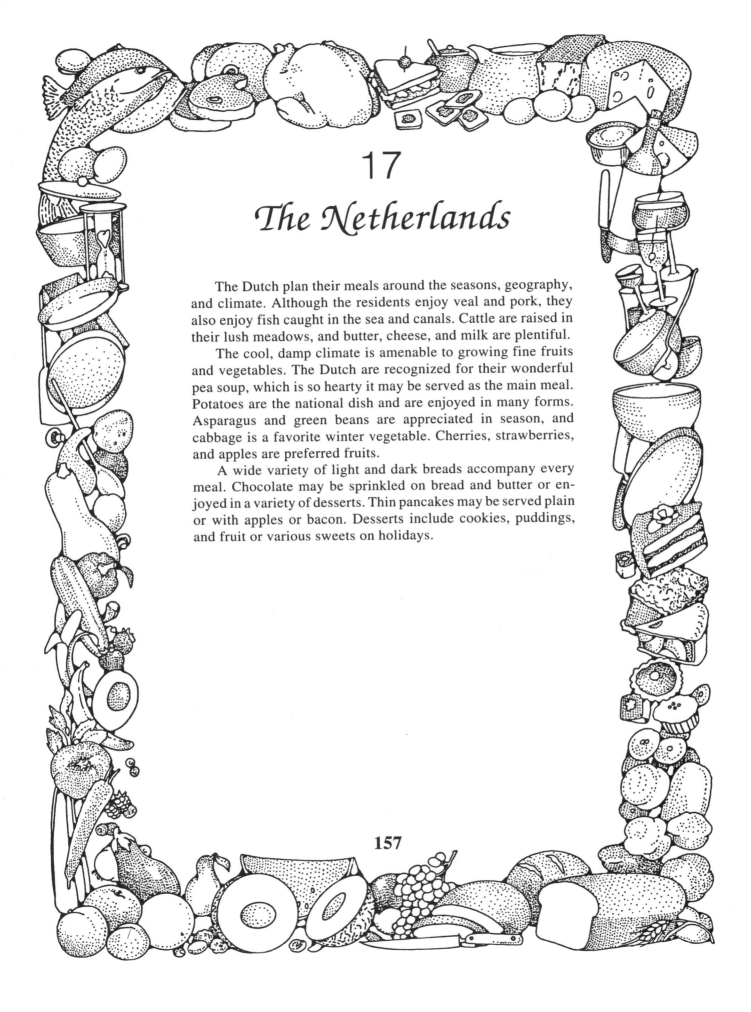

17

The Netherlands

The Dutch plan their meals around the seasons, geography, and climate. Although the residents enjoy veal and pork, they also enjoy fish caught in the sea and canals. Cattle are raised in their lush meadows, and butter, cheese, and milk are plentiful.

The cool, damp climate is amenable to growing fine fruits and vegetables. The Dutch are recognized for their wonderful pea soup, which is so hearty it may be served as the main meal. Potatoes are the national dish and are enjoyed in many forms. Asparagus and green beans are appreciated in season, and cabbage is a favorite winter vegetable. Cherries, strawberries, and apples are preferred fruits.

A wide variety of light and dark breads accompany every meal. Chocolate may be sprinkled on bread and butter or enjoyed in a variety of desserts. Thin pancakes may be served plain or with apples or bacon. Desserts include cookies, puddings, and fruit or various sweets on holidays.

157

OLIEBOL

(New Year's Doughnuts)

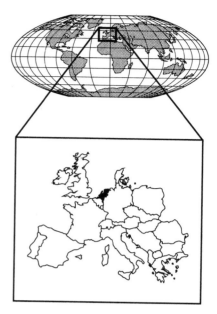

The Netherlands

INGREDIENTS

¼ cup very warm water (110 degrees F.)
1 envelope dry yeast
⅓ cup sugar
½ cup very warm milk (110 degrees F.)
½ teaspoon salt
3 eggs, beaten
3⅓ cups flour
Oil for deep fat frying
¾ cup currants
1 tablespoon grated lemon peel
Powdered sugar
Cooking thermometer

STEPS

1. Put water, yeast, and 2 tablespoons of the sugar in a large bowl. Stir until yeast dissolves.
2. Let stand 5 minutes.
3. Stir in rest of the sugar, milk, salt, and eggs.
4. Stir in 2 cups of the flour.
5. Cover. Let stand 10 minutes.
6. Stir in enough of the rest of the flour to make a soft dough.
7. Turn dough out onto a floured board. Knead for a few minutes.
8. Clean bowl and grease well.
9. Put dough back in bowl. Cover and let rise in warm place until doubled in size.
10. Pour oil into saucepan or deep fat fryer to 3 inches deep.
11. Heat oil to 350 degrees.
12. Punch down dough. Knead in currants and lemon peel.
13. Shape dough into 12 balls.
14. Fry balls in hot oil about 5 minutes on each side or until browned on the outside and cooked through.
15. Drain on paper towels. Sprinkle with powdered sugar.
16. Serve warm.

Serves 6.

📖 **Library Link 1:** Research other breads for special days.

BOERENKASS SOUP

INGREDIENTS

1 tablespoon butter

¼ cup chopped onion

1 cup cauliflower florets

2 potatoes, peeled and cut into small cubes

⅓ cup carrots, peeled and chopped

½ teaspoon celery salt

2 cups water

2 packets chicken bouillon or 2 chicken bouillon cubes

4 slices bacon

2 thick slices white bread

2 ounces Gouda cheese, shredded

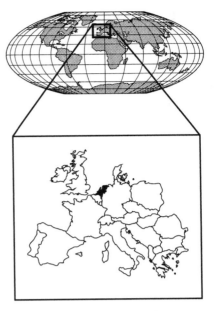

The Netherlands

STEPS

1. Put butter in medium saucepan. Heat over medium-high heat until bubbly.
2. Add onion. Cook until soft.
3. Add cauliflower, potato, carrot, and celery salt. Cook for 5 minutes.
4. Add water and chicken bouillon. Bring to a boil.
5. Reduce heat to low. Cover pan and simmer for 15 minutes or until vegetables are tender.
6. Put bacon in a small skillet over medium-high heat. Cook until crisp.
7. Pour soup into 2 heat-proof bowls.
8. Put 2 pieces of bacon in each bowl.
9. Toast bread and place one slice on top of each bowl of soup.
10. Sprinkle cheese evenly over both pieces of toast.
11. Put bowls under broiler for 3 minutes or until cheese is bubbly. Serve hot.

Serves 2.

📖 **Library Link 2:** Research the Dutch jambless (fireplace).

ERWTENSOEP
(Split Pea Soup)

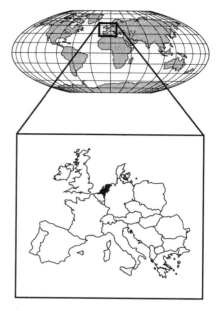

The Netherlands

INGREDIENTS

1½ cups dried green split peas

2 pork hocks

1 teaspoon salt

Water

2 stalks celery, sliced

3 leeks, sliced

2 potatoes, peeled and chopped

½ pound cooked, smoked sausage, sliced

¼ teaspoon pepper

STEPS

1. Put peas, pork hocks, salt, and water to cover in a large saucepan.
2. Bring to a boil over high heat.
3. Reduce heat. Cover and simmer for 25 minutes.
4. Stir in celery, leeks, and potatoes.
5. Cover and simmer for 20 more minutes.
6. Add sausage and pepper. Simmer for 10 more minutes.
7. Remove pork hocks and separate meat from bones.
8. Cut meat up and add to soup. Serve hot.

Serves 4.

📖 **Library Link 3:** Research the equipment found in a seventeenth-century affluent Dutch kitchen.

HUTSPOT

INGREDIENTS

1½ pounds beef brisket

½ teaspoon salt

Water

3 potatoes, peeled and cut into large chunks

4 carrots, peeled and sliced

3 onions, sliced

Salt and pepper to taste

Parsley

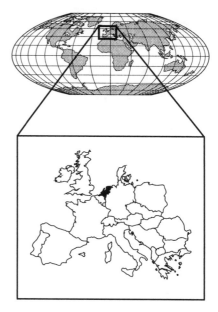

The Netherlands

STEPS

1. Put beef and salt in a large saucepan. Add water to cover.

2. Bring to a boil over high heat.

3. Reduce heat. Cover and simmer for 2 hours.

4. Add potatoes, carrots, onions, salt, and pepper.

5. Cover and simmer for 35-45 minutes or until tender.

6. Remove brisket. Cut into cubes.

7. Stir beef cubes into stew.

8. Add salt and pepper to taste.

9. Spoon into bowls. Sprinkle with parsley to serve.

Serves 6.

📖 **Library Link 4:** *Hutspot* was served as the main meal for the masses in seventeenth-century Netherlands. Research varieties of *hutspot*.

FISH FILLETS

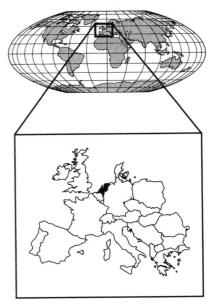

The Netherlands

INGREDIENTS

8 ounces flounder fillets

2 teaspoons lemon juice

2 tablespoons flour

½ teaspoon salt

Dash of nutmeg

¼ teaspoon pepper

¼ teaspoon dill seed

2 slices bacon

2 teaspoons butter

2 tablespoons bread crumbs

½ ounce Gouda cheese, shredded

STEPS

1. Put fillets in a bowl. Sprinkle with lemon juice.
2. Let stand 15 minutes.
3. Put flour, salt, nutmeg, pepper, and dill seed on a paper plate. Mix well.
4. Roll fillets in flour mixture. Set aside.
5. Put bacon in a large skillet with a metal handle.
6. Cook bacon over medium heat until done.
7. Remove bacon and set aside.
8. Put 2 teaspoons butter in skillet. Heat until bubbly.
9. Cook fillets in skillet until browned on both sides.
10. Put bacon, bread crumbs, and cheese on top of fillets.
11. Put skillet under hot broiler. Broil until cheese is melted and lightly browned.
12. Serve hot.

Serves 2.

📖 **Library Link 5:** Research the Twelfth Night Feast.

SPECULAAS

INGREDIENTS

1½ cups flour

2 teaspoons cinnamon

¼ teaspoon crushed anise seed

¼ teaspoon nutmeg

¼ teaspoon cloves

⅛ teaspoon salt

¼ teaspoon baking powder

½ cup butter, softened

⅓ cup brown sugar

2 tablespoons cream

¼ cup almonds, chopped finely

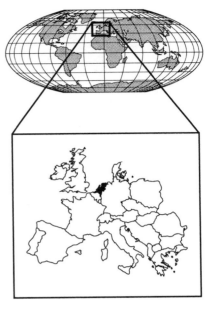

The Netherlands

STEPS

1. Put flour, cinnamon, anise seed, nutmeg, cloves, salt, and baking powder in a medium bowl. Mix well.

2. Cream butter and sugar together in a large bowl.

3. Add cream and dry ingredients. Mix well.

4. Divide dough in half. Put half on a floured board.

5. Using a floured rolling pin, roll dough out into a rectangle about 10 inches x 6 inches.

6. Cut into small rectangles or cut with windmill or St. Nicholas cookie cutters.

7. Grease a cookie sheet and put cookies on pan.

8. Repeat with rest of dough.

9. Sprinkle almonds onto cookies.

10. Bake in a 375-degree oven for 12-15 minutes or until lightly browned.

Serves 8-10.

📖 **Library Link 6:** When is speculaas traditionally eaten?

ANNOTATED BIBLIOGRAPHY

DeJong, Meindert. *The Wheel on the School.* Illustrated by Maurice Sendak. New York: Harper & Row, 1954. Grades 4 and up.
  After Lina's essay about storks leads to an investigation into why storks never nest in Shora, determined children bring storks to every rooftop.

Dodge, Mary Mapes. *Hans Brinker or the Silver Skates.* Illustrated by George Wharton Edwards. New York: Charles Scribner's Sons, 1915. Grades 5 and up.
  Through Hans's adventures, readers learn about the history and culture of Holland.

Frank, Anne. *Anne Frank: The Diary of a Young Girl.* Translated by B. M. Mooyaart. New York: Simon & Schuster, 1952. Grades 6 and up.
  Anne Frank's diary describes the family's life as they hide from the Nazis during World War II.

Green, Norma, reteller. *The Hole in the Dike.* Illustrated by Eric Carle. New York: Thomas Y. Crowell, 1974. Grades preschool and up.
  Peter is on his way home when he discovers a small hole in the dike. He bravely puts his finger in the dike, holding back the sea until help comes.

Krasilovsky, Phyllis. *The Cow Who Fell in the Canal.* Illustrated by Peter Spier. Garden City, NY: Doubleday, 1957. Grades preschool and up.
  Hendrika the cow has a fine adventure when she falls in the canal and floats to the city.

Locker, Thomas. *The Boy Who Held Back the Sea.* New York: Dial Books, 1987. Grades preschool and up.
  Locker uses oil paintings to illustrate the tale of Peter's bravery. (See Green above.)

Oppenheim, Shulamith Levey. *The Lily Cupboard.* Illustrated by Ronald Himler. New York: HarperCollins, 1992. Grades 2 and up.
  During World War II, a family hides a small Jewish girl in a secret cupboard.

Vos, Ida. *Hide and Seek.* Translated by Terese Edelstein and Inez Smidt. Boston: Houghton Mifflin, 1981. Grades 4 and up.
  Rachel is a young Jewish girl during the German occupation. The years of hiding and adjustments to many losses are described.

Williams. *The Wicked Tricks of Tyl Uilenspiegel.* Illustrated by Friso Henstra. New York: Four Winds Press, 1978. Grades 3 and up.
  Tyl is a thief, but he is admired for his clever pranks and daring by the people of Holland. This collection of four escapades will amuse readers.

VIDEOS

Anne Frank: A Legacy for Our Time. Society for Visual Education, 1985. 38:30 minutes. Grades 6 and up.
  This award-winning story of Anne Frank was developed in cooperation with the Anne Frank Center in Amsterdam.

Christmas Time in Europe. Coronet, 1971. 21 minutes. Grades kindergarten and up.
  Visit families in Holland, Belgium, Luxembourg, France, and Great Britain at Christmas time.

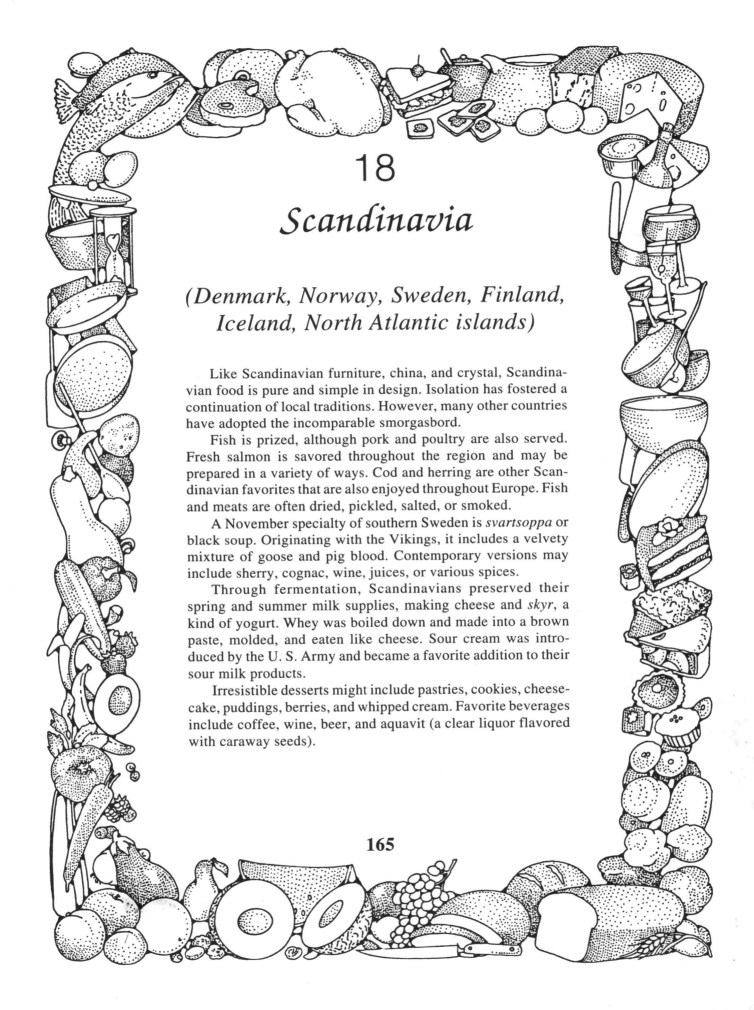

18

Scandinavia

(Denmark, Norway, Sweden, Finland, Iceland, North Atlantic islands)

Like Scandinavian furniture, china, and crystal, Scandinavian food is pure and simple in design. Isolation has fostered a continuation of local traditions. However, many other countries have adopted the incomparable smorgasbord.

Fish is prized, although pork and poultry are also served. Fresh salmon is savored throughout the region and may be prepared in a variety of ways. Cod and herring are other Scandinavian favorites that are also enjoyed throughout Europe. Fish and meats are often dried, pickled, salted, or smoked.

A November specialty of southern Sweden is *svartsoppa* or black soup. Originating with the Vikings, it includes a velvety mixture of goose and pig blood. Contemporary versions may include sherry, cognac, wine, juices, or various spices.

Through fermentation, Scandinavians preserved their spring and summer milk supplies, making cheese and *skyr*, a kind of yogurt. Whey was boiled down and made into a brown paste, molded, and eaten like cheese. Sour cream was introduced by the U. S. Army and became a favorite addition to their sour milk products.

Irresistible desserts might include pastries, cookies, cheesecake, puddings, berries, and whipped cream. Favorite beverages include coffee, wine, beer, and aquavit (a clear liquor flavored with caraway seeds).

165

POTATO SOUP

INGREDIENTS

3 large potatoes

1 small onion

¾ teaspoon salt

Water

2 cups milk

2 tablespoons butter

1 tablespoon chopped parsley

¼ teaspoon pepper

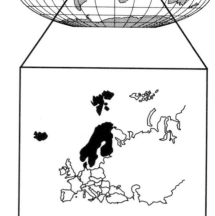

Scandinavia

STEPS

1. Peel potatoes. Cut each potato into 4 chunks.
2. Peel onion. Chop into small pieces.
3. Put potatoes, onion, and salt into a 2-quart saucepan. Add water to cover the potatoes.
4. Boil over medium-high heat for 20 minutes or until potatoes are soft.
5. Remove pan from heat. Mash potatoes, onions, and water together.
6. Stir in milk.
7. Put pan on medium-low heat. Simmer and add butter, parsley, and pepper.
8. Stir well until smooth. Serve hot.

Serves 6.

📖 **Library Link 1:** Dry, mealy potatoes are preferable to moist, waxy types for mashing. How can you determine which kind you have?

BAKED COD

INGREDIENTS

6-8 cod fillets

3½ cups milk

6-8 tablespoons butter

Salt and pepper to taste

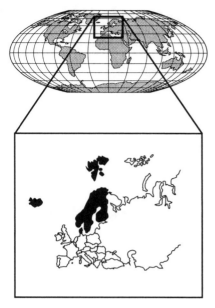

Scandinavia

STEPS

1. Preheat oven to 350 degrees.

2. Grease a shallow baking dish. Lay fillets in the dish. The fillets should be close together, but not on top of each other.

3. Pour milk over the fillets to cover them. (You may not need all of the milk.)

4. Put one teaspoon butter on top of each fillet.

5. Bake for 20 minutes. Fish should flake apart with a fork when done.

6. Sprinkle with salt and pepper.

Serves 4-6.

Library Link 2: What members of the cod family are most popular in the Scandinavian countries? Why do cod have whiter flesh than other fish?

SWEDISH MEATBALLS

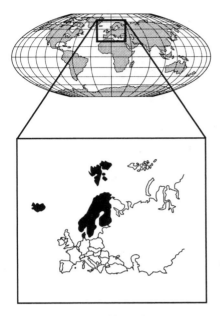

Scandinavia

INGREDIENTS

4 slices white bread

¾ cup light cream

2 pounds ground beef

½ pound ground pork

2 eggs, well beaten

½ teaspoon nutmeg

¼ teaspoon pepper

¼ teaspoon allspice

½ cup finely chopped onion

2 teaspoons salt

2 teaspoons shortening

1 cup light cream

1 tablespoon cornstarch

2 tablespoons cold water

STEPS

1. Soak bread in 3/4 cup light cream until cream is absorbed.
2. Put bread, cream, beef, pork, eggs, nutmeg, pepper, allspice, onion, and salt in a large bowl. Mix well with hands.
3. Shape mixture into 1-inch balls.
4. Put shortening in large frying pan and heat over medium heat.
5. Fry meatballs in the shortening until browned evenly on all sides.
6. Remove meatballs from pan. Pour off excess shortening. Keep other drippings in pan.
7. Add 1 cup light cream to pan.
8. Mix cornstarch and water in a small bowl. Stir until well mixed.
9. Add cornstarch and water to the pan.
10. Stir ingredients in pan while simmering over medium heat. Gravy will thicken.
11. Add meatballs to gravy. Serve hot.

Serves 8.

📖 **Library Link 3:** Swedish meatballs are always part of a Swedish smorgasbord. What is a smorgasbord?

SARDINE SANDWICHES

INGREDIENTS

1 can boneless, skinless sardines, in oil

¼ cup mayonnaise

2 tablespoons chopped celery

1 teaspoon lemon juice

1 teaspoon Worcestershire sauce

¼ cup finely chopped onion

8 slices dark rye bread

¼ cup butter

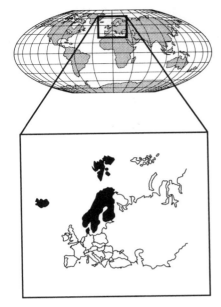

Scandinavia

STEPS

1. Put sardines in a small bowl. Mash with a fork.

2. Add mayonnaise, celery, lemon juice, Worcestershire sauce,
   and onions to the sardines. Mix well.

3. Preheat a griddle or frying pan.

4. Spread sardine mixture on 4 slices of bread. Put rest of slices on top, making sandwiches.

5. Spread butter on outside of both sides of bread.

6. Grill sandwiches on both sides until brown.

Serves 4.

📖 **Library Link 4:** When were sardines first canned?

FATTIGMANDS BAKKELS

(Scandinavian Fried Cookies)

INGREDIENTS

Deep fat for frying

3 egg yolks

1 whole egg

½ teaspoon salt

⅓ cup confectioners sugar

1 teaspoon almond flavoring

1 teaspoon vanilla flavoring

1 cup flour

¾ cup confectioners sugar

Cooking thermometer

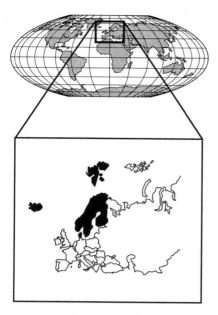

Scandinavia

STEPS

1. Heat deep fat to 375 degrees.
2. Beat egg yolks, whole egg, and salt together until very stiff.
3. Add ⅓ cup confectioners sugar, almond flavoring, and vanilla. Mix well.
4. Add flour. Mix well.
5. Knead dough on well-floured board for 8-10 minutes.
6. Divide dough in half. Roll ½ out until very thin.
7. Using a knife, cut dough in 4-x-2-inch diamonds. Cut a 1-inch slit down the center of each.
8. Pick up one point of the diamond, put it through the slit, and curl it back out.
9. Fry in the deep fat until browned on both sides, about 2 minutes.
10. Drain cookie on paper towel. Sprinkle with confectioners sugar.
11. Repeat with rest of dough.

Makes 2-3 dozen.

📖 **Library Link 5:** Research the importance of salt in the Scandinavian countries.

SPRITZ

INGREDIENTS

2¼ cups flour

1 cup confectioners sugar

¼ teaspoon baking powder

½ teaspoon salt

1 cup butter, softened

3 egg yolks

1 teaspoon vanilla flavoring

½ teaspoon almond flavoring

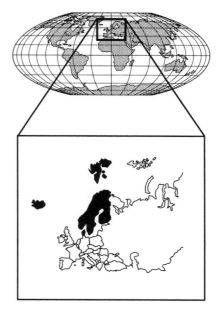

Scandinavia

STEPS

1. Mix flour, confectioners sugar, baking powder, and salt in a large bowl.
2. Mix butter, egg yolks, and flavorings in a medium bowl.
3. Add butter mixture to flour mixture. Blend.
4. Put dough into a cookie press. Press cookies onto an ungreased baking sheet.
5. Bake for 8-10 minutes or until slightly browned on the bottoms.

Makes 4-6 dozen.

📖 **Library Link 6:** What does "spritz" mean?

FRUKTSUPPE
(Fruit Soup)

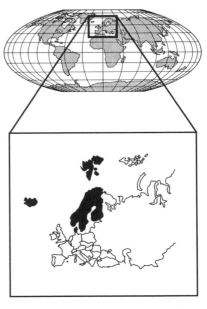

Scandinavia

INGREDIENTS

1 pound pitted prunes

1 cup raisins

6 cups water

6 ounces dried apricots

1 large can unsweetened cherries, with juice

⅓ cup sugar

3 tablespoons quick-cooking tapioca

STEPS

1. Put prunes, raisins, and water in a large saucepan. Cook over medium-high heat until the mixture boils.

2. Reduce heat. Simmer for 25 minutes.

3. Add apricots. Simmer another 15 minutes.

4. Remove from heat. Pour liquid into another saucepan.

5. Add juice from cherries, sugar, and tapioca to liquid.

6. Cook liquid over medium heat for 30 minutes until tapioca is clear and liquid is thick.

7. Pour liquid and cherries into fruit in saucepan. Stir well.

8. Serve hot or cold.

Serves 10.

📖 **Library Link 7:** What is the source of tapioca?

ANNOTATED BIBLIOGRAPHY

Allen, Linda. *The Mouse Bride: A Tale from Finland.* New York: Philomel, 1992. Grades 1 and up.
    Three brothers set out to find wives, and the youngest agrees to marry a mouse. He eventually breaks a spell and discovers his bride is a beautiful young woman.

Andersen, Hans Christian. *The Fir Tree.* Adapted and illustrated by Bernadette Watts. New York: North-South Books, 1990. Grades 1 and up.
    A fir tree learns to appreciate happiness.

_____. *The Snow Queen.* Retold by Amy Ehrlich. Illustrated by Susan Jeffers. New York: Dial Press, 1982. Grades 2 and up.
    Lush illustrations provide a fascinating backdrop for this haunting tale of quest.

_____. *The Wild Swans.* Retold by Amy Ehrlich. Illustrated by Susan Jeffers. New York: Dial Press, 1981. Grades 2 and up.
    A young girl must sacrifice to save her seven brothers from a life as swans.

Anderson, Lena. *Stina.* New York: Greenwillow Books, 1988. Grades preschool and up.
    Stina visits her grandfather's house by the sea and enjoys its treasures.

_____. *Stina's Visit.* New York: Greenwillow Books, 1988. Grades preschool and up.
    Stina hears stories of the sea from her grandfather's friend, Stretchit.

Barlow, Gillian. *East o' the Sun & West o' the Moon.* New York: Philomel, 1988. Grades 2 and up.
    In this variant of "Beauty and the Beast," a white bear takes away a young girl. The bear becomes a man at night, and after she sees him at night she must travel east of the sun and west of the moon to regain his love.

Carle, Eric, reteller. *Seven Stories by Hans Christian Andersen.* New York: Franklin Watts, 1978. Grades 2 and up.
    Carle's brilliant illustrations bring these traditional stories to life.

Donehower, Bruce. *Miko: Little Hunter of the North.* Illustrated by Tom Pohrt. New York: Farrar Straus & Giroux, 1990. Grades 3 and up.
    Miko searches for the truth about King Winter and Ravna in this story from Lapland.

Greene, Carol. *Hans Christian Andersen: Teller of Tales.* Chicago: Childrens Press, 1986. Grades 4 and up.
    This biography includes a timeline and a detailed index.

Hague, Kathleen, and Michael Hague, retellers. *The Man Who Kept House.* Illustrated by Michael Hague. San Diego, CA: Harcourt Brace Jovanovich, 1981. Grades 1 and up.
    A man who thinks he can keep house while his wife works in the field finds that her work is quite difficult.

Hague, Michael. *Michael Hague's Favourite Hans Christian Andersen Fairy Tales.* New York: Holt, Rinehart & Winston, 1981. Grades 2 and up.
    Hague has created warm illustrations for eight familiar tales by Andersen.

Haviland, Virginia, reteller. *Favorite Fairy Tales Told in Sweden.* Illustrated by Ronni Solbert. Boston: Little, Brown, 1966. Grades 2 and up.
    Six charming tales are illustrated.

_____. *The Talking Pot: A Danish Folktale.* Illustrated by Melissa Sweet. Boston: Little, Brown, 1971. Illustrations, 1990. Grades kindergarten and up.
   A poor man trades his cow for a magic pot.

Hurwitz, Johanna. *Astrid Lindgren: Storyteller to the World.* Illustrated by Michael Dooling. New York: Viking Kestrel, 1989. Grades 4 and up.
   This biography will fascinate all readers of Lindgren, who launched her career because of a sprained ankle.

Kent, Jack, translator and illustrator. *The Fat Cat.* New York: Scholastic, 1971. Grades preschool and up.
   In this cumulative Danish tale, a cat eats everything until he meets a woodcutter.

Kimmel, Eric A., reteller. *Boots and His Brothers.* Illustrated by Kimberley Bulcken Root. New York: Holiday House, 1991. Grades kindergarten and up.
   Three brothers set out to make their fortunes, and the youngest is rewarded for his kindness.

Lagerlöf, Selma. *The Changeling.* Illustrated by Jeanette Winter. Translated by Susanna Stevens. New York: Alfred A. Knopf, 1989. Grades 2 and up.
   When a troll exchanges its baby for a human baby, the mother must learn to love the changeling to earn the return of her own child.

Lindgren, Astrid. *Pippi Longstocking.* Illustrated by Louis S. Glanzman. Translated by Florence Lamborn. New York: Viking Kestrel, 1950. Grades 4 and up.
   Pippi Longstocking is not only a nine-year-old orphan but also a remarkable young girl. This is one of many chapter books recounting her adventures.

Lowry, Lois. *Number the Stars.* Boston: Houghton Mifflin, 1989. Grades 5 and up.
   During the German occupation of Denmark, Annemarie helps shelter her Jewish friend.

Magnus, Erica, adapter and illustrator. *Old Lars.* Minneapolis, MN: Carolrhoda Books, 1984. Grades kindergarten and up.
   Old Lars takes his horse, Blakken, to fetch wood, but returns with an empty sleigh.

McKee, David, reteller. *The Man Who Was Going to Mind the House.* New York: Abelard-Schuman, 1972. Grades kindergarten and up.
   In this Norwegian folktale, Ulrik decides to stay at home and do the household chores. The resulting chaos is delightful.

McSwigan, Marie. *Snow Treasure.* New York: Scholastic, 1942. Grades 4 and up.
   In this riveting, fact-based story, Norwegian children sled past Nazi soldiers with bars of gold hidden on their sleds.

Nielsen, Kay. *East of the Sun and West of the Moon.* Garden City, NY: Doubleday, 1977. Grades 2 and up.
   This reproduction of the 1914 edition of six Norwegian stories has lovely watercolor illustrations.

Nilsson, Ulf. *If You Didn't Have Me.* Illustrated by Eva Eriksson. Translated by Lone Thygesen Blecher and George Blecher. New York: Margaret K. McElderry Books, 1985. Grades 4 and up.
   A small boy is visiting his grandparents' farm for the summer while his parents build a house.

Reuter, Bjarne. *Buster: The Sheikh of Hope Street.* Translated by Anthea Bell. New York: Dutton Children's Books, 1980. Grades 4 and up.
   Buster wants to be the lead of a play, but his vivid imagination helps him deal with disappointment.

____. *Buster's World*. Translated by Anthea Bell. New York: E.P. Dutton, 1980. Grades 4 and up.
Buster's magic tricks don't solve all his problems, but they provide flavor to his Copenhagen neighborhood.

Rudström, Lennart. *A Family*. Illustrated by Carl Larsson. New York: G.P. Putnam's Sons, 1980. Grades 3 and up.
The life of Swedish artist Carl Larsson is narrated with text and Larsson's paintings.

Rydberg, Viktor. *The Christmas Tomten*. Adapted by Linda M. Jennings. Translated by Lone Thygesen Blecher and George Blecher. Illustrated by Harald Wiberg. New York: Coward, McCann and Geoghegan, 1981. Grades 1 and up.
When little Vigg is left alone on Christmas Eve, the Christmas Tomten takes him to the Hall of the Mountain King, where he learns the importance of good deeds.

Schwartz, David M. *Supergrandpa*. Illustrated by Bert Dodson. New York: Lothrop, Lee & Shepard, 1991. Grades kindergarten and up.
When the judges will not let 66-year-old Gustav enter the Tour of Sweden bicycle race, he rides the 600 miles to his own victory.

van Vorst, M. L. New. *A Norse Lullaby*. Illustrated by Margot Tomes. New York: Lothrop, Lee & Shepard, 1988. Grades preschool and up.
A family enjoys their warm home while the father comes home on a reindeer-drawn sled.

Wisniewski, David. *Elfwyn's Saga*. New York: Lothrop, Lee & Shepard, 1990. Grades 1 and up.
A curse causes Elfwyn's blindness, but her second sight and internal vision help save her people. Cut-paper illustrations enhance this tale from Iceland.

VIDEO

The Fir Tree. Centre Communications. 28 minutes. Grades 1 and up.
In this version of Hans Christian Andersen's tale, a young girl plants a seedling from the discarded tree.

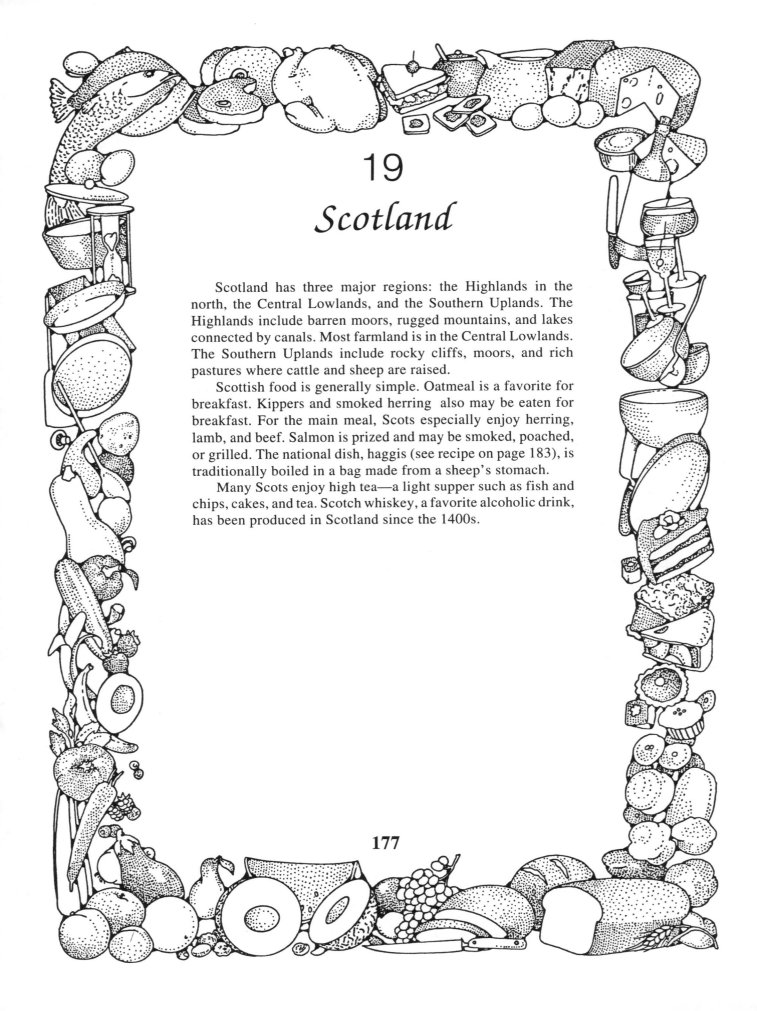

19

Scotland

Scotland has three major regions: the Highlands in the north, the Central Lowlands, and the Southern Uplands. The Highlands include barren moors, rugged mountains, and lakes connected by canals. Most farmland is in the Central Lowlands. The Southern Uplands include rocky cliffs, moors, and rich pastures where cattle and sheep are raised.

Scottish food is generally simple. Oatmeal is a favorite for breakfast. Kippers and smoked herring also may be eaten for breakfast. For the main meal, Scots especially enjoy herring, lamb, and beef. Salmon is prized and may be smoked, poached, or grilled. The national dish, haggis (see recipe on page 183), is traditionally boiled in a bag made from a sheep's stomach.

Many Scots enjoy high tea—a light supper such as fish and chips, cakes, and tea. Scotch whiskey, a favorite alcoholic drink, has been produced in Scotland since the 1400s.

SCONES

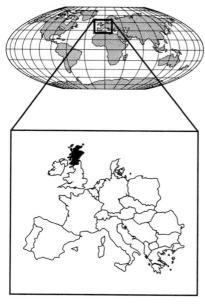

Scotland

INGREDIENTS

½ cup whole wheat flour

1 cup plus 2 tablespoons white flour

Dash of salt

¼ teaspoon baking soda

½ stick butter, softened

1¼ cups buttermilk

Butter or jam to serve with scones

STEPS

1. Put flours, salt, and baking soda in a large mixing bowl. Stir together.

2. Cut in butter with two knives.

3. Add enough buttermilk to make a soft dough.

4. Knead dough gently on a floured board.

5. Roll out dough to ¾-inch thick. Cut with a round cookie cutter.

6. Place round pieces of dough on a greased cookie sheet. Poke tops with a fork.

7. Bake in a 400-degree oven for about 15 minutes or until browned.

8. Serve warm with butter or jam.

Serves 6.

📖 **Library Link 1:** What is the source of the name "scone"?

OATCAKES

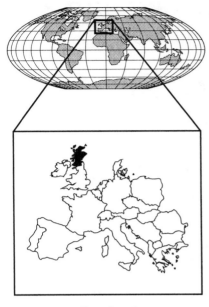

Scotland

INGREDIENTS

1¼ cups oatmeal

Pinch of baking soda

¾ teaspoon salt

2 tablespoons melted lard

4 tablespoons hot water

Ground oatmeal for kneading

STEPS

1. Mix oatmeal with baking soda and salt in a large bowl.

2. Make a hole in the center of the mixture.

3. Pour lard and water into the hole.

4. Stir lightly until dough is mixed. Add a bit more water if dough is dry.

5. Turn dough onto a board sprinkled with ground oatmeal.

6. Roll as thin as possible into a large circle. Use ground oats to keep from sticking.

7. Cut dough into wedges. Curl up edges and poke with a fork.

8. Grease a frying pan. Heat over medium heat.

9. Cook oatcakes on hot pan until browned. Turn and cook until lightly browned on other side.

10. Serve hot.

Serves 6-8.

📖 **Library Link 2:** Research bannocks.

CULLEN SKINK

(Fish Soup)

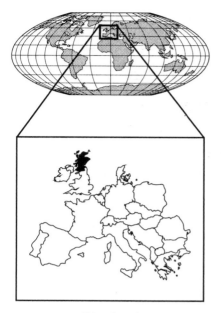

Scotland

INGREDIENTS

1 whole haddock (1½-2 pounds)

1 onion, chopped

1¼ cups water

Salt and pepper to taste

¼ cup chopped chives

3 cups milk

2 tablespoons butter

2 cups mashed potatoes

4 tablespoons cream

Fresh parsley for garnish

STEPS

1. Put haddock, onion, and water into a large saucepan.
2. Bring to a boil over medium-high heat. Simmer 10 minutes.
3. Remove fish from pan.
4. Separate meat from skin and bones.
5. Put skin and bones back in pan of water. Simmer for 1 hour.
6. Remove pan from heat. Strain the liquid (stock).
7. Discard bones, skin, and onion. Put liquid in pan.
8. Separate meat into chunks. Add to liquid.
9. Add salt, pepper, chives, milk, butter, and mashed potatoes to liquid.
10. Bring to a boil over medium-high heat. Reduce heat to low and simmer for 10 minutes.
11. Put soup in bowls.
12. Stir a tablespoon of cream into each bowl. Sprinkle with parsley.

Serves 4.

📖 **Library Link 3:** Research haddock.

SKIRLIE
(Fried Oatmeal)

INGREDIENTS

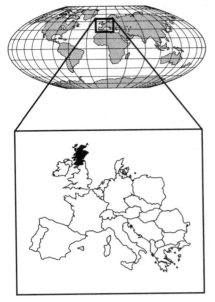

Scotland

¼ cup beef suet, chopped finely

1½ cups onion, chopped finely

1 cup oatmeal

Salt and pepper to taste

¼ teaspoon coriander

¼ teaspoon cloves

½ teaspoon nutmeg

STEPS

1. Put suet in a frying pan over medium heat.

2. Add onions. Cook until brown.

3. Add rest of ingredients. Fry until oatmeal is brown and crunchy, stirring well.

4. Serve as a side dish.

Serves 6.

📖 **Library Link 4:** Research oats.

STOVIES
(Potatoes and Meat)

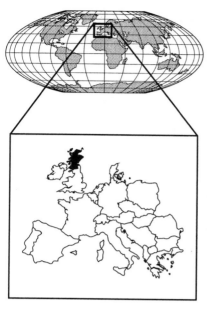

Scotland

INGREDIENTS

2 tablespoons shortening

1 onion, chopped finely

1½ pounds potatoes, peeled and cut into thick slices

Salt and pepper to taste

¾ cup water

¾ pound leftover meat, cut into bite-sized pieces

STEPS

1. Melt shortening in a large saucepan over medium-high heat.

2. Add onion. Cook until lightly browned.

3. Add potatoes, salt, and pepper.

4. Pour water over potatoes.

5. Bring to a boil. Cover and reduce heat. Simmer for 1 hour.

6. Add meat. Cook for 10 more minutes.

Serves 6.

📖 **Library Link 5:** When were potatoes first cultivated in Scotland?

HAGGIS
(Pudding Sausage)

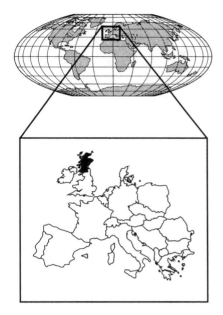

Scotland

INGREDIENTS

¼ pound lamb's liver

1 sheep's heart

½ cup onion, chopped finely

Water

½ cup oatmeal

¼ cup beef suet, grated

¼ teaspoon nutmeg

Salt and pepper to taste

STEPS

1. Put washed liver and heart into a medium saucepan over medium heat.
2. Add onion and enough water to cover.
3. Simmer for 40 minutes or until meat is tender.
4. Drain meat and onion.
5. Put meat into a food processor and grind.
6. Stir onion into meat.
7. Heat a large frying pan over medium heat.
8. Put the oatmeal into frying pan. Stir and cook until it is lightly toasted and browned. Remove from heat.
9. Mix oatmeal, suet, nutmeg, salt, and pepper into meat.
10. Pour mixture into a pudding bowl. Cover with foil and place in a steamer or a pan with water in the bottom.
11. Steam for 2 hours.
12. When pudding is done, add salt and pepper if desired.
13. Serve with crackers or potatoes.

Serves 6.

📖 **Library Link 6:** Haggis may be considered the national dish of Scotland. What entertainment traditionally accompanies haggis?

ANNOTATED BIBLIOGRAPHY

Anderson, Margaret J. *In the Circle of Time*. New York: Alfred A. Knopf, 1979. Grades 4 and up.
Two youngsters find themselves in the future as they hunt for missing stones.

_____. *In the Keep of Time*. New York: Alfred A. Knopf, 1977. Grades 4 and up.
A Scottish tower takes four children into the past and future.

Cooper, Susan, reteller. *The Selkie Girl*. Illustrated by Warwick Hutton. New York: Margaret K. McElderry Books, 1986. Grades 2 and up.
Donallan falls in love with a seal girl and marries her, only to eventually lose her to her life in the sea off the coasts of Ireland and Scotland.

_____. *Tam Lin*. Illustrated by Warwick Hutton. New York: Margaret K. McElderry Books, 1991. Grades 3 and up.
In this classic tale from Scotland, Lady Margaret saves Tam Lin, an elfin knight, from an evil enchantment. Preread for suitability for your students.

Hedderwick, Mairi. *Katie Morag Delivers the Mail*. Boston: Little, Brown, 1984. Grades preschool and up.
Katie helps out by delivering the mail on a busy day, but she mixes up the packages, creating havoc.

Leaf, Munro. *Wee Gillis*. Illustrated by Robert Lawson. New York: Viking, 1928. Grades kindergarten and up.
Wee Gillis has to decide between living in the Lowlands or Highlands of Scotland.

Oram, Hiawyn. *Skittlewonder and the Wizard*. Illustrated by Jenny Rodwell. New York: Dial Press, 1980. Grades 2 and up.
In this Scottish folktale, when Skittlewonder beats a wizard at bowling with skittles, he has to learn the wizard's name or be turned into a set of skittles.

Robertson, Joanne. *Sea Witches*. Illustrated by Laszlo Gal. New York: Dial Books for Young Readers, 1991. Grades kindergarten and up.
A superstitious grandmother tells the tale of ghost sea witches who destroy ships.

Sewall, Marcia. *The Wee, Wee Mannie and the Big, Big Coo*. New York: Little, Brown, 1977. Grades kindergarten and up.
This is a Scottish folktale of a contrary cow that is outwitted by a wee man.

Wallace, Barbara Brooks. *Argyle*. Illustrated by John Sandford. Nashville, TN: Abingdon Press, 1987. Grades preschool and up.
In this fanciful explanation of Argyle knitwear, Argyle is just like all the other sheep until he eats some strangely colored flowers.

Yolen, Jane. *Greyling*. Illustrated by David Ray. New York: Philomel, 1991. Grades 2 and up.
This tale from Scotland tells of a childless fisherman who takes a stranded seal home to his wife. The seal is a selchie, a young boy on land who will return to being a seal if allowed in the sea. Greyling grows to be a beloved young man but chooses to return to the sea forever to save his father in a storm.

VIDEO

Wee Gillis. Churchill Films, 1986. 19 minutes. Grades kindergarten and up.
Wee Gillis tries to decide his future. This video shows the geography and life of Scotland.

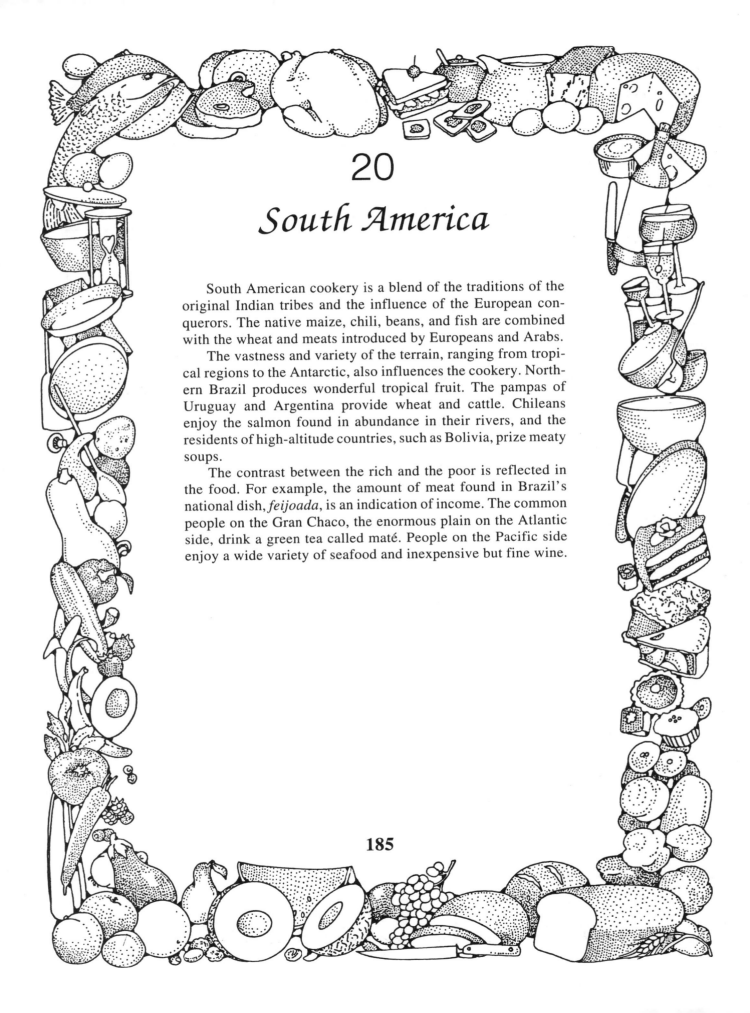

20

South America

South American cookery is a blend of the traditions of the original Indian tribes and the influence of the European conquerors. The native maize, chili, beans, and fish are combined with the wheat and meats introduced by Europeans and Arabs.

The vastness and variety of the terrain, ranging from tropical regions to the Antarctic, also influences the cookery. Northern Brazil produces wonderful tropical fruit. The pampas of Uruguay and Argentina provide wheat and cattle. Chileans enjoy the salmon found in abundance in their rivers, and the residents of high-altitude countries, such as Bolivia, prize meaty soups.

The contrast between the rich and the poor is reflected in the food. For example, the amount of meat found in Brazil's national dish, *feijoada*, is an indication of income. The common people on the Gran Chaco, the enormous plain on the Atlantic side, drink a green tea called maté. People on the Pacific side enjoy a wide variety of seafood and inexpensive but fine wine.

185

STUFFED AVOCADOS

INGREDIENTS

6 avocados

½ pound cooked shrimp, chopped

1 cup chopped lettuce

½ cup mayonnaise

1 hard-boiled egg, chopped

Salt and pepper to taste

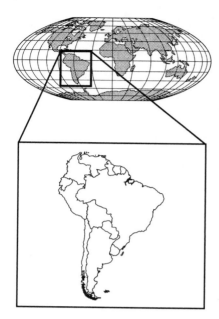

South America

STEPS

1. Peel avocados and cut in half. Remove pits.
2. Mix rest of ingredients.
3. Put shrimp mixture in avocado halves.
4. Serve immediately.

Serves 3-6.

📖 **Library Link 1:** For how many years has the avocado been cultivated?

SEVICHE OF STRIPED BASS

INGREDIENTS

2 pounds striped bass fillets, cut into 1-inch pieces

1⅔ cups lemon juice

1 cup orange juice

1 cup oil

1 hot red chili, chopped finely

1 onion, chopped

2 cloves garlic, minced

Salt and pepper to taste

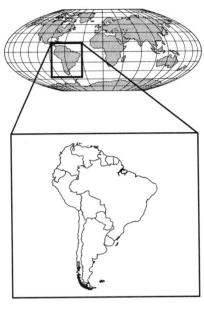

South America

STEPS

1. Put fish in a medium bowl.
2. Pour lemon juice over fish.
3. Cover fish. Put in refrigerator for 4 hours. Turn fish after 2 hours.
4. Drain lemon juice off fish.
5. Add rest of ingredients to the fish. Stir to mix.
6. Let mixture stand in the refrigerator 30 minutes. Serve.

Serves 4-6.

📖 **Library Link 2:** Research nonfood uses of chilies by the Incas, Mayans, and Aztecs.

EMPANADAS

(Meat-Filled Turnovers)

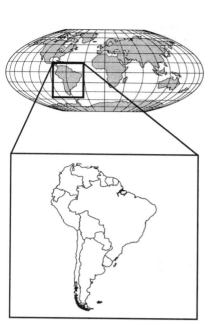

South America

INGREDIENTS

Filling:

½ cup onions, chopped finely

1 tablespoon olive oil

½ cup water

½ pound sirloin steak, cut into small cubes

3 tablespoons currants

1 teaspoon paprika

¾ teaspoon salt

¼ teaspoon pepper

Pastry:

2 cups flour

1 teaspoon salt

⅓ cup plus 1 tablespoon shortening, softened

¼ cup cold water

Garnish:

2 hard-boiled eggs, sliced

12 black olives, sliced

STEPS

1. Put onions, oil, and water in a large skillet.
2. Boil over medium-high heat until water evaporates.
3. Add meat. Cook until browned on all sides, stirring constantly.
4. Stir in currants, paprika, salt, and pepper.
5. Remove filling from heat. Set aside.
6. To make pastry, combine flour and salt in a large bowl.
7. Cut in shortening.
8. Pour in water. Mix lightly with hands.
9. Roll dough onto a floured board to ⅛-inch thick.
10. Cut out circles about 4-5 inches wide.
11. Place about 2 tablespoons of meat filling onto center of each pastry circle.
12. Top with a slice of egg and a few olive slices.
13. Dip your finger into water and rub over the outside edge of the pastry circle.
14. Fold the pastry in half, forming a crescent.
15. Pinch the edges of the dough to seal all around.
16. Heat oven to 400 degrees.
17. Place pastries on ungreased baking sheet.
18. Bake for 5 minutes or until lightly browned.
19. Serve hot.

Serves 6-8.

📖 **Library Link 3:** Research other kinds of turnovers.

SWEET SQUASH

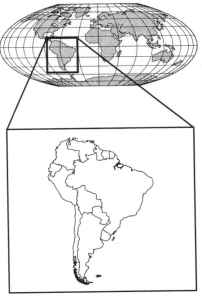

South America

INGREDIENTS

2 large butternut or acorn squash

1¼ cups water

3½ cups dark brown sugar

2 cups whipped cream

STEPS

1. Cut each squash in half.

2. Clean seeds out of center of squash.

3. Put squash in a large skillet.

4. Pour water into skillet.

5. Sprinkle brown sugar over squash.

6. Put skillet on stove over medium-high heat. Bring to a boil.

7. Cover skillet. Reduce heat to simmer.

8. Simmer over lowest heat for an hour. Pour liquid over squash every 10 minutes.

9. When squash is soft, remove skillet from heat. Let cool.

10. To serve, put squash on a plate, spoon liquid over squash, and top with whipped cream.

Serves 4.

📖 **Library Link 4:** Research the parts of South America and contrast the living styles and eating habits.

RICE AND TOMATOES

INGREDIENTS

¼ cup olive oil

1 onion, sliced thinly

3 cups raw, long-grain rice

3 cups chicken broth

3 cups boiling water

3 tomatoes, peeled and chopped

1½ teaspoons salt

Dash pepper

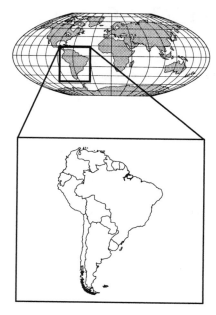

South America

STEPS

1. Put oil in a large saucepan.

2. Add onions. Cook over medium heat for 5 minutes until clear, but not browned.

3. Add rice. Cook for 3 minutes, stirring constantly.

4. Add rest of ingredients. Bring to a boil, stirring constantly.

5. Cover pan. Reduce heat and simmer for 20 minutes or until liquid is absorbed.

6. Serve hot.

Serves 8-10.

📖 **Library Link 5:** Research the history of tomatoes.

CREME DE ABACATE

(Cream of Avocado Dessert)

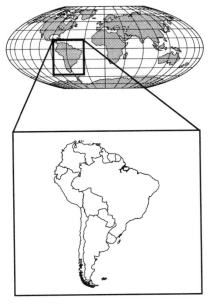

South America

INGREDIENTS

2 large, ripe avocados

¼ cup lime juice

½ cup powdered sugar

½ lime, sliced thinly

STEPS

1. Peel avocados and cut in half. Remove pits.

2. Push avocados through a sieve placed over a bowl.

3. Stir lime juice and sugar into avocado.

4. Put avocado mixture into 4 parfait glasses.

5. Place a lime slice on top of each glass.

6. Put glasses in refrigerator until chilled.

7. Serve cold.

Serves 4.

📖 **Library Link 6:** Avocados, also known as alligator pears, turn brown easily. How can the browning be reduced?

ANNOTATED BIBLIOGRAPHY

Ada, Alma Flor. *The Gold Coin.* Illustrated by Neil Waldman. Translated by Bernice Randall. New York: Atheneum, 1991. Grades 2 and up.
Set in Central America, this is the tale of Juan, who is determined to steal a gold coin.

Alexander, Ellen. *Llama and the Great Flood: A Folktale from Peru.* New York: Thomas Y. Crowell, 1989. Grades 1 and up.
After a llama tells his owner of his dreams of a great flood, the animals and people climb atop a mountain and are safe.

Baden, Robert, reteller. *And Sunday Makes Seven.* Illustrated by Michelle Edwards. Niles, IL: Albert Whitman, 1990. Grades 1 and up.
Carlos and Ana are poor in Costa Rica, until Carlos is rewarded for his rhyme by a group of witches. When Ricardo also tries to get some gold, the witches reward him with two moles on his nose.

Barbot, Daniel. *A Bicycle for Rosaura.* Illustrated by Morella Fuenmayor. Brooklyn, NY: Kane/Miller, 1991. Grades preschool and up.
In this story from Venezuela, a clever man outfits Rosaura, a hen, with a bicycle.

Brusca, María Cristina. *On the Pampas.* New York: Henry Holt, 1991. Grades kindergarten and up.
A young girl spends summer at her grandparents' *estancia* (ranch) on the pampas of Argentina.

Carlson, Lori M., and Cynthia L. Ventura. *Where Angels Glide at Dawn: New Stories from Latin America.* Illustrated by José Ortega. New York: J.B. Lippincott, 1990. Grades 4 and up.
Ten tales from Latin America are illustrated with woodcuts. Includes a glossary.

Delacre, Lulu, selector. *Arroz con Leche: Popular Songs and Rhymes from Latin America.* New York: Scholastic, 1989. Grades preschool and up.
These charming songs are presented in English and Spanish, with musical notation at the end of the book.

_____. *Las Navidades: Popular Christmas Songs from Latin America.* New York: Scholastic, 1990. Grades preschool and up.
Old and new Christmas songs are presented in Spanish and English.

Dorros, Arthur. *Tonight Is Carnaval.* New York: Dutton Children's Books, 1991. Grades 1 and up.
The excitement of Carnaval for people of the Andes is highlighted by *arpilleras*, wall hangings created for the book by members of the *Club de Madres Virgen del Carmen* of Lima, Peru.

Ehlert, Lois. *Moon Rope: A Peruvian Folktale.* Translated by Amy Prince. San Diego, CA: Harcourt Brace Jovanovich, 1992. Grades preschool and up.
Mole and Fox want to go to the moon in this boldly illustrated, oversize folktale presented in English and Spanish.

Frost, Abigail. *Myths and Legends of the Amazon.* Illustrated by Jean Torton. New York: Marshall Cavendish, 1989. Grades 3 and up.
Color illustrations enhance 10 stories plus background information on South America.

Gelman, Rita Golden. *Dawn to Dusk in the Galapagos: Flightless Birds, Swimming Lizards, and Other Fascinating Creatures.* Photographs by Tui De Roy. Boston: Little, Brown, 1991. Grades 3 and up.
Color photographs explore a day in the life of the unusual animals found on the Galapagos Islands west of Ecuador.

George, Jean Craighead. *One Day in the Tropical Rain Forest.* Illustrated by Gary Allen. New York: Thomas Y. Crowell, 1990. Grades 3 and up.
Tepui loves the rain forest of Venezuela, but his world is threatened by bulldozers coming to level the forest. He endeavors to stop the destruction by searching for a nameless butterfly.

Gifford, Douglas. *Warriors, Gods & Spirits from Central & South American Mythology.* Illustrated by John Sibbick. New York: Schocken Books, 1983. Grades 4 and up.
This impressive collection of myths includes striking illustrations and a discussion of the symbols used in the myths.

Griego, Margot C., Betsy L. Bucks, Sharon S. Gilbert, and Laurel H. Kimball, selectors. *Tortillitas Para Mama and Other Nursery Rhymes/Spanish and English.* New York: Holt, Rinehart & Winston, 1981. Grades preschool and up.
Nursery rhymes and lullabies are collected from Spanish communities in the Americas.

Lattimore, Deborah Nourse. *Why There Is No Arguing in Heaven: A Mayan Myth.* New York: Harper & Row, 1989. Grades 2 and up.
Intricate illustrations enhance this creation myth about the Maize God, who proves his worthiness to be seated at Kunab Ku's side.

Lewis, Richard. *All of You Was Singing.* Illustrated by Ed Young. New York: Macmillan, 1991. Grades 1 and up.
In simple style, Lewis tells an Aztec myth of the earth's creation and how music comes to earth.

Pino-Saavedra, Yolando, editor. *Folktales of Chile.* Translated by Rockwell Gray. Chicago: University of Chicago Press, 1967. Grades 4 and up.
This collection includes animal, wonder, religious, romantic, trickster, and cumulative tales.

Pitkänen, Matti A., Ritva Lehtinen, and Kari E. Nurmi. *The Grandchildren of the Incas.* Minneapolis, MN: Carolrhoda Books, 1991. Grades 3 and up.
Brilliantly colored photographs enhance the text about the lives of Inca children.

Shetterly, Susan Hand. *The Dwarf-Wizard of Uxmal.* Illustrated by Robert Shetterly. New York: Atheneum, 1990. Grades 3 and up.
In this Yucatan Maya legend, a boy hatched from an egg becomes ruler.

Volkmer, Jane Anne, reteller. *Song of the Chirimia: A Guatemalan Folktale.* Translated by Lori Ann Schatschneider. Minneapolis, MN: Carolrhoda Books, 1990. Grades 2 and up.
Presented in English and Spanish, this is the tale of a young man who loves a Maya princess.

FILM

Geography of South America. Coronet, 1977. Grades 4 and up.
    Each film in this series explores life in the cities and country. The series includes "Argentina, Paraguay, and Uraguay" (11 minutes), "Brazil" (10 minutes), and "South America: The Continent" (14 minutes).

VIDEOS

Suemi's Story: My Modern Mayan Home. Little Fort Media, United Learning, 1991. 25 minutes. Grades 5 and up.
    This is a documentary about a young girl living in the village of Dzita, Yucatan.

The Tale of the Wonderful Potato. Phoenix/PBA Films and Video. 24 minutes. Grades 1 and up.
    Relating the journey of the potato from South America to Ireland, this video introduces viewers to the history and politics of the potato.

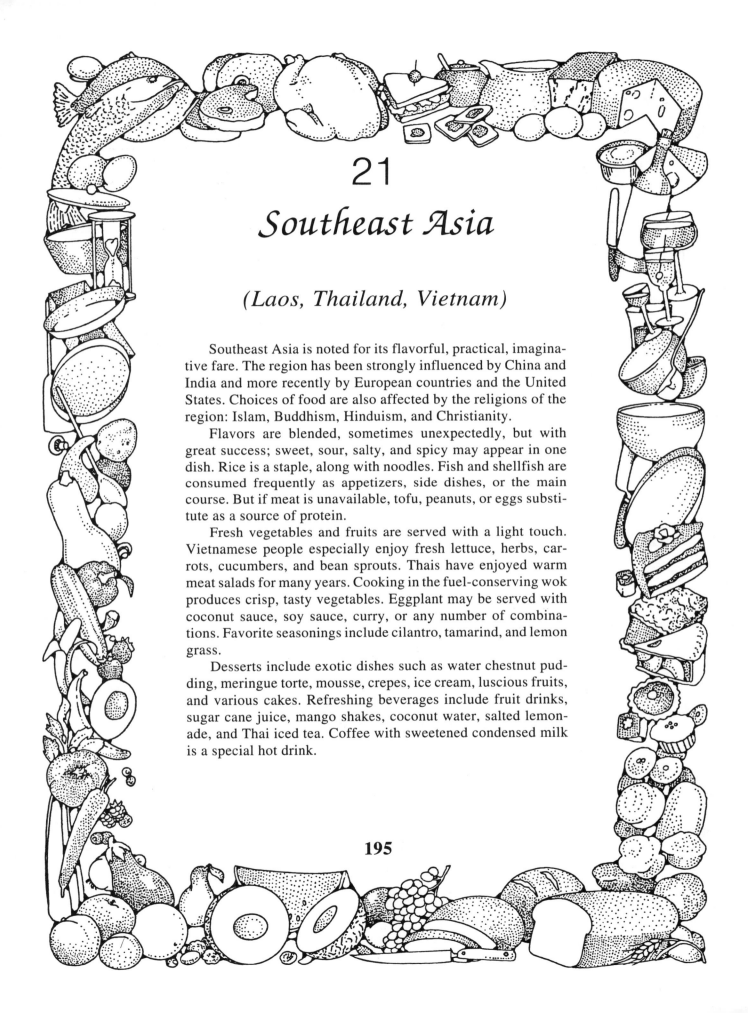

21

Southeast Asia

(Laos, Thailand, Vietnam)

Southeast Asia is noted for its flavorful, practical, imaginative fare. The region has been strongly influenced by China and India and more recently by European countries and the United States. Choices of food are also affected by the religions of the region: Islam, Buddhism, Hinduism, and Christianity.

Flavors are blended, sometimes unexpectedly, but with great success; sweet, sour, salty, and spicy may appear in one dish. Rice is a staple, along with noodles. Fish and shellfish are consumed frequently as appetizers, side dishes, or the main course. But if meat is unavailable, tofu, peanuts, or eggs substitute as a source of protein.

Fresh vegetables and fruits are served with a light touch. Vietnamese people especially enjoy fresh lettuce, herbs, carrots, cucumbers, and bean sprouts. Thais have enjoyed warm meat salads for many years. Cooking in the fuel-conserving wok produces crisp, tasty vegetables. Eggplant may be served with coconut sauce, soy sauce, curry, or any number of combinations. Favorite seasonings include cilantro, tamarind, and lemon grass.

Desserts include exotic dishes such as water chestnut pudding, meringue torte, mousse, crepes, ice cream, luscious fruits, and various cakes. Refreshing beverages include fruit drinks, sugar cane juice, mango shakes, coconut water, salted lemonade, and Thai iced tea. Coffee with sweetened condensed milk is a special hot drink.

195

KAENG CHUED

(Shrimp Soup)

(Thailand)

INGREDIENTS

2 cups coconut milk

3 shallots, minced finely

1 clove garlic, minced finely

1 teaspoon ground coriander

1 tablespoon soy sauce

1½ tablespoons sugar

⅛ teaspoon red pepper

12 whole peppercorns

Grated peel of 1 lemon

1 teaspoon lemon juice

4-5 ounces small shrimp, cooked and peeled

2 teaspoons butter

1 slice white bread, toasted and cut into cubes

Thailand

STEPS

1. Put coconut milk, shallots, garlic, coriander, soy sauce, sugar, pepper, peppercorns, lemon peel, and lemon juice in a medium saucepan.
2. Bring mixture to a boil over medium-high heat.
3. Add shrimp. Boil 1 minute.
4. Reduce heat to low.
5. Melt butter in a small frying pan over medium heat.
6. Add bread cubes. Stir to coat all sides with butter.
7. Cook 3-5 minutes or until browned.
8. Pour soup into bowls. Sprinkle with bread cubes and serve.

Serves 4.

 Library Link 1: Research the political history of Thailand.

CHA GIO
(Vietnamese Spring Rolls)

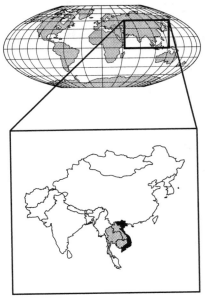

Vietnam

INGREDIENTS

½ package cellophane or rice noodles

2 eggs, beaten

1 pound ground pork, cooked

2 carrots, peeled and shredded

1 onion, minced finely

1½ teaspoons fish sauce (nuoc mam)

½ teaspoon pepper

¼ cup scallions, chopped

1-pound package rice papers or lumpia

1 beaten egg mixed with 1 teaspoon water

Oil for frying

Nuoc cham (see recipe on page 198)

STEPS

1. Soak cellophane noodles by following directions on package. Drain and cut into 2-inch lengths with scissors.
2. Put noodles, eggs, pork, carrots, onion, fish sauce, pepper, and scallions in a large bowl. Mix well.
3. Place 1 rice paper wrapper on a plate. Put 1-2 tablespoons of pork filling in center. Keep other rice papers covered with a damp cloth to keep them from drying out.
4. Fold bottom edge of wrapper up over filling. Then fold over and overlap 2 sides.
5. Brush top edge with egg and water mixture. Roll bottom up toward top. Press to seal. Repeat with other wrappers.
6. Heat oil in a frying pan or wok over medium heat for 1 minute.
7. Put spring rolls in pan. Fry about 8 minutes on each side or until brown.
8. Keep cooked rolls in a warm oven (200 degrees) while frying the rest.
9. Cut each roll into 4 pieces. Serve hot with bowls of nuoc cham.

Serves 8-10.

📖 **Library Link 2:** What countries have influenced Vietnamese cooking?

NUOC CHAM

(Vietnamese Fish Sauce Spice)

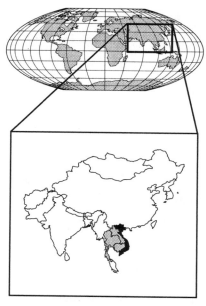

Vietnam

INGREDIENTS

2 cloves garlic, minced finely

½ teaspoon crushed red pepper flakes

3 tablespoons sugar

4 tablespoons vinegar

5 tablespoons fish sauce (nuac mam)

¾ cup water

STEPS

1. Put all ingredients in a small bowl.
2. Stir well until sugar is dissolved.
3. Taste and add a bit more water if too strong or salty.
4. Serve immediately or pour into a covered jar. May be refrigerated 2 weeks.

Serves 6-8.

📖 **Library Link 3:** Which region of Vietnam produces the most food?

OR LAM
(Laotian Quail Stew)

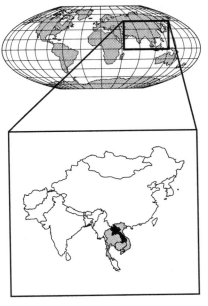

Laos

INGREDIENTS

2 ounces salt pork, cut into 4 pieces
2 small quail, cut into serving parts*
3 cups water
2 small Oriental eggplants, peeled and sliced
3 chili peppers
½ lemon rind, grated
½ teaspoon salt
½ teaspoon anchovy paste
1 pound spinach
15 string beans, ends cut off and cut in thirds
2 sprigs fresh dill
2 shallots, chopped
10 fresh basil leaves
10 fresh coriander leaves (cilantro)
1 cucumber, peeled and sliced
1 small bunch watercress
8 lettuce leaves, torn in half

STEPS

1. Put salt pork in a large frying pan or wok over medium heat.
2. Fry until crisp and oil has been released into pan. Discard salt pork, and retain oil in pan for frying quail parts.
3. Put quail parts in pan. Fry on all sides until browned.
4. Add water, eggplant, chili peppers, lemon rind, salt, and anchovy paste. Bring to a boil.
5. Cover and reduce heat. Simmer for 10 minutes or until eggplant is tender.
6. Remove eggplant and peppers. Place in a blender. Blend until smooth.
7. Pour mixture into stew.
8. Stir well. Cover and simmer for 25-30 minutes more or until quail is tender.
9. Uncover pan. Add spinach, string beans, dill, and shallots.
10. Cover pan. Simmer for 5 minutes.
11. Pour stew into a large tureen. Sprinkle with basil and coriander.
12. Cucumbers, watercress, and lettuce may be used as a garnish or stirred into stew before serving.

Serves 4.

📖 **Library Link 4:** Research quails.

*1 Cornish hen may be substituted; however, it must be simmered longer.

KHAO PHAT
(Rice and Pork)

(Thailand)

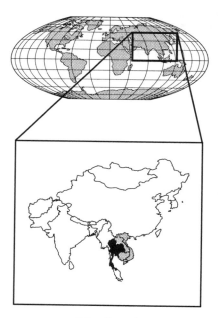

Thailand

INGREDIENTS

¼ cup oil

1 onion, minced finely

2 cloves garlic, minced finely

½ pound boneless pork, cut into thin strips

½ pound medium shrimp, cooked and peeled

2 cups cooked rice

3 tomatoes, peeled and chopped

2 teaspoons chili sauce

1 teaspoon salt

1 teaspoon shrimp paste

3 eggs, beaten

6 shallots, chopped

2 tablespoons parsley

STEPS

1. Put oil in a wok or frying pan over medium heat.
2. Add onion and garlic. Cook until soft.
3. Add pork. Cook until browned.
4. Add shrimp. Cook 4 minutes.
5. Stir in rice, tomatoes, chili sauce, salt, and shrimp paste.
6. Stir well. Cook until heated through.
7. Stir eggs into mixture. Cook for 2 minutes.
8. Stir in shallots.
9. Remove from heat. Put into serving bowls.
10. Sprinkle with parsley and serve.

Serves 4.

📖 **Library Link 5:** What countries have influenced Thai cookery?

CAMBODIAN PINEAPPLE COMPOTE

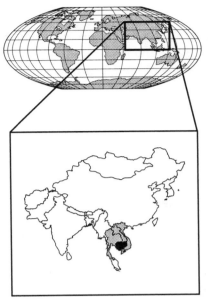

Cambodia

INGREDIENTS

1 can litchis

1 teaspoon lime juice

1 teaspoon lemon juice

2¼ cups fresh pineapple, cut into chunks

1 large orange, peeled and cut into sections

STEPS

1. Drain litchis, saving ½ cup syrup.

2. Mix syrup, lemon, and lime juices.

3. Cut litchis in half. Put in large bowl.

4. Stir in pineapple and orange pieces.

5. Pour syrup over fruit. Toss carefully.

6. Cover and refrigerate 30-60 minutes.

7. Serve cold.

Serves 4.

📖 **Library Link 6:** Research political challenges faced by Cambodians from the 1060s to the present.

ANNOTATED BIBLIOGRAPHY

Baillie, Allan. *Little Brother*. New York: Viking, 1985. Grades 4 and up.
  Vithy and his brother, Mang, are separated when they try to escape from Cambodia to Thailand. Through the efforts of a visiting doctor, they are eventually reunited.

Graham, Gail B., reteller. *The Beggar in the Blanket and Other Vietnamese Tales*. Illustrated by Brigitte Bryan. New York: Dial Press, 1970. Grades 2 and up.
  Eight tales include a Cinderella variant and other stories of romance and intrigue.

Ho, Minfong. *The Clay Marble*. New York: Farrar, Straus & Giroux, 1991. Grades 4 and up.
  Dara and her family flee Cambodia for a border refugee camp. When shelling begins along the border, she is separated from her family and must rely on her inner strength to survive.

Hoyt-Goldsmith, Diane. *Hoang Anh: A Vietnamese-American Boy*. Photographs by Lawrence Migdale. New York: Holiday House, 1992. Grades 2 and up.
  Although set in America, the text and color photographs provide a valuable exploration of the Vietnamese cultural heritage as explored by a young boy.

Lawson, Don. *An Album of the Vietnam War*. New York: Franklin Watts, 1986. Grades 4 and up.
  Text and compelling black-and-white photographs chronicle the war and the U.S. involvement.

Lee, Jeanne M. *Bà-Nam*. New York: Henry Holt, 1987. Grades 1 and up.
  Nan goes with her family to the graveyard on Thanh-Minh Day to honor her ancestors.

Livo, Norma J., and Dia Cha. *Folk Stories of the Hmong: Peoples of Laos, Thailand, and Vietnam*. Englewood, CO: Libraries Unlimited, 1991. Grades 4 and up.
  Folktales are enhanced with color plates of the Hmong dress and needlework and a history of the Hmong people.

Terada, Alice M., reteller. *Under the Starfruit Tree: Folktales from Vietnam*. Illustrated by Janet Larsen. Honolulu: University of Hawaii Press, 1989. Grades 3 and up.
  Historical and cultural notes enhance these translations of traditional tales of Vietnam.

Warren, James A. *Portrait of a Tragedy: America and the Vietnam War*. New York: Lothrop, Lee & Shepard, 1990. Grades 5 and up.
  This is an extensive discussion of the U.S. involvement in the war. Includes black-and-white photographs, a chronology, further reading, notes, and an index.

Xiong, Blia, reteller. *Nine-in-One, Grr! Grr!* Adapted by Cathy Spagnoli. Illustrated by Nancy Hom. San Francisco: Children's Book Press, 1989. Grades preschool and up.
  In this Hmong tale, when Bird hears Tiger sing that she will have nine cubs in a year, Bird tricks her into saying she will have one cub in nine years.

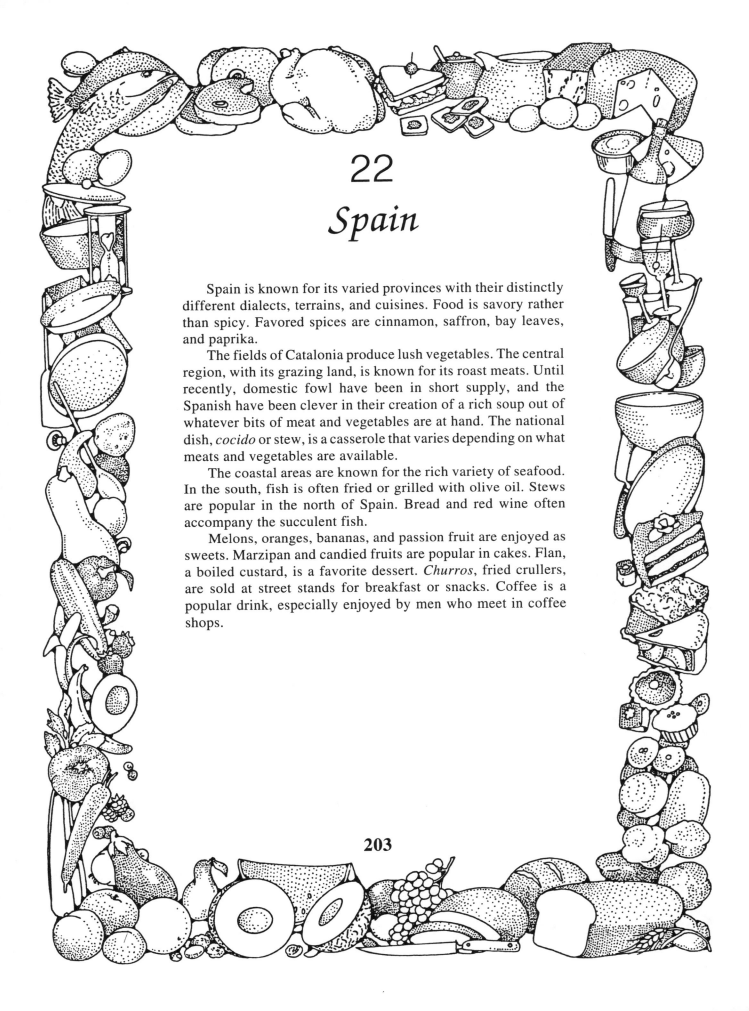

22

Spain

Spain is known for its varied provinces with their distinctly different dialects, terrains, and cuisines. Food is savory rather than spicy. Favored spices are cinnamon, saffron, bay leaves, and paprika.

The fields of Catalonia produce lush vegetables. The central region, with its grazing land, is known for its roast meats. Until recently, domestic fowl have been in short supply, and the Spanish have been clever in their creation of a rich soup out of whatever bits of meat and vegetables are at hand. The national dish, *cocido* or stew, is a casserole that varies depending on what meats and vegetables are available.

The coastal areas are known for the rich variety of seafood. In the south, fish is often fried or grilled with olive oil. Stews are popular in the north of Spain. Bread and red wine often accompany the succulent fish.

Melons, oranges, bananas, and passion fruit are enjoyed as sweets. Marzipan and candied fruits are popular in cakes. Flan, a boiled custard, is a favorite dessert. *Churros*, fried crullers, are sold at street stands for breakfast or snacks. Coffee is a popular drink, especially enjoyed by men who meet in coffee shops.

203

SPANISH OMELETTE

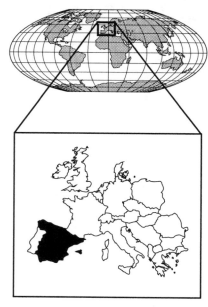

Spain

INGREDIENTS

5 tablespoons olive oil

1 onion, chopped finely

1 large potato, chopped

½ teaspoon salt

5 large eggs, beaten

2 tablespoons olive oil

STEPS

1. Heat 5 tablespoons of olive oil in frying pan over medium heat.

2. Stir in onion, potato, and salt.

3. Stir until cooked through.

4. Pour beaten egg into frying pan.

5. As egg begins to cook, lift up edges and let uncooked egg run underneath.

6. Continue until all of egg is cooked.

7. Lift one side of omelette and pour 2 tablespoons olive oil underneath.

8. Flip omelette onto a plate. Then flip it back upside down onto the pan to cook the other side.

9. Cook just until browned.

10. Serve hot.

Serves 4.

📖 **Library Link 1:** Research kinds of omelettes. Create your own.

GAZPACHO

(Cold Vegetable Soup)

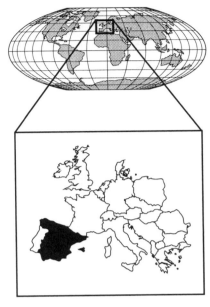

Spain

INGREDIENTS

2 cucumbers, peeled and chopped

4 large tomatoes, peeled and chopped

1 medium onion, peeled and chopped

1 green pepper, chopped

2 cloves of garlic, minced

4 cups chopped stale bread

4 cups water

⅓ cup vinegar

3½ teaspoons salt

4 tablespoons olive oil

1 tablespoon tomato paste

STEPS

1. Mix all ingredients except olive oil and tomato paste in a large bowl. Stir well.
2. Put mixture in a food mill, one cup at a time, to puree.
3. Stir olive oil and tomato paste into pureed mixture.
4. Cover and put in refrigerator for 2 hours.
5. Serve cold.

Serves 8.

📖 **Library Link 2:** Find other Spanish soups and stews and share the recipes for them with the class. Discuss how the Spanish terrain may have contributed to the ingredients of the soup.

PAELLA

INGREDIENTS

½ pound spicy sausage
2 tablespoons olive oil
3 pounds chicken, cut into serving pieces
4½ cups chicken broth
1 small red onion, cut in chunks
1 sweet pepper, cut into strips
¾ teaspoon minced garlic
2 cups uncooked rice
1 can pimento, sliced
½ teaspoon saffron
12 steamed clams
12 steamed shrimp
¾ cup fresh peas

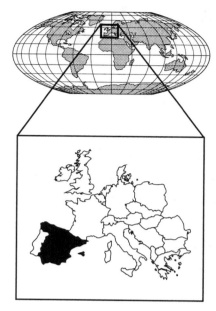

Spain

STEPS

1. Cook sausage over medium-high heat in a large oven-proof skillet until done.
2. Slice sausage. Set aside.
3. Heat oil in the skillet over medium-high heat.
4. Cook chicken pieces in oil about 15 minutes, browning on all sides.
5. Remove chicken. Set aside.
6. Heat chicken broth to boiling in a large saucepan.
7. While broth is boiling, put onion, pepper, and garlic in the remaining oil in the skillet.
8. Cook over medium-high heat until browned.
9. Add rice, boiling chicken broth, pimento, and saffron to the skillet.
10. Bring all ingredients to a boil over high heat.
11. Remove from heat.
12. Arrange chicken, sausage, clams, shrimp, and peas on top of rice mixture.
13. Heat oven to 400 degrees.
14. Set skillet in bottom of oven. Bake uncovered for 25-30 minutes or until liquid is absorbed. Do not stir.
15. Remove paella from oven. Cover with a towel.
16. Let sit for 5 minutes.
17. Remove towel. Serve directly from skillet.

Serves 6.

📖 **Library Link 3:** How did paella get its name?

MEJILLONES A LA VINAGRETA

(Marinated Mussels)

INGREDIENTS

½ cup olive oil

4 tablespoons vinegar

1½ teaspoons capers

1 tablespoon minced onion

1½ tablespoons minced parsley

Salt to taste

½ teaspoon pepper

24 steamed mussels

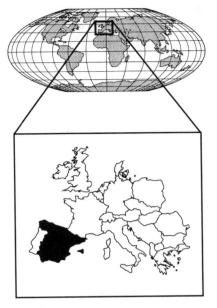

Spain

STEPS

1. Mix all ingredients except mussels in a medium bowl.
2. Remove mussels from shells.* Stir into marinade mixture. Save the shells.
3. Cover bowl. Put in refrigerator overnight.
4. Clean and put shells in refrigerator.
5. When serving, put a mussel in a shell. Pour a little of the marinade mixture over the mussel.

Serves 6.

📖 **Library Link 4:** Research mussel farming.

* Discard any mussels whose shells have not opened.

MANTECADAS DE ASTORGA
(Spanish Cupcakes)

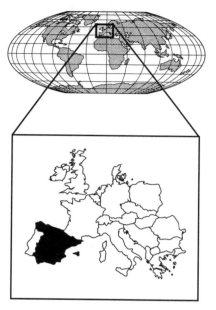

Spain

INGREDIENTS

1½ sticks butter

4 eggs

⅔ cup sugar

1⅓ cups flour

¼ teaspoon salt

½ teaspoon cinnamon

⅛ teaspoon nutmeg

Powdered sugar to sprinkle on top

STEPS

1. Melt butter. Set aside to cool.
2. Put eggs in a large bowl. Beat with a mixer until foamy.
3. Add sugar, a little at a time, while beating.
4. Beat 3 more minutes.
5. Stir in flour, salt, cinnamon, and nutmeg.
6. Lightly fold in the cooled butter.
7. Put paper cupcake liners in 24 cupcake pans.
8. Pour batter in papers about ⅔ full.
9. Bake at 350 degrees for 15 minutes or until light brown.
10. Remove from oven and sprinkle with powdered sugar.
11. Serve while warm.

Makes 24.

📖 **Library Link 5:** These cupcakes are considered "foam" cakes. Why?

CAFÉ CON LECHE

(Coffee with Milk)

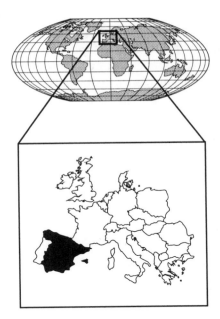

Spain

INGREDIENTS

6 cups milk

6 teaspoons instant coffee

10 teaspoons sugar

STEPS

1. Put milk in saucepan. Heat over medium heat until it boils.

2. Stir in coffee and sugar.

3. Serve hot in glass coffee cups.

Serves 6-8.

📖 **Library Link 6:** Coffee was believed to be a cure and a cause for many ills. Find out what you can on this topic.

ANNOTATED BIBLIOGRAPHY

Anderson, David. *The Spanish Armada*. New York: Hampstead Press, 1988. Grades 4 and up.
An abundance of color photographs, charts, maps, and illustrations enhance this history of the legendary battles of the Spanish Armada.

Duff, Maggie. *The Princess and the Pumpkin*. Illustrated by Catherine Stock. New York: Macmillan, 1980. Grades kindergarten and up.
In this tale from Majorca, a prince and princess find each other in spite of outrageous events.

Griffiths, Helen. *Running Wild*. Illustrated by Victor Ambrus. New York: Holiday House, 1977. Grades 5 and up.
Pablo lives with his grandparents while his parents work in Germany. He loves his new puppy but faces problems when more puppies arrive.

Hancock, Sibyl. *Esteban and the Ghost*. Illustrated by Dirk Zimmer. New York: Dial Books for Young Readers, 1983. Grades kindergarten and up.
A Spanish tinker braves Halloween night in a haunted castle and helps an unhappy ghost.

Leaf, Munro. *The Story of Ferdinand*. Illustrated by Robert Lawson. New York: Viking Kestrel, 1936. Grades preschool and up.
Ferdinand the bull loves to sit and smell the flowers, even in the bullring.

O'Dell, Scott. *The Captive*. Boston: Houghton Mifflin, 1977. Grades 5 and up.
A young Jesuit seminarian fights against enslaving the Indians in sixteenth-century Spain.

Rodari, Florian. *A Weekend with Picasso*. New York: Rizzoli International, 1991. Grades 3 and up.
Photographs of paintings, sculptures, drawings, and masks highlight an imaginary excursion with famed artist Pablo Picasso.

Wilkes, Angela, and Rubí Borgia. *Mi Primer Libro de Palabras en Español*. Translated by Annie Frankland. New York: Dorling Kindersley Children's Books, 1993. Grades kindergarten and up.
My First Word Book gives clear, colorful photographs and corresponding vocabulary for the 1,000 most commonly used words. This is sure to fascinate children and adults.

Wojciechowska, Maia. *Shadow of a Bull*. Illustrated by Alvin Smith. New York: Atheneum, 1965. Grades 5 and up.
Bullfighting and the culture of Spain are explored through the life of a young boy.

Appendix A: Answers to Library Links

1: AFRICA

1. Bananas, which are thought to have come to Africa in C.E. 500, are primarily produced in Africa, Asia, Central America, and South America.

2. Yams are from the tuber of a flowering plant that is related to lilies and grasses. Of the genus *dioscorea*, yams are thought to date from 8000 B.C.E. Yams have a high starch content and can grow to $\frac{1}{2}$ meter long and weigh up to 20 kilos.

3. Okra, a relative of the hibiscus, is native to tropical Africa or Asia and was brought by slave trade to the United States.

4. The coconut, one of the oldest food plants, is the most important commercially grown nut. The palm will grow in poor soil, providing oil, lumber, and charcoal in addition to food. Originating in the Malay Archipelago, it has migrated throughout the tropics. The coconut's face-like appearance inspired its name, which comes from the Portuguese *coco*, meaning goblin or monkey.

5. Papaya or papaw is a small tropical tree with large fleshy fruit resembling melons. Thought to have originated in the West Indies or Mexico, it probably reached Africa in the 1600s. The fruit contains the enzyme papain, which helps digestion and is used in medicines and meat tenderizers.

6. Cookie, derived from the Dutch word *koekje* or *koekie*, means small cake. A cookie is also sometimes referred to as a sweet biscuit.

2: AUSTRALIA

1. Originally, it was baked on a long, green stick over a camp fire that had burned down to coals. The ingredients were contained in a "tucker bag."

2. In some areas, kangaroos compete with farmers' cattle and sheep because kangaroos eat the precious grass down to the roots. In some areas, they feed on golf courses. One protected species is the Big Red kangaroo.

3. Like kangaroos, rabbits compete for scarce grass. The common gray rabbits and the larger, tan-colored hares are considered pests. Some efforts to reduce the populations have proven successful.

4. After the American Revolution, England could no longer send its convicts to America. Convicts were sent to Australia where they became a rugged sort of people who settled this vast continent. Details will vary depending on the research by the students.

5. Reports will vary.

6. Unusual Australian animals include the platypus, kangaroo, koala, kookaburra, and lyre bird.

211

3: CANADA

1. Peas, originally cultivated by the Hebrews, Persians, Greeks, and Romans, are now found throughout the world. They are rich in nitrogen and mucilage and high in protein.

2. European cookery, in particular that of Switzerland, England, and France, has most heavily influenced Canadian cuisine. Answers regarding individual dishes will vary.

3. From the Latin *tortus*, which means making round. *Tourtes* may be filled with French pastry cream, jam, raw fruit, or cooked fruit.

4. The Huron and Iroquois Indians ate beans, a porridge of water and crushed maize, fish, and meat.

5. Prince Edward Island is near Nova Scotia and New Brunswick, with the Gulf of Saint Lawrence to the north.

6. Saskatoons grow near rivers and are small, firm berries resembling blueberries crossed with wild currants.

4: CHINA

1. Answers will vary.

2. Eggs are buried for a few months in a special mixture that turns the shell a marbled black and the insides to a hard-boiled texture with green veins.

3. A banquet may include 20 dishes, but the polite diner may take only a spoonful or two of each dish.

4. Pigs symbolize prosperity.

5. Red cooking is a type of stewing with soy sauce called *hung shao*. The soy sauce provides the red color.

6. Answers will vary.

5: COMMONWEALTH OF INDEPENDENT STATES

1. Caviar, originating from the Turkish word *khavia*, is eggs of the sturgeon.

2. Buckwheat is not a grain, but its kernels are chenes, dry fruits similar to strawberry seeds. Buckwheat originated in Manchuria. The English name means "beech wheat," because the kernels are shaped somewhat like beechnuts. Buckwheat thrives in soil where wheat, barley, or rye will not grow and is considered grain for rural residents.

3. Catherine the Great enjoyed French food and brought French chefs to the country. She especially enjoyed warm appetizers. Ivan the Terrible loved the sherbets, ice creams, and pastries of the Italians. Peter the Great appreciated the vegetable dishes and spiced honeycakes of the Dutch. The first czar, Rurik, was from Scandinavia, and he brought cocktail appetizers with him.

4. Roots are high in carbohydrates, providing energy to consumers. It is thought that humans' search for roots to eat initiated the practice of farming. People used sticks or stones to dig up roots, and eventually developed the hoe and plough. Once soil was dug or moved, the aeration caused more fertility.

5. Cucumbers, perhaps native to India or Africa, were brought to France in the ninth century. They have been cultivated for approximately 4,000 years. During the Middle Ages they were thought to be unhealthy because they were hard to digest.

6. Russians like a strong black China tea made in a samovar. The poorest people would hang a lump of sugar over the table to remind themselves of their bitter lives. The more affluent would take turns sucking a lump of sugar before drinking the tea. The rich would add sugar to their tea.

6: ENGLAND

1. *Platichthys flesus*, a small dextral flatfish, is found not only in the English Channel but also on the muddy bottoms of estuaries and creeks.

2. The Romans brought cabbage to England when they conquered it during the first century.

3. "Pudding" is derived from an Old English word for "swelling."

4. Though popular in England, shortbread is of Scottish origin.

5. Currants were first cultivated commercially in the Low Countries of northern Europe before 1600.

6. "Ladiesfingers" refers to the vegetable okra.

7: FRANCE

1. Strawberries were found by the colonists in Virginia and brought to France in the early nineteenth century. The French have cultivated the highly regarded *fraise des bois*.

2. Sauté is from the French *sauter*, to jump. It relates to tossing the ingredients while cooking them in hot fat.

3. "Soufflé" means to blow up or puff up. It relates to the practice of introducing air into the mixture through beating the egg whites.

4. The wild carrot is Queen Anne's Lace. Its roots are white and can be eaten but are not as flavorful as the carrot. The seeds are also flavorful.

5. Although pears are native to the Middle East and their name is derived from "Persia," their seeds have been found in Stone Age dwellings.

6. *Mousse* means froth.

7. The French and other European clergy campaigned against the use of chocolate, claiming it was tainted by the Spanish, who brought the cacao beans from the Aztecs in Mexico.

8: GERMANY

1. In rural homes breakfast is usually bread, butter, and coffee with milk. Oatmeal or rice with milk, sugar, or raisins may be eaten by children. A larger morning meal in the cities might include bread and beer, a cheese sandwich, bacon on sour rye bread, or meat with a pastry.

2. A ratskeller is a town hall that may be simple or elegant. Food is generally authentic and delicious.

3. The Schnitzel is a slice or cutlet from the veal leg. It is cut in a slight diagonal to the long grain.

4. Bockwurst, a small Weisswurst (white sausage), is made only during bock beer time in the spring. It is served with bock beer. A variation is a smoked red sausage similar to the hot dog.

5. The terrain of Germany includes the lush forests of the south, the warmth of Rhine country where wine is produced, and the mountains of Bavaria.

6. On Holy Thursday one might eat new spinach, a creamed green soup, or eggs on creamed new spinach. Good Friday is meatless and people eat various fish dishes. On Easter children enjoy the universal colored eggs and candy, plus tempting chocolate. Breakfast includes a sweet yeast coffee cake.

7. Germans love cakes and cookies, and the variety is endless. Favorites are deep-fried cakes such as doughnuts and crullers, puff pastry, sweet tart pastry, torte or round cake, and sponge cakes. Cookies include individual tarts, tiny cake rolls, and waffles with creams. Such treats are typically between-meal snacks and not desserts.

9: GREECE

1. Feta cheese is a soft, salty white cheese made from goat's milk.

2. Native to the eastern Mediterranean region, the olive has been cultivated since at least 3000 B.C.E. In addition to cooking, it is used for lamp oil and cosmetics.

3. Lamb is generally slaughtered at less than 14 months, veal at less than 3 months, beef at less than 42 months, and pork from 6 to 7 months.

4. Eggplant is a member of the nightshade family, which also includes the potato, tobacco, jimson weed, and nightshade, a deadly plant.

5. Pythagoras believed that beans contained souls of the dead and forbade his followers from eating them.

6. The first Greek breads and cakes were baked in embers or under a dome-shaped device. The Greeks invented the bread oven, which could be preheated and opened in the front.

10: INDIA

1. Turmeric is used in Asian ceremonies as a cosmetic and as a dye. It is also used as a charm, with a bit of root hung around a newborn baby's neck.

2. Chutney is eaten to refresh the palate and to add accent to a meal.

3. Yogurt is a Turkish term. Yogurt probably originated in Central Asia. It is made from whole sheep's, goat's, or cow's milk.

4. Accounts vary, but probably wheat has been cultivated more than 6,000 years. Grain transactions have been recorded since 3000 B.C.E.

5. Saffron is made from the stigmata of saffron crocuses (*Crocus sativus*). It takes 75,000 crocuses to make 1 pound of leaf saffron. Therefore saffron is the most expensive spice. It is also common in Spanish cooking.

6. Cardamom grows in shaded, moist areas of mountain slopes in India. It also grows in Sri Lanka. Cardamom was valued by Greeks and Romans for food and medicines more than 2,000 years ago. The Vikings carried it to the Scandinavian countries.

11: IRELAND

1. As long as 2,000 years ago, outdoor cooking sites included a hearth, a well, and a trough in which water was heated. Stones were heated in the hearth and dropped in the water, quickly bringing the water to boil.

2. The potato stores energy as starch, contains approximately three percent protein, and provides vitamin C.

3. Europe had made the potato an important food source in the sixteenth and seventeenth centuries. When the potato blight struck in 1845, more than 1 million people died. Another 1¼ million emigrated, most of them coming to America.

4. The candle is a sign to the homeless that the residents are willing to give a warm welcome to visitors, unlike that received by Mary and Joseph in their search for an inn.

5. Caffeine is an alkaloid that stimulates the cortex of the brain. Small doses improve concentration, attention span, and coordination. Caffeine increases water elimination and gastric secretions; it also stimulates the heart and makes skeletal muscles less susceptible to fatigue. Excessive amounts can cause adverse reactions.

12: ITALY

1. Chickens were first bred in Southeast Asia or India and spread to the West. Eggs have been commonly eaten in the West since Roman times. Cockfights were popular in Rome almost as early as fifth century B.C.E.

2. Spinach, thought to be Persian in origin, was probably brought to the Romans by Arabs. Other examples of the spinach family include mountain spinach, lambs quarters or pigweed, amaranth, fenugreek, and Malabar nightshade.

3. Macaroni was mentioned in records as early as 1200. What appeared to be pasta-making devices were found in Pompeii.

4. Anise was a favorite during Julius Caesar's day. It was used as a flavoring, as an antidote for scorpion bites, as a safeguard against the evil eye or nightmares, and as perfume or in sachets.

5. Some historians believe lemons originated in India, but no one is sure. They may have been brought to Europe by the Crusaders.

6. Ice cream was probably invented in the East and brought to Northern Italy. It was later taken by an Italian cook to France in the 1500s. Italians brought ice cream to the United States in the 1800s.

13: JAPAN

1. The *okonomiya* are omelet shops where there is a wide variety of omelettes.

2. Answers will vary. Consult *Cultures of the World: Japan* (see series information on page 349) for examples.

3. Tofu became popular as a protein source when Buddhism discouraged eating meat.

4. Favored fish include sea bream, tuna, carp, turbot, and mackerel.

5. *Cha-no-ma* is the Japanese term for tea room.

14: KOREA

1. Soup may be served as a main dish at any meal. The breakfast soup is usually a light, clear soup. Heartier soups are served at lunch or dinner.

2. In spite of political differences, the people of Korea share a common cuisine. The food preferences and cooking practices have remained essentially the same.

3. For Sol, a three-day feast for greeting the new year, foods might include rice soup, egg rolls, meat dumplings, fried fish, kimchi, and various sweets and fruit. For Shusok, the harvest observation, foods would include seasonal fruits and vegetables. On Shampoo Day people might have a picnic after bathing.

4. Traditional colors include red, green, yellow, white, and black.

5. Chicken, fish, and soybean products, including tofu, are beef substitutes commonly used in Korea.

6. Briefly, both North Korea and South Korea wanted to rule the peninsula. North Korea invaded South Korea in 1950, and the United States became involved in this three-year war. The two countries continue to maintain an uneasy relationship with very different governments.

15: MEXICO

1. *Sopa seca* is a dry soup made with rice, pasta, or tortillas. *Cocido* is a stew-like soup with meat and vegetables. Menudo is tripe soup. *Calco de queso* is cheese soup.

2. The Mayas believed man was created from *masa* or corn. The Aztecs worshipped corn gods. Although Mexicans no longer worship corn, it is highly respected for providing sustenance.

3. Many foods use tortillas, including enchiladas, tacos, burritos, *totopos*, and quesadillas.

4. The chayote or custard marrow is a vegetable from a climbing plant. Native to Mexico and the Antilles, it is now a primary crop of Algeria.

5. Of the species *Phaseolus vulgaris*, the common bean is native to southwest Mexico. Cultivated more than 7,000 years ago, the species now includes hundreds of varieties.

6. Examples include *capirotado* or bread pudding for Lent, flan, a caramel-colored custard, *arroz con leche* or rice pudding, and *chongos* or sweetened curds and whey.

16: MIDDLE EAST

1. Almonds are the seed of a plum-like fruit (drupe). They are native to west India and a relative of the plum and peach.

2. Seeds and rhizomes are boiled, dried, and ground into flour. They are also used for perfume.

3. Matzo balls are eaten by Jews on Passover.

4. Paprika comes from a sweet pepper. Mild paprika comes from the seeds. Strong paprika comes from the whole fruit, which is dried and ground.

5. Bulgur is made from boiling and drying the grain.

6. *Shekar polo* is sugar pilaf, a sweet rice pilaf served at weddings and on holidays.

7. Yeast originally meant the froth or sediment of a fermenting liquid. In Egypt beer froth was used.

8. Figs are not bee or wind pollinated but are only pollinated by a certain kind of wasp about $\frac{1}{8}$ inch long.

17: THE NETHERLANDS

1. Examples might include various breads. The *duivekater* (diamond shaped) is baked from December to New Year's Day. Three Kings Bread is baked for Epiphany and contains a bean. It is thought that the pretzel was created when a baker who was jailed for making bitter bread was told by the king that he must

bake a see-through bread to regain his freedom. Another theory for the pretzel is that it represents the wheel of the sun king's wagon.

2. The jambless fireplace was primitive with no sides. A large kettle might hang over it. Spits for roasting would be placed in front of the fire. Pans might have feet or be placed on a trivet over the coals.

3. A seventeenth-century kitchen might have a variety of pans, wooden lids, spits with dripping pans, an iron, a chafing dish, knives, a cleaver, a rasp, spoons, a skimmer, a variety of bowls and bottles, earthenware or tin plates and platters, cups, and glasses.

4. Varieties of *hutspot* might include mutton and carrots or prunes or a *hutspot* of ground beef with currants. A more elaborate variation with more meats is the *olipodrigo*.

5. A typical Twelfth Night Feast might include a capon with sauce, waffles, and bread baked with a bean. The person who gets the bean is king for the night. Entertainment might include music, carolers, or a jester. Children play a game of jumping over candles.

6. *Speculaas* is traditionally eaten in December in honor of the St. Nicholas celebration.

18: SCANDINAVIA

1. Add 1 part salt to 11 parts water. Place the potato in the water. The waxy potato will float; the mealy potato will sink.

2. Hake, pollock, and whiting are most popular. Cod rest on the ocean floor more, using less dark muscle than an active hunter fish such as mackerel.

3. A smorgasbord is a buffet table where people help themselves to hors d'oeuvres.

4. Sardines, which swim in shoals, were first canned in 1834.

5. Because salt was historically rare, it was very expensive. It was also critical for the preservation of fish. Once it became available to everyone, people used it with abandon. Scandinavians continue to enjoy the flavor of salt.

6. "Spritz" is from the German and means to squirt.

7. Tapioca is derived from the root of a tropical plant, the manioc or cassava.

19: SCOTLAND

1. The name "scones" originated in a parish in Perthshire, the site of a historic abbey and palace where kings were crowned on the Stone of Destiny of Scone.

2. Bannock is the Gaelic term for oatcake. Bannocks traditionally are served with fish, cheese, or marmalade. A Scottish soldier of days gone by often existed on bannocks.

3. Haddock is of the cod family but smaller than true cod. It is a white fish.

4. Originating in Europe or Asia, oats were originally considered weeds good only for medicine. Oats were cultivated in the wet climate of northern Europe. Of the oat production, approximately 95 percent is consumed by animals, with the balance eaten by humans.

5. Potatoes were first cultivated in 1683.

6. Bagpipes escort haggis during large banquets.

20: SOUTH AMERICA

1. The avocado has been cultivated for approximately 7,000 years in Central America. It was brought to the Old World tropics in the nineteenth century. It was highly esteemed by the Mayas and Aztecs.

2. Chilies were used for torture, and arrows were dipped in their juice. Chilies were put in water to kill fish. Chilies were also used as an antiseptic and to fumigate a room.

3. Answers will vary.

4. Answers will vary.

5. Tomatoes were indigenous to the Andes, cultivated in Mexico, and brought to Europe in 1523. They were called love apples in England in the late sixteenth century but were believed to be poisonous by most Europeans until the nineteenth century.

6. Avocados turn brown from enzymatic action. This can be slowed down by adding lemon juice or vinegar.

21: SOUTHEAST ASIA

1. Briefly, Thailand was known as Siam. It is now a constitutional monarchy. It has never been colonized by a foreign power.

2. China, which ruled Vietnam for a thousand years, continues to influence the food. After becoming part of French Indochina, the country absorbed French practices into its cuisine. Other countries of Southeast Asia also have contributed to Vietnam's cookery.

3. The southern region of Vietnam is the richest, with most food produced there.

4. The common quail, *Coturnix vulgaris*, comes from Europe. Exotic species are in Asia. The American quail is larger and part of the partridge family. Quails are migratory birds.

5. Thailand is mostly influenced by nearby Vietnam and China in addition to the surrounding countries of Burma, Laos, Cambodia, and Malaysia.

6. Answers will vary depending on the depth of research.

22: SPAIN

1. Possible omelettes include Denver, Western, Charentière, and hollandaise.

2. Answers will vary.

3. Paella is named for the two-handled iron frying pan in which it is cooked and served.

4. Mussel "parks" may be developed on sea beds, which must be in calm water and on a firm bed or the mussels will stir up mud. Rows of stakes (*bouchots*) with hanging nets can be used successfully. In deep seas or tides, mussels can be grown on ropes attached to crossbeams.

5. They are considered "foam" cakes because they are leavened by beating the eggs into an air-filled foam.

6. Information will vary, depending on the historical records. Coffee has been believed to cure consumption, dropsy, gout, and smallpox. When mixed with milk, it was believed to cause leprosy.

Appendix B: Measurements

HOW TO MEASURE ACCURATELY

Flour

Spoon into a measuring cup. Level off extra with a knife.

Sugar (granulated or confectioners)

Dip measuring cup into sugar. Level off with a knife.

Brown sugar

Pack brown sugar into a measuring cup. It should hold its shape when turned out of the cup.

Shortening

Use a spatula or scraper to pack it into a measuring cup. Level off with a knife.

Liquids

Pour into cup. A glass liquid-measuring cup allows extra room at the top, preventing spills. Molasses and syrup "round" up, so pour slowly. Use a spatula or rubber scraper to scrape out cup.

Nuts, coconut, bread crumbs, cheese, and so forth

Pack measuring cup lightly until full.

Spices, baking powder, salt, and so forth

Stir. Fill measuring spoon and level off with a knife.

MEASURING EQUIVALENTS

Dash	=	less than $\frac{1}{8}$ teaspoon
3 teaspoons	=	1 tablespoon
4 tablespoons	=	$\frac{1}{4}$ cup
$5\frac{1}{3}$ tablespoons	=	$\frac{1}{3}$ cup
8 tablespoons	=	$\frac{1}{2}$ cup
$10\frac{2}{3}$ tablespoons	=	$\frac{2}{3}$ cup
12 tablespoons	=	$\frac{3}{4}$ cup
16 tablespoons	=	1 cup
1 cup	=	$\frac{1}{2}$ pint
2 cups	=	1 pint
2 pints (4 cups)	=	1 quart

Butter or Margarine

4 sticks = 1 pound = 2 cups

1 stick = $\frac{1}{4}$ pound = $\frac{1}{2}$ cup

$\frac{1}{2}$ stick = $\frac{1}{8}$ pound = $\frac{1}{4}$ cup

$\frac{1}{8}$ stick = 1 tablespoon

Eggs

Whole Medium	Whites	Yolks
1 = $\frac{1}{4}$ cup	2 = $\frac{1}{4}$ cup	3 = $\frac{1}{4}$ cup
2 = $\frac{1}{3}$ to $\frac{1}{2}$ cup	3 = $\frac{3}{8}$ cup	4 = $\frac{1}{3}$ cup
3 = $\frac{1}{2}$ to $\frac{2}{3}$ cup	4 = $\frac{1}{2}$ cup	5 = $\frac{3}{8}$ cup
4 = $\frac{2}{3}$ to 1 cup	5 = $\frac{2}{3}$ cup	6 = $\frac{1}{2}$ cup

Appendix C:
Altitude Adjustments

CAKES

At high elevations up to 3,000 feet:

Raise the baking temperature about 25 degrees.
Underbeat the eggs.

At high elevations above 3,000 feet:

Raise the baking temperature about 25 degrees.
Underbeat the eggs.
Reduce the double-acting baking powder or baking soda by about ⅛ teaspoon for each teaspoon called for in
the recipe.

At 5,000 feet:

Raise the baking temperature about 25 degrees.
Underbeat the eggs.
Reduce the double-acting baking powder or baking soda by about ⅛ teaspoon for each teaspoon called for in
the recipe.
Decrease sugar 1 to 2 tablespoons for each cup.
Increase liquid 1 to 2 tablespoons for each cup.

For all high altitudes:

Grease and flour all baking pans well. Cakes tend to stick.

WATER

Boiling temperatures (Fahrenheit)

Sea level	212 degrees
2,000 feet	208 degrees
5,000 feet	203 degrees
7,500 feet	198 degrees

CANDY

For each increase of 500 feet above sea level, cook candy syrups 1 degree lower than indicated in the recipes.

BREADS

Reduce the baking soda or baking powder by one-fourth.

Glossary of Cooking Terms

Bake. To cook in an oven.

Beat. To mix with a vigorous over-and-under motion with spoon, whip, or beater.

Blend. To mix thoroughly.

Boil. To cook liquid until bubbles break on the surface.

Chill. To allow to become thoroughly cold, usually by placing in a refrigerator.

Chop. To cut in fine or coarse pieces with a knife.

Coat. To cover with a thin film, such as with flour, crumbs, or sugar.

Cool. To allow to cool to room temperature.

Core. To remove the core of a fruit.

Cream. To work shortening and sugar against the side of a bowl with a spoon or to beat with a mixer until thoroughly blended and creamy.

Cut in. To mix fat into flour using a pastry blender, a fork, or two knives.

Devein. To use a knife to remove the thin dark vein from the back of a shrimp.

Dice. To cut into small (about 1/4-inch) cubes.

Dissolve. To stir granules into a liquid until the granules are no longer visible.

Dot. To place small chunks of butter in several places on the top of ingredients.

Fold in. To cut through the center of batter with a spoon, scraper, or spatula, bringing the spoon up close to the bowl, and cutting down through again, around the bowl, until blended.

Frost. To cover with icing.

Fry. To cook in a skillet or frying pan in shortening or oil over medium to medium-high heat.

Grate. To reduce to small particles by rubbing against a grater.

Grind. To cut or crush with a food or nut grinder.

Hull. To remove the stem or hull of a fruit.

Knead. To work dough by pressing, folding, and stretching with the hands.

Mash. To mix or crush to a soft form.

Mix. To combine ingredients by stirring.

Pare or peel. To remove the outside skin.

Pit. To remove pits or seeds from fruit.

Puree. To push fruit or vegetables through a sieve or to whip food in a blender or food processor until it becomes a thick liquid.

Rinse. To wash lightly, usually with water.

Roast. To cook by dry heat, usually in an oven.

Roll. To place on a board and spread thin with a rolling pin.

Sauté. To cook or fry in a small amount of oil, shortening, or butter in a skillet.

Scald. To heat to temperature just below the boiling point until a skin forms on top.

Score. To cut narrow gashes partway through the outer surface.

Shred. To cut or tear into small slices or bits.

Shuck. To peel off the outer layer.

Sift. To pass through a sieve to remove lumps.

Simmer. To cook over low heat in liquid just below the boiling point.

Skewer. To place chunks of food on a long metal or wooden spear for cooking.

Skim. To remove foam or grease with a spoon from the top of a mixture.

Slice. To cut a thin, flat piece off.

Soak. To immerse in liquid.

Steam. To cook in steam that arises from a pan of boiling liquid.

Stir. To mix with a spoon.

Stir-fry. To cook quickly over high heat in a wok or skillet while stirring constantly.

Strain. To remove excess liquid, perhaps with a strainer or sieve.

Toss. To lightly mix ingredients.

Whip. To beat rapidly to incorporate air into the batter.

Annotated Bibliography: Resources About Foods and Cultures

BOOKS

Ancona, George. *Bananas: From Manolo to Margie.* New York: Clarion Books, 1982. Grades kindergarten and up.
The journey of bananas from Honduras to the market is described with text and photographs.

Blackmore, Vivien, adapter. *Why Corn Is Golden: Stories about Plants.* Illustrated by Susana Martínez-Ostos. Boston: Little, Brown, 1984. Grades 2 and up.
Mexican tales are told of corn, sunflowers, chocolate, and other foods in this richly illustrated collection.

Burns, Marilyn. *Good for Me: All About Food in 32 Bites.* Boston: Little, Brown, 1978. Grades 3 and up.
This informative book discusses a wide range of food-related topics from biting and tasting to apples, ice cream, breakfast cereals, and health issues.

Ceserani, Gian Paolo, and Piero Ventura. *Grand Constructions.* New York: G.P. Putnam's Sons, 1983. Grades 3 and up.
Structures around the world are illustrated and described.

Dooley, Norah. *Everybody Cooks Rice.* Illustrated by Peter J. Thornton. Minneapolis, MN: Carolrhoda Books, 1991. Grades kindergarten and up.
As Carrie searches for her little brother, she samples rice at each neighbor's house in her wonderfully multicultural neighborhood. Recipes are included at the back of the book.

Dorros, Arthur. *This Is My House.* New York: Scholastic, 1992. Grades preschool and up.
Houses of a variety of materials are portrayed from all over the world. Includes "This is my house" plus pronunciation guide for 13 languages.

Hautzig, Esther. *In the Park: An Excursion in Four Languages.* Illustrated by Ezra Jack Keats. New York: Macmillan, 1968. Grades preschool and up.
Read about a trip to the park in New York, Paris, Moscow, and Madrid in the respective languages of these cities.

Hughes, Paul. *The Days of the Week.* Illustrated by Jeffrey Burn. Ada, OK: Garrett Educational, 1989. Grades 4 and up.
In addition to information about the traditions and festivals associated with each day of the week, Hughes discusses songs, rhymes, and a variety of facts.

Kalman, Bobbie. *The Food We Eat.* New York: Crabtree, 1986. Grades 1 and up.
Each double-page spread includes a colorful illustration and a discussion of how a food is grown, harvested, prepared, or collected. Includes some cultural discussions such as vegetarianism and a Japanese meal.

Koch, Frances King. *Mariculture: Farming the Fruits of the Sea*. New York: Franklin Watts, 1992. Grades 4 and up.
  Provides a fascinating overview of mariculture with excellent photographs and detailed text. Younger children will enjoy the photographs.

Morris, Ann. *On the Go*. Illustrated by Ken Heyman. New York: Lothrop, Lee & Shepard, 1990. Grades kindergarten and up.
  Color photographs from around the world illustrate how people move.

Spier, Peter. *People*. Garden City, NY: Doubleday, 1980. Grades preschool and up.
  People and their homes, languages, and customs are portrayed from around the world.

FILMS

Foods Around the World. Coronet, 1966. 11 minutes. Grades kindergarten and up.
  Describes how land conditions and climate determine the kinds of food people eat.

VIDEOS

Farming. National Geographic Society, 1985. 16 minutes. Grades 2 and up. (Also available in film.)
  Follows the activities of farmers throughout the year.

Folktales from Two Lands. Churchill Films, 1988. 17 minutes. Grades kindergarten and up.
  Two animated folktales from opposite sides of the globe show that themes are similar throughout the world.

Kids Get Cooking. KIDVIDZ. 25 minutes. Grades 1 and up.
  Focuses on cooking eggs through clever lore, science, and ethnic treats and customs.

Kids' Kitchen: Volume 1, Cookies. Auntie Lee's Kitchen. 23 minutes. Grades 1 and up.
  Although the subject is solely cookies, the instruction is entertaining and useful.

The Tale of the Wonderful Potato. Phoenix/PBA Films and Video. 24 minutes. Grades 1 and up.
  The history and politics of the potato are revealed through the journey of the vegetable from South America to Ireland.

Teeth: The Better to Eat With. National Geographic Society, 1990. 15 minutes. Grades kindergarten and up. (Also available in film.)
  Topics include the role of teeth in animals plus the need for dental hygiene in humans.

Tommy Tricker and the Stamp Travelers. FHE. Distributed by Live Home Video. 101 minutes. Grades 2 and up.
  Tommy shrinks and travels around the world on a stamp.

Annotated Bibliography: Resources in Series

The following bibliography includes series of books, films, and videos from many cultures. They are not listed in the bibliographies of the individual countries in this book. Check your library's nonfiction section for availability. Authors, copyright dates, and illustrators will vary with the individual titles.

NONFICTION BOOKS

The Ancient World. Englewood Cliffs, NJ: Silver Burdett Press. Grades 2 and up.
Photographs and illustrations explore the history and culture of early civilizations such as those of the Aztecs, Chinese, Egyptians, First Africans, Greeks, Incas, Israelites, Japanese, Mayans, Phoenicians, Romans, Sumerians, and Vikings. Each title includes an index, a glossary, and profiles of famous people.

Children of the World. Milwaukee, WI: Gareth Stevens. Grades 2 and up.
Bright color photographs and simple text make this a good choice for young readers. The background notes, maps, activity suggestions, and indexes add to the utility of the series.

Cooking the . . . Way. Minneapolis, MN: Lerner. Grades 2 and up.
This excellent series includes background information on the country, recipes, and information about the recipes. Color photographs enhance the text.

Count Your Way Through. . . . Minneapolis, MN: Carolrhoda Books. Grades kindergarten and up.
Number words from one to 10 describe key elements of the country's culture. Color illustrations, pronunciation guides, and introductory notes lend interest to the series.

Cultures of the World. North Bellmore, NY: Marshall Cavendish. Grades 3 and up.
With lavish color photographs and interesting text, these volumes provide an excellent starting point for research. See the chapters on food and drink and festivals.

Discovering Our Heritage. New York: Dillon Press. Grades 3 and up.
The history and culture of a wide variety of countries are discussed. Color photographs, a glossary, an index, and lists of useful information are included.

Enchantment of the World. Chicago: Childrens Press. Grades 3 and up.
Rich color photographs add interest to discussions of geography, ancient and recent history, commerce, daily life, and people. An index, a variety of maps, and fact lists provide useful information.

The Everyday Life of. . . . London: Macdonald. Grades 3 and up.
Sample titles in the series include *An Ice Age Hunter, A Celtic Hunter, An Egyptian Craftsman.* Color illustrations.

A Family in. . . . Minneapolis, MN: Lerner. Grades 2 and up.
   Color photographs, maps, and text explore family life in a variety of countries around the world.

Food and Drink. New York: Bookwright Press. Grades 3 and up.
   The country's people, culture, food, regional specialties, and special occasions are described. A glossary, booklist, and index are included. These provide an excellent introduction and companion to any cooking experiences.

Great Civilizations. New York: Franklin Watts. Grades 2 and up.
   Maps, illustrations, charts, and text provide insights into civilizations such as the Aztec and Inca empires, Greece, Rome, China, Egypt, and Japan.

Imagine Living Here: This Place Is. . . . New York: Walker. Grades 1 and up.
   Colorful illustrations accompany a narrative about special places. The series includes places that are lonely, cold, wet, dry, and high.

The Land and People of. . . . New York: J.B. Lippincott. Grades 4 and up.
   This series explores each country's regions, people, government, literature, arts, holidays, sports, and current world role. Bibliographies for print and film, a discography, and detailed indexes are particularly useful features.

The Lands, Peoples, and Cultures Series. New York: Crabtree. Grades 4 and up.
   Three books for each country cover the land, people, and culture. Each double-page spread includes beautiful color photographs and text on a variety of topics. Each volume includes a glossary and an index.

Original Peoples. Vero Beach, FL: Rourke Publications. Grades 3 and up.
   Photographs, maps, a glossary, a booklist, and an index enhance the text about cultures such as the Aborigines of Australia, Eskimos, Plains Indians, South Pacific Islanders, Andes Indians, and South African Zulus.

Passport to. . . . New York: Franklin Watts. Grades 3 and up.
   Color drawings and photographs are artfully arranged with text to encourage easy sampling of information. Several "Fact Files" provide useful details, maps, and graphs. The contents and indexes are useful for the early researcher.

Places and Peoples of the World. New York: Chelsea House. Grades 3 and up.
   Both black-and-white and color photographs enhance the texts, which describe the history, people, economy, cities, arts, and culture of a variety of countries. Titles include a glossary and an index.

Recent American Immigrants. New York: Franklin Watts. Grades 3 and up.
   Color photographs, maps, sidebars, graphs, sources, and an index are some of the informative components that explore the heritage of our recent immigrants.

Vanishing Cultures. San Diego, CA: Harcourt Brace Jovanovich. Grades 1 and up.
   Rich color photographs and simple text provide a fascinating glimpse of vanishing cultures. Titles include: *Down Under* (1992), *Far North* (1992), *Himalaya* (1991), and *Sahara* (1991).

We Live in. . . . New York: Bookwright Press. Grades 2 and up.
   Each country is explored through portraits of the lives of residents. Each volume includes color photographs, background facts, an index, and a glossary.

Where We Live. Austin, TX: Steck-Vaughn. Grades kindergarten and up.
The color photographs and simple text provide introductory information about each country. These titles are appropriate for reading aloud or use by independent early readers. Each includes a short index.

World Leaders: Past and Present. New York: Chelsea House. Grades 5 and up.
This series includes 157 biographies of leaders from around the world. Each biography includes further reading, a chronology, and an index.

FILMS

Families of the World. National Geographic Society, 1986-87. 14-18 minutes. Grades 4 and up.
A child from each country or region describes life in that culture: Australia, Central America, the former East Germany, Egypt, Israel, Japan, Mexico, the former Soviet Union, the former West Germany, and the former Yugoslavia.

Global Geography. Agency for Instructional Technology, 1991. 15 minutes. Grades 4 and up.
Various cultures are compared. Titles include "East Asia: Why Do People Live Where They Do?", "Soviet Union: Why Does Planning Occur?", "Australia/New Zealand: Why Is the World Shrinking?", "Central and South America: Why Do People Move?", and "Europe: How Do People Deal with National Hazards?"

Journey to Understanding. Beacon Films, 1991. 25 minutes. Grades 4 and up.
Comparisons are made among topography, religions, languages, and cultures around the world.

Physical Geography of the Continents. National Geographic Society, 1991. 25 minutes. Grades 4 and up.
Each film focuses on the major landforms, climate, plants, and animals of Africa, Antarctica, Asia, Australia, Europe, and South America.

VIDEOS

Although the following series are for adults, they would be valuable for older students and for background information.

Tour Europe on Your VCR. Rand McNally. 60 minutes.
These touring videos give a close-up view of the locales, festivals, and folklore of each area. Titles include "Touring Austria," "Touring England," "Touring the Great Festivals of Europe," "Touring Ireland," "Touring Italy," "Touring London, Paris, and Rome," "Touring Scotland," and "Touring the Stately English Homes and Castles."

Video Visits. Rand McNally. 45-58 minutes.
Countries, cities, and regions included on the visits are: Austria, the Baltics, the former Czechoslovakia, Denmark, England, France, Finland, Germany, Greece, Hungary, Ireland, London, Norway, Poland, Scandinavia, Scotland, Spain, Sweden, Switzerland, and Wales.

Index

About the Authors

Patricia Marden

Suzanne I. Barchers

Patricia Marden received her bachelor of science degree in elementary education and master's degree in reading from the University of Delaware. She was a primary school teacher and administrator in Delaware for 12 years before moving to Colorado in 1982.

Patricia is involved in many aspects of school reform. She has worked extensively in the areas of alternative assessment, the writing process, literature-based reading, animals in the classroom, cooperative groupings, multiaged groupings, computer use in the classroom, multicultural education, and parent-school partnerships. She also works on the Children's Museum of Denver's advisory council.

Patricia was a recipient of the 1991-1992 Milken Family Foundation's National Educator Award. She co-authored *Cooking Up U.S. History: Recipes and Research to Share with Children* (Teacher Ideas Press, 1991).

Patricia resides in Aurora, Colorado, with her husband, Chris, and teaches in the Cherry Creek School District in Englewood, Colorado.

Suzanne I. Barchers earned her bachelor of science degree in elementary education from Eastern Illinois University, her master's degree in reading from Oregon State University, and her doctorate in education from the University of Colorado, Boulder. Formerly a teacher, administrator, and editor, Suzanne currently serves as Deputy Director of the Children's Museum of Denver, writes for *Learning* magazine, and teaches graduate classes at the University of Colorado, Denver.

Suzanne is the author of *Creating and Managing the Literate Classroom* (Teacher Ideas Press, 1990); *Wise Women: Folk and Fairy Tales from Around the World* (Libraries Unlimited, 1990); *Cooking Up U.S. History: Recipes and Research to Share with Children* (with Patricia Marden, Teacher Ideas Press, 1991); *Readers Theatre for Beginning Readers* (Teacher Ideas Press, 1993); and *Teaching Language Arts* (West Educational Publishing, 1994).